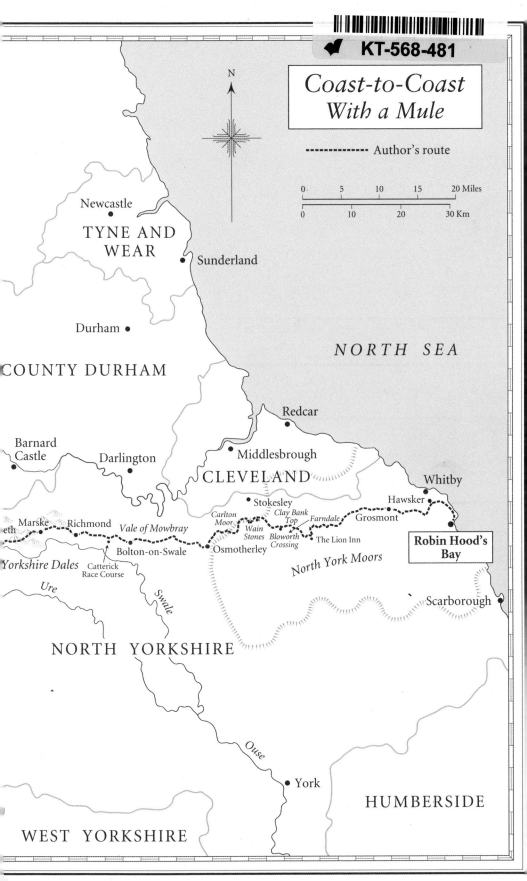

KT-568-481

# Coast-to-Coast
# With a Mule

------------ Author's route

0      5      10      15      20 Miles

0      10      20      30 Km

N

Newcastle

TYNE AND
WEAR

Sunderland

Durham

NORTH SEA

COUNTY DURHAM

Barnard
Castle

Darlington

Redcar

Middlesbrough

CLEVELAND

Whitby

Hawsker

Stokesley

Carlton
Moor

Clay Bank
Top        Farndale    Grosmont

eth    Marske    Richmond    Vale of Mowbray    Wain
Stones    Bloworth
Crossing    The Lion Inn

Robin Hood's
Bay

Yorkshire Dales    Catterick
Race Course    Bolton-on-Swale    Osmotherley

North York Moors

Ure

Swale

Scarborough

NORTH YORKSHIRE

Ouse

York

HUMBERSIDE

WEST YORKSHIRE

# One Man and a Mule

**Please return/renew this item by the last date shown**
Tillibh/ath-chlaraibh seo ron cheann-latha mu dheireadh

# High Life Highland
914.2704 Libraries

Tel. 01463 235713
www.highlifehighland.com/libraries

Also by Hugh Thomson

*The White Rock: An Exploration of the Inca Heartland*

*Nanda Devi: A Journey to the Last Sanctuary*

*Cochineal Red: Travels through Ancient Peru*

*Tequila Oil: Getting Lost in Mexico*

*50 Wonders of the World*

*The Green Road into the Trees: An Exploration of England*


*At The Captain's Table: Life on a Luxury Liner* (Kindle Single)

*Two Men and a Mule: The Last City of the Incas* (Kindle Single)

# Hugh Thomson

# One Man and a Mule

### Across England with a Pack Mule

preface

1 3 5 7 9 10 8 6 4 2

Preface Publishing
20 Vauxhall Bridge Road
London SW1V 2SA

Preface Publishing is part of the Penguin Random House group of companies
whose addresses can be found at global.penguinrandomhouse.com.

Penguin
Random House
UK

First published by Preface Publishing in 2017

www.penguin.co.uk

A CIP catalogue record for this book is available from the British Library.

ISBN 978 1 84809 469 7

All images in the photo sections are courtesy of the author with the following exceptions;

section 1 page 6 (*Seagull Rising I*) © Jason Gathorne-Hardy
section 1 page 8 (Bowderdale Valley) © Jasper Winn
section 2 page 1 (Amanda and Clive Owen) © Amanda and Clive Owen
section 2 page 4 (Hugo Hildyard) © Florencia Clifford
section 2 page 6 (Steampunks and Goths) © Bryan Ledgard
section 2 page 7 ('*Still talking after 200 miles*') © Jasper Winn

Map by John Gilkes

Typeset in 12.85/15.25 pt Centaur MT by Jouve (UK), Milton Keynes
Printed and bound in Great Britain by Clays Ltd, St Ives PLC

Penguin Random House is committed to a sustainable future
for our business, our readers and our planet. This book is made
from Forest Stewardship Council® certified paper.

MIX
Paper from
responsible sources
FSC
www.fsc.org     FSC® C018179

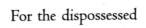

For the dispossessed

# Contents

# Contents

# Introduction

Those who have travelled with me before – along *The Green Road into the Trees* or through any of the South American books – know what to expect. But others might require a health warning on the packet.

This book is unashamedly personal. It is more interested in people than landscape, and in farmers than animals. Those wanting a pure bit of 'nature writing' should look elsewhere – and without great difficulty, as there has been a plethora of such books over the last few years.

Writers' courses always tell you that you should make a 'contract' with the reader. While I won't bother you with all my clauses, one is significant – that I will try to avoid bedazzling you with rare botanical names or birds you've never heard of.

There is always a sort of reader who needs to join up the dots: to know exactly how you get from A to B, where you spent the night, what you had for breakfast and the price of a coffee in Kirkby Stephen. They should not buy this book just to get from coast to coast. There are plenty of suitable guidebooks which will do that job for you. Indeed, I would go further – this book might actually get you lost.

It is perfectly possible to drive across the north of England very fast – say, on the A66 past Barnard Castle, as long as the

*Introduction*

Appleby Horse Fair isn't taking place. Even on a bike it can be done in two days, as my friend Jeff Ford has done. But this is a more discursive journey that goes at mule pace, chats over gates to farmers and takes in byways as well as highways. I have tried to unpick the threads of what is really happening in the rapidly changing countryside, far from London and the metro-politan conversation.

Nothing beats walking for taking the temperature of a country. I was inspired to make this journey by Robert Louis Stevenson's *Travels with a Donkey in the Cévennes*. As Stevenson wrote:

The great affair is to move; to feel the needs and hitches of our life more clearly; to come down off this feather-bed of civilisation, and find the globe granite underfoot and strewn with cutting flints.

There is a song I found useful to sing while travelling and the reader might like to hum it too if at any point they need accom-paniment. For some reason, Jethro never seemed to appreciate it.

Oh I got plenty o' nothing,
An' nothing's plenty fo' me.
I got no car, got no mule,
I got no misery.
'I Got Plenty O' Nuttin', as sung
by Frank Sinatra

*

A visitor to the British Isles usually disembarks in lowland England. He is charmed by its orderly arrangement and by its open landscapes, tamed and formed by man and mellowed by 1,000 years of human history.

There is another Britain, to many of us the better half, a land of mountains and moorlands and of sun and cloud, and it is with this upland Britain that these pages are concerned.

It is equal in area to lowland Britain, but its population is less than that of a single large town. It lies now, as always, beyond the margins of our industrial and urban civilisations, fading into the western mists and washed by northern seas, its needs forgotten and its possibilities almost unknown.

W. H. Pearsall, *Mountains and Moorlands*,
New Naturalist Series (1950)

# Chapter 1

# The North Crossing

Of all pack animals the mule is the favourite, and although frequently employed as a draught or riding animal, it is as a pack carrier that he is known best.

The War Office, *Animal Management* (London, 1923)

'You're not what I thought you'd be.'

Jimmy Richardson gave me a hard look. He was a big man but had small eyes like currants, set in a broad white face. I had arrived while he was still on the phone. He had plenty of time to assess me as he sat on a sofa surrounded by the spillage from a multi-pack bag of crisps; nor had he been in any hurry to finish the call.

We were in the end house of a terraced street south of Newcastle, close to where they filmed *Billy Elliot*. An area where shops were shuttered with security blinds, and both men and boys wore their hair shaved to the bone.

Maybe that was the first problem about me. I needed a haircut. But I could tell that Jimmy also liked to weigh up a man and disconcert him a little – both useful tactics for a horse dealer. Or in this case, mule dealer.

He had heard I wanted one. I had put word out along the very small network of mule fanciers in England, and soon learned there were only a handful of the animals in each county. This was the first I had been offered.

Jimmy was a few years older than me. He had established his seniority before I arrived, when we had spoken on the phone.

Jimmy always carried two mobiles, for backup, and was seldom not talking on one of them. The phrase 'if I can give you a little bit of advice' was a favourite.

'So what is it *exactly* you want to do?' As if he already knew, but could not quite compute it.

I had explained when I rang that I was looking for a mule to take right across England; that I'd worked with mules in Peru and fancied the idea of doing the same in a country in which muleteering had almost died out. And that the north of England, where the tradition of pack animals had lasted longest, was the obvious place to do it. Even if, as he quickly surmised, I was a soft southerner.

What Jimmy was interested in was my route – 'I know all the bridleways between here and Appleby' – and how much I knew about mules. 'Like I always say, you can make a horse, you can ask a donkey. And you can let a mule do whatever it wants.'

We drove over to see his mule; or rather, I drove and Jimmy gave directions around the desolate mini-roundabouts that led to Seaham where, as Jimmy was quick to remind me, Michael Caine had ended up dead on the beach in *Get Carter*.

Jimmy told me he had ridden right across the same route I was going to take. More impressively, when he arrived at one coast from the other, he had turned straight around and ridden all the way back. But he had done it in the conventional way, on a horse not a mule; he also had a friend to help him, mainly to get down and open gates, as 'I'm getting a bit heavy to be jumping on and off a saddle.'

'I'm not being funny,' said Jimmy, 'but I need to know what level of horsemanship you have. Particularly if you're on your own. That's two grand's worth of mule you'll be dealing with, if I lend or sell you mine.' So a marker for the price had been put down. We had not yet discussed money.

I murmured that I'd worked a lot with mules in Peru – which was true. Although to be fair, I'd also worked a lot with muleteers in Peru helping me.

The mule was in a field off a roundabout, with a couple of horses for company. She was a big raw-boned grey brute, at over sixteen hands: big, even if she had been a horse. Jimmy led her out from the field on a length of scraggy rope. The mule looked down at me like a haughty Russian model who'd been asked out on a date by a man wearing trainers.

'You better get on.'

I eyed up the mule. I wanted one as a pack animal to carry my gear, not to ride across England. But Jimmy wasn't going to let that stop him. This was a test of that horsemanship he had been concerned about.

There were no stirrups, let alone a saddle. I felt I could do with a crane to hoist me aboard. And Jimmy had been unclear as to whether anyone had ever ridden this mule before.

But needs must. He gave me a leg-up, complaining I didn't angle my knee in precisely the right way. Then I was riding bareback on the grey mule over a great deal of concrete near a mini-roundabout. A couple passing in their Skoda looked on askance and gave us a wide berth.

The mule seemed fine, if surprised by the turn of events.

'What's her name?' I asked Jimmy.

Jimmy paused, as if this was a question he had never considered. Or expected to be asked.

'I believe . . . I believe she's called Diamond.'

It wasn't clear if this was a recollection or a christening.

If Diamond was strong enough to carry eleven stone of human — a charitable estimate — she could carry any pack a considerable distance. The problem would be getting that pack on her, particularly single-handed. The mules I had worked with in the Andes were around fourteen hands, so on the borderline between pony and horse. Manageable.

Whether I wanted to deal with sixteen hands' worth of mule clattering around me for weeks was another matter. It would be like going out with a woman who was taller.

'I can see you're intimidated,' said Jimmy. There was a hint in his voice that he was pleased about this. 'Let me give you a little bit of advice. If the mule doesn't think you're the master from the off, you never will be.'

Thanks for that, Jimmy.

'Get down and I'll show you how she leads. That's what you want her for anyways.'

We led the mule along a desolate bit of edgeland that skirted the roundabout. Given there were cars passing, the mule seemed calm and well behaved. Until one of the horses we'd left in the field gave a whinny, and she bolted hard enough to leave me with rope burn.

The mule ran onto the centre of the mini-roundabout. It was midday and there weren't many cars about. But there were some.

Jimmy sent me one way and he took the other, so we came at her in a pincer manoeuvre. We tried this several times without success. A mule running around at speed on concrete or tarmac is a hard thing to stop. She was using the small central island of the roundabout to give her jumps extra spring.

A man approaching on the dual carriageway pulled his car up dead to come and help — which we needed. Someone had to hold the gate to the adjoining field open so we could herd the mule inside without letting the other horses out.

'Fuck this for a game of soldiers,' said Jimmy. He was sweating. Rounding up a mule that refuses to follow the Highway Code is hard work. I could tell he was struggling also with a rare emotion. He was embarrassed.

'I'm really sorry,' he said. 'I'm really sorry. I don't feel I've been much help at all. But at least this happened here, not on a Yorkshire moor twenty miles from Whitby when it was pissing down with rain.

'But I tell you what . . . '

I looked at him impassively. I felt I now had all the cards.

' . . . I've got a lovely donkey I can loan you.'

He eyed me up to see how receptive I might be to this idea.

'Jack donkey. Might need a little shoeing. And my lads can give him some training. Been standing in a field for years so he's a little out of condition. Just a little. But he would carry your gear, easy. There's even a packsaddle I could throw in as well.'

We drove to see the donkey in another of Jimmy's pocket fields, which were scattered around the edgelands of Seaham like an archipelago of lost meadows amidst a sea of light industrial waste. He had lovely markings of a dappled grey. Even though a jack donkey, he was also very small.

'How old is he?'

Jimmy looked vague again. I was beginning to get used to this look. The light in his small eyes went out.

'I think about seven.'

That was the same age he'd said the mule had been. A default age. I remember trying to buy a used car once from salesmen in Texas, and having much the same experience with Chevrolets and their mileage.

After the mule, the donkey came as a welcome bit of docility. But I wasn't sure if I saw myself leading a dwarf donkey across England. It felt like a nativity play. And would *One Man and a Donkey* have quite the same ring on the cover of a book? Or would people think it was a comedy special, like that guy taking his fridge around Ireland?

Donkeys needed more shelter than mules, as their coats weren't so weatherproof. That much I knew. And I worried that if the donkey wasn't accustomed to walking, he could get sores.

I asked Jimmy.

'It's not that he *could* get sores or that he *might* get sores. I can absolutely guarantee you – he *will* get sores.

'You'll have to change donkeys along the way. But that's not a problem. We can get a new donkey over to you regular like, for a bit of petrol money.'

While negotiating the mini-roundabouts in the car, we had established that 'a bit of petrol money' for other services – like a van to drop the mule off – would be fifty quid a trip. So a constant relay of donkey reinforcements was an expensive and complicated proposition. Since Jimmy only had one donkey, it would also be a tricky one to fulfil.

Jimmy realised he had talked himself out of a deal.

'OK, let me give you a little bit of advice. Why don't you go to Scarborough and see if they have any donkeys they'd be willing to sell at the end of the season? They'll be used to walking up and down the beach, an' that.'

I felt my quest for a mule was spiralling out of control. The last thing a beach donkey needed was to walk hundreds of miles from one coast of England to the other. Come the end of the season, they would be looking forward to a winter spent in comfortable lodgings, far from pesky kids feeding them Pringles. With their feet up.

'I'm just trying to help, mind. Although I don't feel I've been any help at all.'

We went back to his house for a cup of tea.

'Good luck,' said Jimmy, when I said goodbye. He paused for a beat, to re-establish control.

'You're going to need it.'

*

I travelled all over the north of England from Lancaster to Hartlepool looking for a mule, with no success. My search led me to the annual Appleby Horse Fair. In the Hare and Hounds, one of the pubs on the hill, a tall saturnine man started talking to me over a drink. He was a traveller.

'I've a mule with the horses I'm selling,' he told me. 'But you'll have to walk down to see it. They won't let us bring the horses into town any more.'

A short journey later and I was presented with the animal, standing by the side of the road. He was a fine, sturdy beast who looked like he could carry a good load. He was also, incontrovertibly, not a mule but a pack pony.

I made this point to the tall man, who waved it off as an irrelevance. Indeed, as something of an impertinence.

'Same difference. He'll carry just as good a weight. He'll do the same job of work as a mule. So what's the problem?'

And it was true that pack ponies had carried the bulk of the ore and the provisions in the north for centuries. But that wasn't the point. I wanted a mule.

The tall man looked disappointed, as if a child had wilfully refused an arranged marriage.

'You're making a mistake. Mules are hard to come by. And finding a good mule is even harder. Almost impossible. Whereas there are plenty of these. And they're cheaper. Just tell me how much you'd be willing to pay?'

But I wasn't about to play that game. Not only because I wasn't very good at the rules, but also because, in a suitably stubborn way, I had set my sights on a mule.

I had my reasons. Darwin had eulogised the mule as being a perfect example of the energy of a hybrid: that it took the best qualities of both its parents, the donkey and the horse, to produce an animal with greater vitality and strength than either. They can easily grow taller than both parents. As Lorraine Travis put it in her excellent little handbook, *The Mule*, 'Weight for weight they are stronger than horses, and much longer lived with longer working lives, although maturing slightly later. They rarely become ill or lame or suffer wounds, can withstand extremes of temperature, can live on frugal rations, have tremendous stamina and resilience and are exceptionally surefooted.'

I knew all the arguments against mules as well. Particularly the old chestnut about them being stubborn. A good deal of that came from the mule's intelligence and talent for self-preservation. You can't fool a mule into doing anything, as you can sometimes with a horse, and they are less likely to do anything stupid. There's a reason they use mules, not horses, to lead tourists down into the Grand Canyon. A mule will look after itself and therefore your cargo — or indeed you, if you are riding it.

There was another attractive element to this reputation that mules had for being stubborn. They were sensitive animals. They were also animals that needed to trust you before they would cooperate, so you needed to win that trust. Not least because there was a very physical manifestation of one not trusting you. The phrase 'a kick like a mule', often applied to cocktails of dubious alcoholic provenance, doesn't come from nowhere. They could lash out with incredible accuracy, as I remembered from Peru, where an entire expedition had disintegrated into chaos after one of its leaders had been kicked by his mule.

*

The idea of taking a mule across England had come about in the same focused way as so many of my projects: some long-entertained half-thought (like trying to find an Inca ruin, or running a black-market car from Texas to Central America) crystallising into action, without at any stage being examined for plausibility, possibility or sheer bloody stupidity.

As my wife Irena pointed out, 'You haven't really thought how you're going to do this, have you?'

This was rhetorical, as married conversations often are. We both knew I hadn't.

But then if you don't occasionally jump out of planes, you

never land. For some reason, I've often found this argument appeals more to the masculine than to the feminine mind. Women are equally adventurous — often more so — but they like to see where they are putting their feet. Or in this case, where they are putting their animal's hooves.

I had started with the assumption that I would easily find a mule. Perhaps not quite as easily as in Peru — where you can turn up in a village and book a mule like a taxi — but surely there were plenty around?

No, there weren't. A few chance and choice encounters — as with Jimmy near Newcastle — had put me right on that one.

Unlike Peru, the rest of South America, the United States, France, Spain, and elsewhere in Europe, there were, for complicated reasons, very few mules in England. Plenty of horses, of course — and a surprising number of donkeys — but no mules.

Would I have to import one? Sure to be time-consuming, expensive and complicated. I had heard horror stories about the difficulty of bringing a mule over from Spain. Or buy an American riding mule at several thousand quid?

I did discover there was a British Mule Society. One thing about this country is that it has a specialist society for just about everything even if, in this case, one with an extremely small membership.

By happy chance, the society was holding a 'Mule Fair', their annual big get-together, in Kent a week or so after I discovered its existence. It promised to be an ideal opportunity to meet some of the members who, I imagined, often brought their mules with them. I pictured a scene in which dozens of mules flocked into fields under the North Downs.

The membership secretary, Helen, put me right.

'There will be three mules. If we're lucky.'

This didn't seem a lot to choose from; moreover, those three would already be taken. Was there not some great mule trading market, the equivalent of Appleby Horse Fair, where mules were bought and sold?

'No, there isn't. Not unless you go to Morocco,' one of the ladies at the Kent gathering told me. She was, like everybody else, wearing a cowboy hat. The Mule Fair that year was billed as 'western-themed'. Apart from some old riding boots, I felt underdressed beside the cheery display of Stetsons and fringed buckskin jackets.

Maria, the Mule Society's publicity secretary, had outdone the others. She was got up in a rubber inflatable panto-mule that protruded in front of her. It was the sort of costume that demanded an outgoing personality, and Maria had that in spades. A Colombian who came from a family that bred mules near Medellín, she couldn't understand why there were so few of the animals in this country.

I asked for advice.

'If you're looking for a mule, the first thing is *not* to get one from a donkey sanctuary. You'll find it easier to adopt a baby. *¡Es una locura!* It's madness. They have so many forms to go through.'

Sarah agreed. Tanned and cheerful, she was one of the few members to have brought a mule with her, a small one, which she sometimes rode. 'The thing about mules is that they're intelligent. Whereas horses can be just so – bloody – *stupid*. As can their owners. Which is one of the things I like about mules. You don't get all that stuck-up stuff you do with horses. All those Range Rovers and showing off. Mules are more down-to-earth. And so are we.'

And it was true that the vibe at the barbecue felt more Essex than Badminton Horse Trials. We were in the shadow of the M25 and there was a cheerful karaoke session blaring out from the local pub. 'Bohemian Rhapsody' wafted across the July night.

Some thirty members of the British Mule Society were clutching bottles of beer and chatting over a barbecue. They had a direct, straightforward quality which I liked immediately; and a willingness to help.

I was told to go and look for Yvonne, 'who was wearing a big cowboy hat'. This didn't narrow the search. But when I found her, she was the one who told me about Jethro.

'He's perfect. Very sociable, likes humans. Small, with lovely colouring. And he's not at a donkey sanctuary. He's at an RSPCA rescue centre, who are much easier to deal with.'

I was sold. But would the RSPCA be?
The lady at the rescue centre was helpful when I rang.

'Jethro has been with us for three years. He's eight. Before he came to us he had been badly treated, so he's needed a lot of patience to get to the point he is at now. And he could still need a lot *more* patience.'

This was a warning of sorts, which I chose to ignore. By this stage, I was ready to take any mule who was short of psychopathic.

'Also we don't ride any of our animals, so he's been standing in a field for the last three years and hasn't taken much exercise. And like donkeys, mules can be prone to, uh, "weight-gain issues".'

As soon as I met him, I could see Jethro had a bit of a spare tyre. If anything, this made me sympathetic. Just another middle-aged mule/male. Moreover, Jethro had been gelded late in life, so retained the energies and inclinations, if not the abilities, of a stallion.

He was larger than the donkey Jimmy had once offered me, but still small – about twelve and a half hands – with striking colouring, a freckling of white and beige like an Appaloosa, and an enquiring and appraising gaze which I came to learn was characteristic.

Our first meeting in the stable yard at the RSPCA was cordial, if not effusive; so English in the best possible sense.

I noticed his eyes: dark, soulful and thoughtful. His unusual colouring was not like anything I had seen in Peru, where mules tended to come either bay or skewbald.

Anna, the lady from the RSPCA, asked if I wanted to groom and lead him around. I didn't. For I knew that, like Jimmy, they were asking not only so I could see what Jethro was like; they wanted to know if I would make a suitable foster parent. It was a test, which was fair enough. But I deferred it for two good reasons: I wanted to take things slowly and not rush Jethro on our first date; I hadn't a clue how to groom a mule.

This was not because I hadn't spent many hours with them. It was just that in Peru there had always been a muleteer to do all the grooming and feeding. I either rode the larger mules or walked with the smaller ones as pack animals.

My teenage step-daughter Pippa gave me a crash course at our local stables. The girls mucking out were amused to see a man in his fifties going back to Pony Club – or in my case, going for the first time. I had been more into motorbikes than horses as a teenager, like many an English boy; only later had I learned to enjoy Western-style riding in South America, where the best way to get to many places was on a saddle.

There were no mules at the stables, of course, but plenty of horses on which to practise. Pippa taught me to use a dandy brush, a curry comb and a hoof-pick. This last was the trickiest. Getting a large cob to lift his hooves took a certain nerve.

In Peru, I had led mules in the simplest possible way: with a lead rope, often only draped over my shoulder. Most were so well trained they stayed together in a pack as we trudged over the Andes. 'You can't do that for the RSPCA,' Pippa told me. 'You need to stand on the mule's left, with the lead in your right hand and the rest of the rope coiled in the other.' It sounded like a barn dance.

After a couple of sessions, I was ready to go back and take Jethro for a walk. Pippa came for support and lent me her horse-grooming kit so that, together with my riding-boots and gloves, I looked the

part. A well-brushed Jethro behaved beautifully when escorted by
me around the RSPCA yard with a carefully coiled lead-rope,
although less well with Pippa; as she led him past some other horses,
he bolted, spooked (as he often would be later) by equine interest
or competition. But that was clearly his fault, not ours.

They got out the fostering forms for me to sign. I arranged
to borrow Jethro for enough time to train him and do the journey, although I did not have the stabling facilities to keep him
more permanently.

'The thing about Jethro,' said Alice, one of his RSPCA carers,
'is that he either likes you or he doesn't.'

This seemed straightforward, and Jethro had showed no sign
of taking against me.

'The other thing is ... he's very intelligent. He'll only do
something if he wants to.'

We had 200 miles ahead of us to test this. Alice's tone implied
that Jethro's intelligence was not always a helpful quality.

✻

And now, with the shock of all departures, we are on the far
north-west coast of England, at the small town of St Bees in
Cumbria – 'we' being my friend Jasper Winn, Jethro, and me. The
seafront has a windswept, municipal feel of bollards and concrete.
To the south lie the towers of the nuclear plant at Sellafield, which
glitter in the autumnal sun. And I'm looking out at the wide
Atlantic Ocean from a beach which, being October, is almost
deserted. Although not quite.

A brave family are pretending it is still summer and have spent
the morning building an epic sandcastle: a sandcastle that looks
like a Maya temple, with steep sides, square-cut ditches and a
turret, the whole elaborate ensemble decorated with feathers. It's
a surreal, surprising but also auspicious sight, given how many
of my journeys have been in South America.

They in turn are surprised to see a mule suddenly appear on
the beach. The children ask whether they can stroke his head. Is
he friendly? I say they can stroke anything except Jethro's ears,
which I have already learned are sensitive.

Their parents tell me they are on honeymoon, which I take in
my stride without asking any complicated or intrusive family
questions. But anyway, it's time to get Jethro's feet – and indeed,
our boots – wet in the traditional way before embarking on the
Coast-to-Coast.

Jethro is understandably hesitant at the prospect. He is also
confused. He has probably never seen the sea before. He sniffs
the seaweed but then jumps back in alarm as a wave comes in.

The children come to his rescue and distract us. 'Why are you
collecting those three pebbles?' they ask Jasper.

'Because we're going to take them from this coast to the east
coast on the other side of the country. In Jethro's saddlebag.'

The kids waved goodbye as we headed down the beach, and
started up the headland to the south of St Bees. Jethro set off at a
smart pace. I had discovered during previous training sessions near
my home in Oxfordshire that he often, like a wilful teenager, began
with great verve and enthusiasm which tailed off as he got bored.

We climbed fast. Jasper pointed out that we were heading the
wrong way, as the headland went even further west out to sea
from St Bees. I assured him this would be the first time of many,
at least while I was responsible for the route, so he should get
used to it. Two women we met wondered if Jethro was a donkey

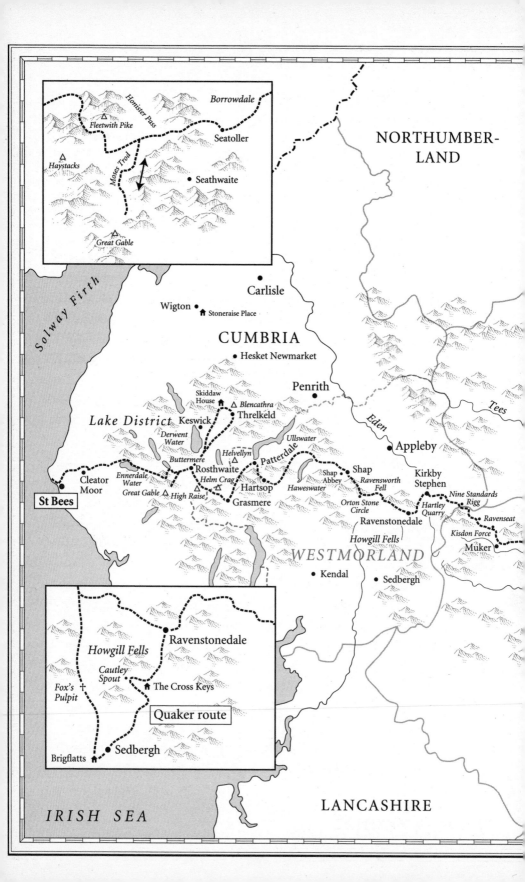

### Inset map (top left)

Borrowdale

Honister Pass

Fleetwith Pike

Seatoller

Moses Trod

Haystacks

Seathwaite

Great Gable

### Main map

NORTHUMBER-
LAND

Solway Firth

Carlisle

Wigton

Stoneraise Place

CUMBRIA

Hesket Newmarket

Penrith

Skiddaw
House

Blencathra

Threlkeld

Lake District

Keswick

Derwent
Water

Ullswater

Appleby

Eden

Tees

Helvellyn

Patterdale

Buttermere

Rosthwaite

Shap
Abbey

Shap

Kirkby
Stephen

St Bees

Cleator
Moor

Ennerdale
Water

Helm Crag

Hartsop

Haweswater

Ravensworth
Fell

Nine Standards
Rigg

Great Gable

High Raise

Hartley
Quarry

Ravenseat

Grasmere

Orton Stone
Circle

Ravenstonedale

Kisdon Force

WESTMORLAND

Howgill Fells

Muker

Kendal

Sedbergh

IRISH SEA

LANCASHIRE

### Inset map (bottom left)

Howgill Fells

Ravenstonedale

Cautley
Spout

Fox's
Pulpit

The Cross Keys

Quaker route

Brigflatts

Sedbergh

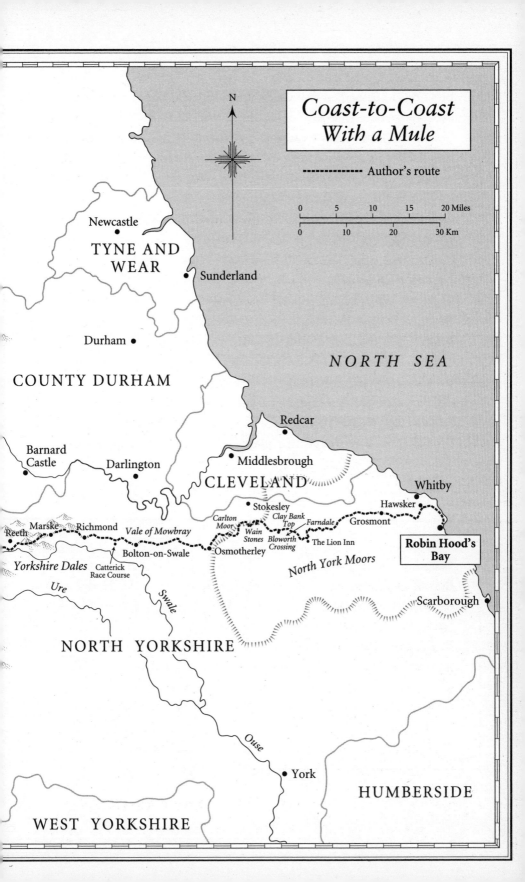

N

# Coast-to-Coast
# With a Mule

------------ Author's route

| 0 | 5 | 10 | 15 | 20 Miles |
|---|---|----|----|----------|
| 0 | | 10 | 20 | 30 Km |

*NORTH SEA*

Newcastle

## TYNE AND
## WEAR

Sunderland

Durham

## COUNTY DURHAM

Redcar

Barnard
Castle

Darlington

Middlesbrough

## CLEVELAND

Whitby

Hawsker

Stokesley

*Carlton
Moor*

*Clay Bank
Top*

*Farndale*

Grosmont

Reeth

Marske

Richmond

*Vale of Mowbray*

*Wain
Stones*

*Bloworth
Crossing*

The Lion Inn

**Robin Hood's
Bay**

Bolton-on-Swale

Osmotherley

*Yorkshire Dales*

Catterick
Race Course

*North York Moors*

*Ure*

*Swale*

Scarborough

## NORTH YORKSHIRE

*Ouse*

York

## HUMBERSIDE

## WEST YORKSHIRE

or a horse. I informed them that he was neither. Jasper prophesied, accurately, that this would happen a lot. He also pointed out how well Jethro was managing on the thin, winding track. A mule's feet are closer together than a horse's, so they can follow a narrow contouring path better.

This was a symbolic first stage of the walk with Jethro. As we were on a footpath, not a bridleway, stiles lay ahead at the top of the hill, and while you can always wrestle a mountain bike over a fence, you can't do that with 300 kilos of mule. We would have to turn inland.

Before we did so, I looked back down on the small town of St Bees. It had the simple clarity of all good beginnings: the breakwaters dividing the beach into neat segments; the buildings clustered in radial lines; the coastline extending away to the south with lucidity and enticement.

I felt that familiar tingle of excitement at the onset of a new project, almost as if I had dived off the headland and the water was rushing up to meet me. A new journey is always a birthing of sorts.

*

Planning the trip – and finding Jethro – had been complicated. But an extraordinary piece of good luck, or rather of kindness, had also come my way. I had managed to persuade my Irish friend Jasper Winn to accompany us.

This was providential. After collecting Jethro from the RSPCA, it soon became clear that trying to get a mule across the country was not going to be easy, with either carrot or stick. During training sessions before we left for the North, he had proved a handful, to say the least, bolting off and chasing local mares. The patience of my kind sister Katie had been considerably tested while hosting him in her Oxfordshire field.

So to have someone like Jasper, who had ridden horses all over the world from Kyrgyzstan to Andalusia to Argentina – and had once bought a mule at a market in Morocco – was a gift from heaven. He had grown up with horses in County Cork and learned the Irish way of managing them, a combination of straight-talking and sweet-talking.

Not only that, but he was delightful company: a rover and a traveller, whose home was wherever he set his hat (a beret, usually at a rakish angle). Jasper had somehow managed to get through life without any of the usual responsibilities – family, property or job – and could live free as a bird, writing and playing music. A true bohemian.

I had met him when he was house-sitting for some friends of mine, something which he enjoyed doing. I had not realised quite what a demand there was for this particular service in the countryside. If you live in a large house with a lot of animals, you can't just go away and leave them on their own. Jasper had therefore acquired a devoted following as a man trusted to walk dogs, look after horses or livestock and keep the home fires burning.

As soon as he agreed to join me on this journey, he had proved endlessly resourceful and versatile. Did we need a packsaddle? He had an old Iranian one stashed at his mother's, which was both practical and stylish. Girths to secure it to Jethro? No need to buy them, he would sew some together from sofa-webbing fabric and the belt from an old leather trunk.

Moreover, he took a much sterner line with Jethro than I did. While liking our teenage mule – and admiring his spirit – Jasper felt he had been living too much on the fat of the land at the RSPCA and 'getting away with it'. He thought we should, in a firm but fair way, put Jethro through 'Mule Camp'. He would be well looked after, fed and cared for – but not allowed to behave with quite the truculence he had shown at the RSPCA, where his carers had needed a special Monty Roberts Dually halter to control him.

One reason for delaying our departure to October was that, while late in the year, so risky with the weather, it was the first time Jasper was able to join me, and I was sure the journey would be more successful – indeed, perhaps only possible – with him.

By the start of our journey, we no longer needed to use the Dually halter on Jethro unless crossing roads. While he could still be difficult – especially when it came to being caught, a tedious task at the start of each day – the pre-match training had generally gone well, and he had been a good and patient passenger in the horse lorry as we drove north.

There was plenty of petrol in his own tank as he frisked up the headland. 'Easy, boy,' said Jasper. 'You've got 200 miles still to go.'

At the point of the St Bees coast where we turned inland, memorial headstones and flowers had been placed on a small headland that jutted out to sea. Some touching remembrances had been engraved on the stones: 'See you again'; 'Your favourite place'.

'Do you think people have wanted their ashes to be scattered here because it's the start of the Coast-to-Coast?' I asked Jasper.

'I think they must have. Amazing how important walking becomes to people – particularly the elderly, when it can be their only form of exercise. One of the few ways they can still enjoy themselves, get out and about.'

'Yes, and people can become hefted to places, like sheep. Like Wainwright having his ashes scattered in the Lake District. I always find memorial benches moving, whether in a municipal park or with some fabulous view, like this one out over the Atlantic. That sense of coming back home . . . '

'I think so, and some people find walking has been the best part of their life.' Jasper paused to adjust Jethro's head collar. 'And something, moreover, they've always done. That has continuity.

They may have walked a place as a child, an adult and when old. And for complicated people – and most of us are – walking has a simplicity to it that is very compelling. You just keep putting your feet in front of you.'

✻

The thin strip of land between the coast and the Lake District is a quiet and gentle bit of countryside with a handy bridle path converted from an old railway line: an uneventful stretch before you enter the fairy-tale castellations of the Lake District, which has always been a place of enchantment for me.

But the Lakes would have to wait. There was something I had to do first a little to the north of our route – and something I needed to do on my own.

Leaving Jasper and Jethro in a snug farmhouse, I went to a quiet bit of unassuming countryside near Wigton. It was not a place I had ever visited before. Nor was it an area to attract tourists, being both remote and relatively flat compared to the neighbouring Lake District. But it had a huge emotional pull for me.

It was where my mother's ancestors had come from.

The signpost to Stoneraise Place was on a small country lane. I approached nervously down the drive, both because I had not been able to contact the current owners beforehand and because there were a lot of dogs barking. A handsome Georgian farmhouse lay up ahead, with modern agricultural buildings behind it.

A St Bernard bounded towards me, followed by a large young man in wellington boots.

'Sorry, we're in the middle of moving cattle. Don't worry, he won't bite. What can I do for you?'

I noticed a memorial stone on the front wall of the farmhouse to help me out: to William H. Bragg, my great-grandfather, who had been born here and gone on to become a successful physicist. I explained I was a descendant.

'Oh, OK. Well, have a look round. But you'll have to do it all on your own, I'm afraid. We're a bit busy.'

I wandered off into the garden in front of the house; overhanging trees cast deep shadows over the long grass and there were wood pigeons cooing overhead. Half-buried in the border was a rusting old ploughshare. The letters punched out in metal across the yoking band proclaimed it to have been made by Nicholsons of Newark. It looked suitably nineteenth-century, although abandoned farm machinery ages fast.

A woman's voice ambushed me.

'It wasn't theirs.'

She came bustling out of the house. 'Sorry, I'm Lorna – we're in the middle of everything but my son said you were here. The ploughshare. It isn't theirs. We brought it with us as an antique. As soon as my son said you were looking round the garden, I guessed you'd find it and think it had been lying in the grass ever since the Braggs left.'

I knew from old family records that Robert Bragg had bought this house in 1858. The Bragg family is a big one in this part of Cumbria. Robert's side of the family had a long tradition of going to sea, unsuccessfully. His father and grandfather had both drowned as merchant seamen. Notwithstanding this daunting precedent, Robert signed up as a sixteen-year-old and sailed to India. He was made First Mate within a few years. However, after a spectacular shipwreck off Calcutta, when he was one of the few survivors, he decided it was time to stick to dry ground and came home.

He was only twenty-five but had somehow acquired enough money to buy Stoneraise Place, whether through a lucky inheritance or some smart bit of trading in India. While the farmhouse was a handsome building, it only had a small amount of agricultural land attached. Since then the farm had expanded considerably: Lorna and her husband now had some 600 acres, which they either owned or rented.

Lorna was interested in the Braggs, which was lucky as I had been able to discover very little about them from family records. She had even gone to the nearby churchyard to copy out Robert's gravestone, as she was worried that it was becoming eroded. She suggested I go over to the church to have a look for myself.

As I walked over the field in his footsteps, in the clear sunlight, the whole of what must have been Robert Bragg's compass seemed visible: the farm, his fields, the church and the hills of the Northern Fells beyond. The grass on the long sloping hill was speckled with tufts of sheep's wool, carded white against the green.

A story came back to me, one that my mother had told me many times when I was a child and which had always fascinated me.

Robert had often taken this route, and not only to attend services. After buying the farmhouse, he successfully courted the vicar's daughter, Mary, who played the organ at the church. On the day of their wedding he would have taken this same path.

I could imagine him on that day in May 1861. Once he had crossed oceans, at the mercy of heavy seas and vulnerable ships. Now he was on top of the world: a master of his own destiny, walking on his own land towards the woman he was going to marry.

Yet somewhere along the way, he managed to drop the new gold wedding ring he had bought for the occasion. Bought with most of his year's earnings, but more importantly, bought as a token of his affection and love. He had inscribed it with their interlinked initials.

Poets over the millennia have covered many acres of paper with laments over lost love. Very few have written about the pain of lost possessions. That clutching of the lungs: how could I have been so stupid? Why did I not value more something that was so precious to me and allow it to be mislaid? The overconfidence that comes when something matters to you so much that you assume it will stay connected, as if by an umbilical cord.

Perhaps he lost the ring because he was so happy. It was the sort of thing I could have done myself. I can imagine him rubbing it in his pocket, talismanic. Taking it out to feel the reassuring weight. Only for it to slip when he put it back.

One of his brothers, as best man, gamely offered his own ring as a standby. Then after the service, Robert had another one made. By that time, there was much joking and jollity about the wedding that needed three rings – although when it happened, and given the cost of the ring for a farmer who had scant resources, it was a calamity.

The first years of the marriage were happy ones. Mary was by all accounts a gentle and kind person, much loved. A letter survives that Robert sent to his wife on one of their rare separations, when he went with his brothers to attend one of the Great Exhibitions in London. The tone is teasing and affectionate: 'I do hope you will take every care of yourself and do please be lazy, that's just what I want you to be, at least for the present . . . '

Three sons quickly followed – the oldest, William, my future great-grandfather. But a fourth pregnancy proved fatal. A combination of pneumonia and pleurisy caused a dreadful protracted and premature labour, which lasted for nine days and ended in Mary's death.

'To be honest,' Lorna had told me, 'and I know this might sound funny, I've always sensed the ghost of Mary in the drawing room. That must be where she would have been confined. And where she passed away.'

I wondered if that was why Lorna had gone over to trace the gravestone. I found Mary's tomb where Lorna had described, on the overgrown slope beside the path up from the fields. I was glad she had told me, as the engraved writing had worn smooth. Husband and wife had been buried together. Mary had been just thirty-seven when she died. Robert survived for another two decades, before dying at fifty-four – my age. Still young, as far as I was concerned.

When I got back to Stoneraise Place, the cattle had been put in their sheds. The cheerful sound of afternoon Radio Two mixed with the echoing hooves of heifers shunting around on the concrete. Along with the cattle, Lorna told me, she and her husband Peter took in sheep over winter to fatten them up for the fells.

Now that she had more time, she added, there was something else I should see. She sent me up to the top of the old wheelhouse. The building was full of all the detritus that accumulates in a farm – rusting machinery, canvas sacks, even an old shoe beneath layers of dust. It was dark, but using the torch application on my phone I could see up the stairs and across the rafters which, just as Lorna had warned me, were partially rotten.

Right at the end was a long roof-beam with the names of three boys carved into the wood: James Bragg, J. W. Bragg and William Addison – Robert's two younger boys and their cousin. But not the name of my great-grandfather William.

For after his mother's death, he was, for reasons that family history has never quite satisfactorily explained, sent away. His father ended up selling the farm and going to live on the Isle of Man, and arranged for William to go and live with an uncle hundreds of miles distant in Leicestershire. He was only seven.

Perhaps it was too much for Robert to look after all three boys – although in that case, would he not have sent away the youngest, rather than the older one who could have helped? Or it may have been thought that William, who was already showing promise, would benefit from the better schools in Leicester.

Certainly his uncle, who was a pharmacist, encouraged him in his scientific studies, to the extent that he managed to get to

Cambridge, where he became a good mathematician and even better physicist, going on to win the Nobel Prize. But the emotional damage of losing both his mother and, effectively, his father (for he rarely saw Robert again) seems to have been heavy for William. His own daughter always said that he found close relationships impossible.

He inherited some of his father's restless, seafaring streak, travelling to Australia. But he also returned to the farm at least once in later life. I know because, almost unbelievably, I discovered that there was still someone living locally who remembered him.

George Bainbridge was eighty-four and lived in a small bungalow nearby with his wife Isabel. When I went to see them, George had only recently returned from a long stay in hospital and was frail. Isabel was not sure whether he would be able to see me as he was sleeping. But he came down to join us when he heard voices in the hall.

George's family had bought Stoneraise Place from the man Robert Bragg had sold it to, as that farmer had gone bankrupt. George had grown up in Stoneraise Place and was there when my great-grandfather returned in October 1936. William H. Bragg, who by then was very old himself, had afterwards sent a book he had written for children to the young George. George looked it out to show me.

'I remember him well,' George told me, 'when he came back, as an old man. He was very reserved. And by then he was moving slowly. But he wanted to see everything. It must have been hard, that farm, back when he was born. They only had a scraggy bit of land. No wonder it made farmers bankrupt or broke their spirits. The house was big – a huge house, I always think – but they had less than a hundred acres. Quite a lot less – just eighty. Amazing, though, that people in the old days managed to make a living from so little. Some people could live off twenty acres. Don't know how they did it, I really don't . . . '

George's family had expanded the farm over the generations they had been there. By the time he retired, they had a herd of 100 cows. But living conditions had still not been easy. As Isabel told me, mains electricity only arrived at Stoneraise Place in 1957. Up until then, they had used the cellar for refrigeration, curing pigs on one side of it and making butter on the other. George's mother had sold her butter on market day in Wigton, as Mary Bragg had once done.

I asked if the countryside had changed a lot in their time.

'Not much,' said George. 'The high communications mast on the hill, of course. But most of this is what your great-grandfather would have seen.' He waved out of the window.

'Although perhaps not the llamas,' I suggested.

George and Isabel, who were supposed to have retired – 'but you've got to do something, haven't you?' – had started breeding llamas. Ten or so of them were in the paddock. This was after a brief experiment with ostriches, who had proved volatile and 'had claws that could rip you up', according to Isabel.

That said, the llamas brought their own concerns. When they had recently got in a stud to impregnate the females, George was worried the male had not shown himself up to the job.

'A feller let us have him on the cheap. To be honest, I think he was just getting him going as a stud, which is why he didn't charge too much. But the male looked a bit lost. Hadn't a clue what he was doing, as far as I could see.' He paused. 'I have my doubts anything will come of it.'

'Ah well,' Isabel added wisely. 'Only time will tell.'

I said my goodbyes and headed off down the lane. When I

came to the gate that led over from Robert's farm, I stopped again. I could see the church clearly, lying over the fields in a little dip of the valley below. My heart gave a lurch. For the part of the story about the lost ring that had always caught at me when my mother told it – the part that seemed out of a Thomas Hardy novel – was the coda.

Many years after the wedding, Robert had again taken this same route across the fields, as he did so often. Yet this time, he had seen something glinting in the mud, near a stile. It was the lost wedding ring, engraved with Mary's and his initials. A particular angle of the sun had picked it out. Miraculously, he had found it once more – but by that time, Mary was dead.

As I drove back in the last rays of sunlight to meet up with Jethro and Jasper, I thought that in some ways I was undertaking this journey to find something I had myself lost or, as can happen along the way, a core truth I needed to rediscover.

There were parts of England – like the Lakes – that were familiar, although it was many years since I had first experienced their vertiginous rush. Others, like the Yorkshire Dales and Moors, I knew less well, for no good reason other than laziness. And some I had never been to at all. After a restless life, I needed to get to know my own country once more. To find the ring glinting in the mud.

✲

# Chapter 2

# The Naked Muleteer

In the matter of water, mules are somewhat dainty and if the
supply is not to their taste will, unless extremely thirsty, decline
to drink.

The War Office, *Animal Management* (London, 1923)

The Honister is the first big pass you reach when coming
into the Lake District from the north-west. It lies at the
top of a narrow, steep valley, with quarries to one side. As we
breached the pass we could see the gentler slopes of Borrowdale
descending ahead.

I wanted to take Jethro along the old pack pony path that
wound from the quarries over towards the spectacular ring of
mountains of the Western Fells, centred on the domed anvil of
Great Gable. The path was called Old Moses Trod after a
nineteenth-century quarryman who had designed the route to
contour beautifully around the slope ahead of us, run for some
fifteen miles across the Western Fells through Wasdale Head, and
arrive at Ravenglass for the ships.

The only way to get the slate down from quarries like the
Honister was to carry it in panniers on pack ponies. And very
fine slate it was too. I have always loved the unusual deep green
hidden in the grey of the stone which is only visible in certain
lights, the result of the ferrous oxide content in the fine volcanic
dust and ash. The slate from quarries further east, like Kirkby,
is more blue, while that of Wales is a far plainer grey, to my eyes
at least.

The non-porous, non-staining qualities of Lakeland slate have always been thought desirable. From at least the seventeenth century, when local records began, and probably from long before, it was mined at the Honister and other local sites to cover the roofs of northern England. First, the slate was blasted out of the quarry; then it was 'docked up' – turned into manageable lumps – before workers called 'rivers' would with great skill use a wedge-ended hammer to split the rock neatly down the cleavage plane. It was a source of considerable pride to the 'rivers' that they never needed to use a chisel. Finally, the slate would be dressed and polished before a line of pack animals would take it away and over the mountains.

We had a welcome cup of tea at the small café by the quarry workshops and I commissioned, for a modest fee, something I had long wanted: an engraved nameplate for my house, with the slate surface polished but the edges left rough-hewn. The lady at the shop showed me some samples, with script ranging from Old English to the wild Century Gothic. I settled for the more sedate Times New Roman.

'You're not from Wales, are you?' she asked, with concern. 'You don't sound like you are. Not that I've got anything against the Welsh. But some of their house names are so long. It means we have to charge extra.'

Some people find the Honister Pass grim and the quarries ugly. It holds the record as the wettest place in Britain, and when the rains come down it can be miserable. But we had arrived on a day of clear sunshine.

We were only a little into the journey, yet Jethro was already walking quietly and calmly as we set off from the quarry shop; his ears set back, he looked engaged and interested. Jasper thought he had already lost a bit of weight. His cinches were fitting better and he was a smartly turned-out mule as well, in a striped

Colorado riding blanket I had borrowed from Pippa, together with some leather saddlebags.

'If we let him loose now when we were having a picnic, would he just take off or hang around?' I wondered idly to Jasper.

'He wouldn't take off at all. He's decided we're his herd. Not a very pleasant herd, and decidedly lacking in intelligence, with terrible ears, but about as good as he's going to get, so he's making the best of it.'

There were different ways up to the high ground, but Jasper suggested we might as well take the full-frontal approach up the steep and stony old miners' tramway. This was how the slate was originally lowered from the quarries.

Some school kids were sitting with their teacher on the track eating sandwiches, and we were a welcome diversion. They had come all the way from Gateshead – a long four-hour round journey to make for a school geography outing. But then the people of Tyneside have always loved the Lake District.

The teacher was telling them that the nearby pile of stones had once been a drum house which operated the cable of the tramway back down to the cutting sheds, so that the loads could be lowered. Like most industrial archaeology, it was the sort of detail more likely to appeal to an adult than a child. I could tell that he had lost his audience, who were preoccupied with who had got what flavour sandwiches and crisps.

'So, are you a business?' the teacher asked us, with the direct tone of someone used to getting prompt answers from the class – and perhaps as a way of getting back his own class's attention.

'What do you mean?' I was puzzled. My wife pointed out to me on a regular basis that writing could in no way be considered a business. More a lifestyle with benefits.

'Are you a business? Do you carry picnics up for people?'

It wasn't such a bad idea – except that Jethro was unwilling to carry very much. He had the smallest saddlebags I'd ever seen on a mule: no bigger than the clutch bags carried by ladies who lunch. We were, as we pointed out to him occasionally, carrying far more on our own backs. He would never have made the grade carrying slate from the quarry. I hadn't even been able to fit my new slate nameplate into his saddlebag to give him a spurious sense of historical validity.

The school kids asked about Jethro. By now I had a good brisk description of the difference between a horse, a mule and a donkey down pat. And they were impressed he had his own Facebook page – an idea of Jasper's; for someone who liked to imply he would have been far happier living on horseback in the nineteenth century, Jasper was an avid user of social media. Although we were both irritated that Jethro had in a short space of time acquired more 'likes' than either of us.

'So does that mean,' said one chubby kid, with the kind of leer that even though I have never been a teacher I could tell was trouble, 'they can't have children themselves? I mean, you know, can mules have *sex* and that?'

The class dissolved in titters and gave muffled snorts through their bags of crisps. It was time to move on. I left their teacher to explain things. He was, after all, the professional. Although for any readers who are wondering, the answer to that last question is 'yes'.

For a late October day, it was unseasonably mild and sunny, giving us views of the sea through the gaps in the mountains. Wordsworth always claimed that October was the best month in the Lakes. To the north, I could even make out the faint glimmer of wind farms far offshore in the Atlantic.

Below us was the strange geological formation of Haystacks.

Even in the clear sunshine it was a confusing mass of upturned rock formations, an extended plateau which commanded the valleys to either side like an enormous aircraft carrier.

It was impossible to look down on Haystacks without remembering it was the final resting place of Britain's best-loved mountain guide. Alfred Wainwright's beautifully produced volumes have become so iconic – there can be few walkers in Britain who have not held one – that we sometimes forget what an extraordinary achievement they were. Handwritten and hand-drawn, these are books made with the love and dedication of a medieval monk; and for Wainwright, his descriptions of each Lake District climb, along with maps and the odd trenchant comment, were worthy of a lifetime's devotion.

The quality of his draughtsmanship was legendary. He used a special set of 1901 OS maps with the outrageous scale of six inches to the mile to make sure he got every detail right. Having spent the better part of a year on his first guide, he scrapped the lot and started all over again because he wasn't satisfied with the right-hand margin. But there is also a quiet underlying wit which has helped many a walker through bog and mist.

I once heard of a woman who had designed her wedding invitation to look like a Wainwright illustration. There were dotted lines to lead guests from car park to church to marquee, 'where *hopefully* the best man will keep his speech short'.

Alfred Wainwright was born in Blackburn in 1907. Despite doing well at school, he left early, at the age of thirteen, and worked as a clerk first in Blackburn's council offices and then Kendall's. In 1930, when he was twenty-three, he went to the Lake District for the first time, and began what he later described as 'a love affair with the Lakes', producing a prodigious number of books celebrating their landscape. He died in 1991.

Nor did he stop at the Lakes. He devised and published *A Coast to Coast Walk* from St Bees on the Cumbrian coast to Robin Hood's Bay on the east coast, a walk that has now become one of the most popular in the world. Although we were not following the exact route of Wainwright's Coast-to-Coast — for the obvious reason that he used footpaths while we needed bridleways — I had charted a rough approximation across country.

But however far he wandered, the heartland of the Lake District for Wainwright was these Western Fells, the mountains that fan out from Great Gable between the lakes of Wastwater and Buttermere. It was the area about which he wrote the last and most personal of his acclaimed series of seven Lakeland books ('guides' is surely an inadequate term) in 1966, when he was falling in love with the woman who was to become his second wife; and it is where he chose to be remembered after his death. Not coincidentally, it is one of the least visited corners of the Lakes, furthest from the M6 and the tourist magnets of Grasmere and Dove Cottage. You have to work to get here, and I'm sure that appealed to him. Wainwright did not go into the hills for company.

It is also the area I know best, which is why it felt like a homecoming.

✳

For many years, I have had a recurring dream. I stand on the top of Fleetwith Pike in the early morning. Below me, coming up the Honister Pass and fanning out, are the hunters. I stand deliberately on the very top of the peak so they can see me silhouetted against its chiselled ridge. Then I blow the horn. The noise carries and echoes off Great Gable, Haystacks, Kirkfell. And the hunters start moving with renewed purpose towards me.

I turn and run back off the Pike and along the narrow edge that drops sharply down towards the lake of Buttermere. It feels as if I am running off the top of the world. I run with both adrenaline and the horn beating against my chest. I can no longer see my pursuers, but I sense they are behind me. Buttermere seems to be under my feet, but also miles away. The hunters follow me and although I can no longer see them, I hear their voices over the bluff of the hill, echoing in the slate quarries of the Honister Pass.

The dream comes from the days when I took part in fell-running man-hunts across this area. A few runners were selected each day to be chased down by the rest of the pack. As a way of getting to know every last twist and turn of the landscape, it was hard to beat. Runners would deliberately access the most remote and difficult terrain, from scree slope to hidden high ravine. The broken tussocks of Haystacks, right in the centre of the hunting area and the Western Fells – and Wainwright's favourite place 'for a man with a persistent puzzle on his mind' – could hide a determined 'hare' for hours, as the hunters circled round their prey, hearing his horn but never seeing him in the geological maze.

I tried to explain the hunt to Jasper, with only a modicum of embarrassment at the antics of supposedly grown men chasing each other over the hills.

'But this is a huge area.' Jasper gave a sweep of his hands at the twenty square miles in front of us, from the Honister Pass to Wasdale Head. 'Surely, the hares just get lost. So it must be frustrating to be a hunter.'

'The hares wear red sashes which are visible for a long way. And everyone can hear the horns they blow for miles. There are usually three or four hares each day, criss-crossing the area, so the hunters have a good chance of finding one – as long as the hares give good sport and keep running rather than hiding, which would be too easy.' My much faster and fitter brother Ben had once gone and hidden for some time under a log in Ennerdale Forest, about which I occasionally teased him (not least because at the time he was being chased by me).

'And what happens when they catch you? If they catch you,' asked Jasper politely, and unnecessarily, as I have always been very thoroughly caught.

'Uh – we all stop for a sandwich.'

For this being a very English affair, instead of ripping me apart in bacchanalian fashion after the passions of the chase, my pursuers would then pause for some genial conversation – before I would set off again, blowing my horn to lead on a new set of hounds.

It was something I had done in college, and then later at intermittent intervals through every decade of my life, so it had provided continuity; even if it was also a measuring stick by which to gauge my increasing slowness of speed. The last time the Master of the Lake Hunt had asked me to be a hare, I had refused on the grounds that, at fifty, I would be caught so often my entire day would be spent eating sandwiches and discussing the weather with jubilant hunters. I might even put on weight, which would defeat the whole point of the exercise.

Just across from Fleetwith Pike, where I had often led the hunters, we could look back to see the Honister quarries more clearly from afar. A few years previously, they had been at the centre of a controversial attempt to attract younger visitors to the Lakes. Mark Weir, a flamboyant local entrepreneur who flew to work in a helicopter, had already built a *via ferrata*, a climbing route with fixed holds and aids, in the old quarry workings. He had also reopened part of the site, making it the only working slate quarry in the entire country, and set up the shop. Now he wanted to add a zip-wire, so that those of an adventurous disposition could swing down and across for 4,000 feet from the summit.

There was uproar. The Friends of the Lake District, a local pressure group, declared, 'This is just the wrong place for a new visitor attraction aiming to attract large numbers of people.' But

I disagreed, very publicly, in a piece for *The Times*. It seemed to me that without just this sort of expansion of tourist activities, the area could die on its leather-booted feet. Not all children get excited at the idea of a day's walking in the hills with a packed lunch. And the Lake District can't live on sheep, tea-shops and Beatrix Potter dishcloths alone. Moreover, the original quarry would have had pulley wires slung all over the place, so in some ways, I argued, Mark was attempting a restoration; the council should have given him a grant.

The zip-wire never happened, and Mark died tragically in a helicopter accident not long afterwards. Many locals remember him as someone who, while controversial, tried his best to bring much-needed employment to the area.

Would A. W. (he would have thought it overfamiliar to call him plain Alfred) have approved of the project? Wainwright was not sentimental – and was always interested in the industrial archaeology he came across on his walks – so might have been sympathetic, at least to the idea of employment. Perhaps not to the zip-wire, however: he would have seen that as an abominable way of getting down a mountain, although the thought of him taking one is agreeably comic. And I also liked to play out a fantasy in my head in which some fell-running hare, cornered by a set of baying hounds, would take to the zip-wire and swing like Douglas Fairbanks Jr over the heads of his pursuers with a merry quip, the horn tucked into his bright red sash. 'Some hare'? I must, as always, be honest with my readers. In any such fantasy, it would of course have been myself.

As we got closer, Haystacks unfolded her many layers of fascinating complexity below us. It is possible to wander for hours around those heather-clad knolls and never quite take the same route twice: a delight for a hare trying to hide from his pursuers, and a great spectator sport if you happened to be, as we were now, above Haystacks. I had seen a hare run up to the top of one of the mounds, toot a horn cheekily at his pursuers, and then be away and up another mound before the hounds had even reached the first one, a game that could continue for some time.

At the centre of Haystacks was Innominate Tarn, a lake that some argue Wainwright named (if you can be said to name something that is innominate). On earlier maps – like my old OS map from the 1970s, which cost £1.50, dating it considerably – it is anonymous. More recent ones have followed the name he gave in his guide: 'nameless tarn'.

That it was a special place for him is clear. In *Fellwanderer*, his autobiography, he made a very public wish to have his ashes scattered 'where the water gently laps the gravelly shore and the heather blooms and Pillar and Gable keep unfailing watch. A quiet place, a lonely place. I shall go to it, for the last time, and be carried: someone who knew me in life will take me and empty me out of a little box and leave me there alone.' And this is indeed what happened.

Looking down at the heather-rimmed tarn, in the bowl of what Wainwright called 'the sunset side' of the Lakes, I also remembered the typically self-deprecating comment with which he had followed this rare statement of emotion: 'And if you, dear reader, should get a bit of grit in your boot as you are crossing Haystacks in the years to come, please treat it with respect. It might be me.'

Jethro chose that moment to disturb my contemplation by bolting sharply. Quite what it was that alarmed him, I'm not too sure; nor was this the first or last time it happened on our journey. It may have been a walker with a dog who was approaching, and was now amused to see two grown men running after the rope trailing behind Jethro, like balloonists who had lost their balloon.

'You need to keep that donkey under control,' he said helpfully, with a laugh.

Jasper and I were too out of breath to respond.

A little later that day, despite having walked and run this route many times, and even with the Wainwright guide to hand, I managed to get lost contouring around Moses Trod. The paths had divided over the years, without the cohesion any more of being a pack-pony route. Humans are more prone to wander than animals led in teams. Or at least, that was my excuse.

At one point, therefore, Jasper and I found ourselves retracing our steps uphill, never good for morale. It was a reminder of the complete illusion that you somehow get wiser when old. This was an area I was supposed to know 'like the back of my hand'; but then, as I told myself, I didn't often study the back of my hand – in fact, would challenge anyone to draw the back of theirs without looking, and would find it slightly sad if they could.

In my defence – as I pointed out to Jasper, who at this early stage in the walk still assumed I might know what I was doing – the route had changed in many places to negotiate a newly strengthened boundary fence, which in the old days, as Wainwright attested, was broken and not much of an obstacle. The boundary fence was a rude reminder of something I had managed so far wilfully to ignore. Despite Moses Trod having always been a bridleway in the past, constructed for pack ponies, it had now reverted to footpath status; so when we came to the boundary fence, there was a quite legitimate – and impassable – stile. This was something we would encounter right along our journey.

We did what any expedition from the Andes to the Himalaya does when faced with a problem. We stopped for lunch.

While Jethro munched on some carrots and grass, Jasper and I made do with chunks of chorizo and Cheddar, with the odd sandwich. It reminded me of being caught in the middle of a lake hunt.

Jasper and I discussed how many obstacles we had already encountered in trying to get a mule across the countryside. For I was beginning to realise that to take a pack animal across

England, which once would have been so natural as to attract no notice, was now working against the lie of the land; that the route was bifurcated with everything from stiles to boundary fences to the six lanes of the M6. The process of enclosure, begun so controversially in the eighteenth century, was still continuing.

＊

Just then a woman came down the hill. She was in her forties, with a warm, approachable face. We asked if there was any way of getting Jethro over the fence higher up – which there wasn't. But we did get to talking. There's nothing like having a mule to provide a conversation point.

Sarah was attempting to 'do the Wainwrights' – all the hills and mountains described in his guides, of which there are 214, so a considerable undertaking. But that was only the start of her adventure.

'I've given up my job. Given up work completely. I've moved out of my house and I'm living in a camper van. In a few weeks' time, as the weather gets bad, I'm heading south. To Spain, maybe Morocco. England's just going to be my summer holiday destination from now on. So it may take a while before I finish the Wainwrights. A few years at least.'

She was talking in a rush, in the way of someone who has pent up a great deal.

'At the moment I don't always know where I'm going to sleep. I could just stay over this evening in the Honister car park. Although I could do with buying a bottle of wine to keep warm. At least I've got a camper van. I met someone yesterday who was just going to put up a tent on Haystacks. Now that would be chilly in October.

'I don't have heating in the van. It's not really a camper. It's just an old panel van. I mean it's lovely, it looks more like a gypsy boat on the inside. It's got a curved roof and the cupboards are all home-made and look slightly Moroccan. So it's beautiful. . . but cold!'

Sarah asked what the plan was with Jethro and where we were heading; in return, I wondered why she'd made the decision to leave everything behind and start a life on the road.

'Because I was sick of working to pay the rent, the council tax, the bills, the water rates and everything. My happy times were snatches of weekend here and there. I wanted more. More time. My life was a constant rush, always. Now I just want to be free. It's only two weeks since I packed in my job, so it's all come as a bit of a shock.

'I like your idea of travelling with a mule. I used to know this old couple who were in their seventies and had gone right off-grid. Gone solar, grew their own produce. Had nothing to do with the council. And the woman, Ruth, told me that when they were younger, they travelled right across country with a mule and a goat, stopping wherever they could and picking up odd jobs. And they did that for about seven or eight years before settling down. But they're still off-grid. Completely off-grid.

'Ruth told me that sometimes the mule would let her ride him, because she had a bad back, but the mule would always sense if her back was really giving her trouble or not. If she tried to ride him when she was actually OK, he wouldn't let her.'

Jasper gave what I was beginning to recognise as his patented wise muleteer's look.

'Ah yes, well, they're very intelligent, mules.' This sounded even more definitive with his soft, slow Irish accent.

He paused politely. 'So what were you doing before?'

'I worked in a school with special-needs students. Still keep in touch with some of them. Although they can only get in contact when they turn eighteen. I had to be strict about that. Wonderful job – I really loved my students. I had a text from one of them today who's just turned eighteen, saying "great, I can talk to you now!" I'll miss all that side of it, but I won't miss the stress.'

I asked how she would get down to Spain.

'Probably down through France, maybe staying for a while in the Dordogne, and over the Pyrenees into the Picos mountains. Then down through Portugal to the south of Spain. I was going to carry on into Morocco, but I'm a little bit . . . my brother is ex-army, but he still has to do with intelligence and he was telling me it's not really a good place to be travelling at the minute, with all the ISIS threats and everything. We'll see.'

'I guess you have to be careful,' I said. 'But it all sounds good and adventurous.'

'Slightly terrifying. I think, though, you have to push yourself out of your comfort zone in life. You have to. What's the alternative? Just wait for your retirement and die? I don't want to look back on my life and think, "What did I do for half of it? Worked and was tired and never had any time."'

Sarah went silent. I sensed there was more to the story, which all of a sudden came pouring out.

'The thing is, I started doing this all with my boyfriend. But before we were due to go, just before, he decided he didn't want to do it. And he didn't really want *me* either. So, you know, we split up. Which has been a shock, really. I keep thinking about it as I'm walking. This was going to be the thing we did together. Now I'm doing it on my own, which is much more difficult.

'Also it's his van, but I said I was taking it anyway.'

While Jasper and I absorbed this last revelation, she told us the van had a shallow space cut out at the back for a shower. 'It's great if I'm on my own and can have a shower in the open. And can sing for happiness. But if I need to keep the back door shut, it's a little claustrophobic.'

Sarah reminded me of Vashti Bunyan, the folk singer who had travelled north from London to Skye in a horse-drawn caravan in 1968, composing the songs that went into her album *Just Another Diamond Day* — songs I had played as we drove north with Jethro. Sarah was another remembrance of a time when there was still a yearning to be free, even if there was always the danger, in Janis Joplin's words, that 'freedom's just another word for nothing left to lose'. We wished her well on her adventure.

✳

Open country, indeed, it was. At this time it was scarcely cultivated save in a few fields round Seathwaite or Rosthwaite. It lay in purple shadows with splashes of glittering sunlight, a lost land, untenanted by man, no animal anywhere visible, dominated entirely by the mountains that hemmed it in. To David's right ran the path up to Honister, where the mines were; this country was forbidden ground, for here all the rascals and outcasts of the neighbourhood would congregate to scrape among the mine refuse and then sell the scraps of plumbago to the Jews in Keswick, who would meet them at 'The George' or 'The Half-Moon' and then bargain with them.

The stories were that titanic battles were fought above
Stye Head and on Honister between rival bands of robbers,
disputing their plunder, and it was true enough that many
a time, walking up Honister, you would find a dead man
there, by the roadside, his throat cut or a knife in his belly
and often enough stripped naked.

Hugh Walpole, *Rogue Herries*

Hugh Walpole's novel is an enjoyable bit of hokum about the
Western Fells. Published in 1930, *Rogue Herries* received rapturous
accolades from critics. John Buchan said it was the best novel in
English since *Jude the Obscure*; a judgement so delightfully absurd
that it needs to be viewed against the literary politics of the time,
when established figures like Buchan, Wells and Arnold Bennett
were fighting the forces of modernism in a rearguard action.

Walpole is now an almost forgotten figure, with few of his books
in print. Well considered in his day, he was knighted for services to
literature – and was more popular on lecture tours of the United
States than Charles Dickens had been. The *Herries Chronicles* performed for the Lake District what *Poldark* did later for Cornwall:
ripped open the bodices and celebrated a family of 'drunken,
robbing freebooters'. The books chart the fortunes of the Herries
family, beginning with the 'Rogue' of the first book, a swashbuckler
who chases wild gypsy women and challenges any man who crosses
him to a duel.

Some contemporaries were amused that it should be
Walpole – a gay aesthete and avid collector of fine books and
antiques – who championed the wilder shores of the Lake District. He had, said Anthony Powell, 'that exacting brand of
homosexuality which drew him towards middle-aged married
men'. The Rogue's son David is a quieter, more reflective figure,
more in the author's own image, who is uncomfortable with
women, and the sagas continue right up to the twentieth century
in a sweep that attempts the epic.

But Walpole was appealingly self-deprecating. He described his *Rogue Herries* more accurately than Buchan as 'a fine, queer book in the big manner', and confessed he had allowed himself to be, for the first time in his adult life, 'what I really am – a little boy telling stories in the dormitory'. He was well aware that it was no longer possible to be successful with both the public and modernist critics: 'There is at the present time the superstition far too general among clever people, that if a book has any large sale, it cannot be good literature.'

'It was true enough that many a time, walking up Honister, you would find a dead man there' is a delightful conceit, not made any more likely by the corroborating detail: ' . . . his throat cut or a knife in his belly and often enough stripped naked'. It is not at all 'true enough', even though the plunder they were disputing, plumbago – which we would now call graphite – was of exceptional quality and some of the finest in the world. Walpole was just trying to animate a dramatic landscape with events that lived up to its operatic scale: Rogue Herries sells his mistress at an auction, a woman accused of being a witch is drowned and there are brigands behind every bush.

But in a way, what makes the Lake District so sublime is the very mundanity of its inhabitants. It is from the humble bus trundling up the Borrowdale valley – the one that Wainwright took at the end of his visits to his beloved Haystacks – or for that matter when trudging along with a mule, that the scale and grandeur of the peaks are at their most magnificent.

\*

There was another drovers' road I wanted to explore in the Lake District.

An old pack-horse route leads up from Threlkeld into the

Northern Fells around Skiddaw. My old friend Jeff Ford, who lived locally, told me it had been preserved as a bridleway, so we would not have the same difficulties we had experienced on Moses Trod. Jeff knew the area well and agreed to accompany us.

He went even further: he offered to put us up for a couple of nights. As I should explain to the reader who is interested – and apologise to the reader who isn't – there were some complicated logistics involved in getting Jethro cross-country. In Peru, you could simply stop for the night wherever you got to that day, and park your mule next to the tent – but I realised this might be unpopular in England, unless I had made prior arrangements. Instead, I had to set up a relay of bases where we could stay between stages of the walk, ferrying Jethro back and forwards in the Dodge horse van. This meant we could always carry on where we had left off before – or, as now, accommodate a small diversion.

We met Jeff near Threlkeld. He was duly impressed by our horse lorry (all five and a half tons of it). The Dodge was so old that it had a rope you pulled on to lower the ramp at the back, as if lowering a stage prop. And the whole process seemed theatrical, revealing the pantomime mule within, who sashayed down the ramp with great aplomb, as if it were a red carpet. I felt like the husband of some glamorously dressed starlet, keeping at a respectful rope's length from Jethro's left shoulder. A couple of other assembled walkers in the small car park gave an appreciative ripple of applause which Jethro pretended not to notice.

Jeff was a reassuringly large and steadfast presence. I had always liked him, since we first met on an expedition to the Nanda Devi Sanctuary in the Himalaya – not least because, among a bunch of mountaineers who often took themselves seriously, he had a well-developed sense of humour.

It was partly for that reason I had invited him to join me on an expedition to the Andes a few years later, an expedition for which we had both horses and mules. And on which, as he now reminded me, as leader I had got them all lost. Several times.

It was those expeditions in the Andes which had made me fall in love with the idea of a mule train: a line of mules, their bells tinkling, winding up a track, with the muleteers calling out instructions in a Spanish rich with imprecations and affection.

Clearly I was going to be more limited with just Jethro. And tempting as it was to let out the odd cry of '¡Mula, Mula, carrazo!', it might alarm the Lake District natives. But there was still a certain romance to walking through the hills with a pack animal: Jethro in his white and red horse blanket with the Iranian saddle and Jasper, about as near to a professional muleteer as the British Isles would allow.

Jasper's first question to Jeff as we started off was how the going would be up towards Skiddaw House: would there be grass verges to the track to give Jethro's feet a break after the rocky surfaces near the Honister slate quarries?

Jeff assured him that this part of the Lake District was less hammered from stone than Great Gable, and we soon settled into a relaxed pace as Jethro found the comfortable grass verges. We came to a small waterfall tumbling off the side of Blencathra and Jasper stopped.

'This is a dead ringer, with that little stream coming down and the curve of the hill, for a track I used to take in Morocco when I lived in a village there – must have taken it every day with a mule, so some sixty times.'

There were two ravens turning somersaults over our heads for the fun of it, having a dogfight with each other. What with the rowan trees by the waterfall, it felt very Celtic.

'Yes, like a scene Gavin Maxwell might have written,' Jasper suggested. '*Raven Seek Thy Brother* meets *Ring of Bright Water.*'

One of the things I liked so much about Jasper was that in addition to his fine mulemanship, he was a fine writer with a wide knowledge of travel literature. The reason he spent so much time house-sitting on a commercial basis was that he could write comfortably from those houses, as if enjoying a long series of holiday lets while being paid for it at the same time – ideal for an author. The houses tended to the large and luxurious side, and I teased him occasionally that he was used to gracious living; not something I could offer on this trip across England. But then he still did plenty of the rough stuff as well. He had recently walked from Munich to Paris in the footsteps of one of his heroes, the German film director Werner Herzog. And his book about canoeing around the entire coast of Ireland was both epic and enterprising.

On a fine summer's day before this journey began, we had wandered along the Thames from Wittenham Clumps and swum out into the river, not far from one of those gracious houses, talking of Roger Deakin and putting the world to rights. Jasper had also been in demand as a guest at local parties in Oxfordshire for his Irish gift for telling a story and the slightly glamorous, rakish air he had about him.

We had come to a rivulet running down off the hills. As this was the last stream for a while, we wanted Jethro to drink. But as with horses, you can only lead a mule to water. Only after Jasper gave a peculiar noise of encouragement, like a kettle running dry, did Jethro bend his head and begin.

'It's a curious thing. A descending whistle for some reason makes a mule want to drink. You hear muleteers doing it all over the world. And they haven't learned that from each other. Each country's worked it out for themselves. The whistle tells the mule this might be the last bit of water for the next few hours.'

'So how does that work?'

'No idea. Some sort of mental structure they have.'

Jasper was settling into a familiar role for him, that of mule whisperer.

'I always find that walking with an animal is like a marriage – without the sex, of course,' he pronounced.

I refrained from reminding Jasper, a lifelong bachelor, that for many, 'marriage is like a relationship – without the sex, of course.' I could tell he was, anyway, just warming up.

'Of course a mule is carrying your provisions for the trek, for a brief period. For the rest of the time, you're constantly worrying about him. Whether he's happy, about his feet, his clothing, his rugs, his straps and his girths.

'And then you have to worry about his food, whether he's eating the right stuff, whether he's eating the wrong stuff, whether he's in a field and not eating enough, has he got water, does he like the water? They can be fussy and quite often won't drink if they're suspicious of something.'

Jasper looked up at the cruel and empty sky and scratched his head under his beret.

'You have to worry about any rubs or sores, you have to worry about his ears, about his teeth and his gums. It's bloody *endless*.'

He sighed. Jeff and I tried hard to look sympathetic.

For it was true. One thing I had noticed about the equine world was the constant state of anxiety from which horse owners seemed to suffer. Any horse, and to a certain extent any mule, was always waiting to go wrong. Whenever we were settling Jethro for the night in a pasture next to neighbouring horses, the conversations with their owners revolved around a litany of problems:

ringworm, ragwort, hooves, bone spurs and every horse extremity which needed attention.

Over the last few years, I had spent more time on a bicycle than a horse. A bike had the great advantage that if you left it in the garage, it was unlikely to break down. Whereas the more you left horses alone, the more prone they were to malfunction. At least we were giving Jethro constant attention — which, I was beginning to suspect, he rather liked. And so far he was proving easy to maintain, with low mileage and running costs. A few carrots aside, he was perfectly happy with grass and some pony nuts.

It was still a strange thing to be travelling across England with a mule: strange, because while once the whole landscape would have been filled with pack animals and it would have been unusual to meet anyone who wasn't carrying goods, now these drovers' roads were like motorways without any cars.

And that also made it exhilarating: the sense of reanimating a landscape. Already I found the way that Jethro pulled us along — or held us back — gave a different rhythm to the way we walked. I was enjoying the difference.

Some way on from the little waterfall, we came to heather uplands that stretched ahead of us into the Northern Fells. The heather was in flower, one of the glories of late summer in the Lake District. Jasper described the heather-filled landscape in a lovely phrase as 'tweedy — full of bobbles and burrs and umber colours and knobbles and roughness'.

We met an older man striding across the heather towards us, lean and wiry, who had an attractive tensile strength to the way he phrased his sentences. 'I've come from Mungrisdale Common. The long way round. I know these fells so well, my navigation is getting sloppy.'

Jeff was sympathetic. 'There aren't many paths on Mungrisdale.'

The man had got lost on a few of the more anonymous-looking slopes. 'Difficult to tell if they're concave or convex.' Rather, as

I reminded Jasper later, what had happened when I managed to take the wrong twist óf Moses Trod – still an embarrassment.

I asked the walker about the disappearing bridleways.

'There's a reluctance these days to allow too many bridleways. Because a bridleway doesn't mean a horse, it means a cycle. And that can be controversial. A lot of people don't like the way you get close to the top of Helvellyn and meet a peloton coming down.

'Not just a lot of people. *I don't like it.* And some old bridleways have off-road vehicles using them. Quad bikes as well. They've carved out deep ruts in the grass. I'm surprised they're not down to the axles.

'So you're right, a lot of bridleways have been declassified. And I can see why.'

The man was intrigued by Jethro, although he kept his distance; I had noticed that it was women who instinctively went up to stroke him.

'I haven't seen a mule here for decades. Well – I haven't seen a mule anywhere for decades, to be honest. Last one I saw was in 1976, in Wales. It was a bit curious.'

He paused until he had our attention.

'There was a man and a woman. They were both naked.'

Jasper, Jeff and I – and probably Jethro – tensed a little as it was unclear where this story was going to go.

'So the man put on some sort of loincloth and approached us from about a hundred yards away, demurely, to see if we had any cigarettes. And he had a mule.'

We waited. But that seemed to be the end of the story.

The walker quickly made his apologies and left, as if realising his story had run out of steam. I never learned his name. But for some reason, Jasper and I remembered this story of the mysterious naked muleteer, and would refer to it for the rest of our journey, inventing plausible ways it could have played out. Or even begun. It reminded me of a basic precept of storytelling. Think of an odd and engaging scenario; try and work out how the characters got there.

✳

Skiddaw House lay ahead of us. It looked like something out of a Harry Potter film, a house that a witch forgot, encircled by trees on bleak moorland and with the wide expanse of the Northern Fells stretching away like the steppes. Once a shooting lodge and shepherd's bothy, it was described by Wainwright as being 'at the back o' beyond'. This, from Wainwright, was an affectionate term. But then he didn't like people.

At 1550 feet, Skiddaw House is the highest youth hostel in Britain. It is also one of the most remote. Normally these two statistics would make it an appealing prospect. But it had an unloved, unforgiving quality. Perhaps it was something about the grey stone. Without even stepping inside (which we couldn't, as it was closed during the day), I suspected it would have a shower worthy of 'Cell-block Number Nine'.

We stopped for a lunch that was fast becoming our standby: some oatcake biscuits (Jasper's healthy idea), great slabs of chorizo sausage (my less healthy one) and Cheddar. To be supplemented when possible by any locally available pies, although Skiddaw House looked the sort of place where Oliver would have asked for more. My keen instincts for foraging in the wild told me that, even if it had been open, pies would not have been available.

As we lounged against the low stone wall that surrounded the grounds of Skiddaw House, enjoying the autumn sun and our picnic, Jeff told us about the Bob Graham race, which began over the same fells we were now crossing.

The Bob Graham race is an epic of endurance. It's not only that the runners have to cover sixty-six miles in a day, hard enough in itself; each contestant also makes a cumulative ascent of nearly 27,000 feet by the time they've finished. That's like running up Everest.

And the running surface is not exactly tarmac-smooth. As Jethro had found, even on a bridle path the going is by no means easy, let alone when you're running the wrong way up a remote hill. So the roll-call of local athletes who have successfully completed the Bob Graham is a list of some considerable honour.

Bob Graham was the owner of a Keswick guest-house. In 1932, he decided to celebrate his forty-second birthday by traversing forty-two fells within a twenty-four-hour period – there's a lovely symmetry to that – and the race was born. It starts and finishes in the Moot Hall at Keswick, and has a carefully prescribed route. Almost 2,000 people have now completed it, although to qualify for the Bob Graham Club – which must be a scarily competitive place – you need a relay of companions to verify that you have ticked off each summit. And, although this is an unspoken assumption, in case anything goes wrong.

The fastest time ever set was that of Billy Bland of Borrowdale, who in 1982 completed the circuit in a breathtaking thirteen hours and fifty-three minutes, beating the previous record-holder by nearly four hours. His name still dominates the board in a drinking hole I'm fond of round the back of Rosthwaite, the Riverside Bar. And a short while before, Nicky Spinks, a farmer from Yorkshire, had set a new women's record of eighteen hours and six minutes – aged forty-seven, and after recovering from cancer.

It was clearly an event at which you got even better when older.

Local sheep farmer and fell-running legend Joss Naylor decided that for his seventieth birthday, he would complete seventy peaks, which he did in under twenty-one hours. Being a farmer, though, brought with it occupational hazards that other sportsmen might not face: over the years, Joss had to deal with injuries from inhaling sheep dip and having a railway sleeper dropped on his foot.

'I had a friend in my local pub who tried to do the Bob Graham,' Jeff told us. 'He failed to get within the twenty-four hours by a whisker. I think he was a minute and a half late.'

We contemplated this as we munched our oatcakes and chorizo, and watched Jethro grazing.

'Almost broke him,' said Jeff. He sighed. 'Sad, really.'

My immediate resolve when Jeff had started telling us about the Bob Graham — that I would never even contemplate an attempt — was seeming an even more sensible decision by the minute. I celebrated the thought with a pork pie I had found at the bottom of my backpack.

'Then he tried again a couple of years later. But when he got to the Honister and realised how far ahead the Blands were, he just ran out of energy. He was *demoralised*. That's what he was. Completely demoralised.'

Like the tale of the naked muleteer, there was nowhere left for this story to go and we fell silent.

'I still think it's odd,' I said, 'for Joss Naylor to spend his leisure hours running up and down the same hills he's been farming all day.'

Jeff pondered. 'I think it's simply a love for the hills. The whole Bland family are fell-runners. Although Billy Bland's more into cycling these days.

'Most Bob Graham runners set off from Keswick late at night and in midsummer, so as to get as much daylight as possible up to the end of the run. The first thing they do is come off the back of Skiddaw past this house and head over to Great Calva. Then down across the A66 to the whole of the Helvellyn range – in the dark.'

'When they're still fresh?'

'The sad thing is, Hugh, that compared to us, they *stay fresh* – right through the twenty-four hours. Or they wouldn't attempt it in the first place. And remember, these guys have support runners and a strict regime of food and clothing. They'll have practised for years.'

I felt lazy by comparison as we ambled back towards Threlkeld at mule-at-the-end-of-the-day pace. Although I did notice – and felt duty-bound to point out – that when we got to an incline, Jeff became out of breath faster than I did. So maybe some distant vestige of a competitive fell-runner still lingered somewhere in my make-up, like junk DNA.

*

# Chapter 3

# Of Blacksmiths and Poets

The ordinary distance of which mule transport is capable is 20 to 25 miles a day, carrying 160lbs and the saddle.

The War Office, *Animal Management* (London, 1923)

I t was late afternoon by the time we got back to Threlkeld. The October sun was going down over Derwent Water. From our position in the Northern Fells, we could look south across the whole of the Lake District. Line upon line of summit ranges receded away from us, all with different shades and densities from the way the light was falling on them, like the soft blurrings of a Japanese watercolour. I thought of Alice Oswald's wonderful lines about how 'you can feel by instinct in the distance / the bigger mountains hidden by the mountains, / like intentions among suggestions'.

In the foreground, the much softer green of the fields and the forest fell away from the skyline where, as if pencilled in, a thin file of trees strode across the horizon.

It was the sort of view that gave a man a thirst. We were in the right place. The Horse and Farrier was an old drovers' pub in Threlkeld that still had a dismounting block outside for getting off a horse. I was only sorry that I was leading not riding Jethro — although he would not have taken kindly to having me aboard; to swing off a mule and enter a pub would have been quite an entrance.

And I would also have had an audience. At 4.30, so the earliest of 'early hours' by any standards, the large, long pub was already packed.

'Well,' said Jasper as he stood at the bar in his best Irish manner, 'they have an excuse to be drinking. They've been up on the
fells like us. And once it starts getting dark in autumn, there's
nothing to do but drink.

'And we've all started early, come to that,' he added. 'If you
start at first light, you should end at first light.'

This was a cue. I got the drinks in, buying a pint of 'Sneck
Lifter' for myself, partly on the grounds it was the strongest and
darkest beer they had, partly beguiled by the absurd name. Jasper
thought it had something to do with the latch on a gate: 'you
know, the type you pull up from above'. But with the benefit of
Google, I discovered that 'sneck lifter' was Cumbrian dialect for
'one who goes from door to door, first footing, on New Year's
Eve. A burglar or ghost'. How did pub arguments ever get settled
before the internet and mobile phones? Either by the landlord
or a fight.

The etymology of 'sneck lifter' resolved, we got to talking with
the girl behind the bar, as you do. Although she was more interested in Jethro than us; he had already attracted a gaggle of
admirers outside by the horse box.

As everywhere in Britain, the bar conversation soon turned to
property and the difficulties of finding any on a lower wage.

'A lot of local flats and cottages have local occupancy clauses –
both for buying and renting,' the barmaid told us. 'Which at least
keeps the prices down. But it's a real problem. When I started
working at the pub, I had to travel for miles each day to get here.'

The first pint of Sneck Lifter had inspired me, along with our
meeting with Sarah the previous day.

'Why don't you buy our horse box when we've finished the
journey and convert it? You could just keep it outside the pub.
A lot cheaper to live in. There's plenty of space inside a

five-and-a-half ton lorry. And it's easily big enough inside to take a wood-burning stove.'

Converting the Dodge was something Jasper and I had already discussed. A garage owner near Bassenthwaite had taken one look when we'd driven up in all the van's mock-Tudor glory and suggested we had not realised its potential. And that he was the man who could. I had to explain that we needed it to get a mule across England.

But ever since, I had been imagining the van as a fine writer's mobile shed, with its fold-down ramp at the back for unloading horses – or in our case, a solitary mule. You could drive up somewhere with a view, lower the ramp and reveal a writer's desk permanently installed in the back of the lorry – from which you would have no excuse but to describe the landscape in all its glory. Indeed, so integral could it be to a travel writer's craft that I could probably put it down against tax.

'Depends if you'd throw in the mule as well?' asked the barmaid, and laughed.

What was it about women and mules? Everywhere we went, Jethro got a horde of adoring female admirers, both equine and human. Whereas Jasper and I would be lucky to get a second glance.

We went to sit by the fire with Jeff and nurse our drinks. As I looked into the flames, lulled by another Sneck Lifter, I remembered that I had been here before. And that this was one of those rings of memory I wanted to reclaim.

*

Thirty years ago, I had come here with a friend called Fred who was a blacksmith. We had bought some meat pies from the butcher in Keswick and climbed Blencathra so fast that the pies were still warm when we ate them on the summit. Just as now, we had drunk at the Horse and Farrier when we came down, although in those days there was little food on offer. All the barman could suggest was a Ploughman's lunch, the ubiquitous default option.

'What sort of cheese comes with it?' I had asked, knowing that a Ploughman's could appear in all shapes and sizes, some of them shrink-wrapped and unappetising.

The barman looked puzzled by this question. 'Not sure I can tell you. All I know is that one of the cheeses is red and the other one yellow.'

We were in the Lake District on a quixotic mission: to buy up a blacksmith's forge so Fred could transport it lock, stock and anvil back down to Bristol, where he and I were then living. Fred was my age, in his twenties, and about to be married to my cousin Rachel.

He was an American who I had become fond of, not least for the way in which he had transformed himself from his East Coast preppie origins into a blacksmith working in England. I liked a man with a true obsession. And Fred had become captivated by metal. He showed me round the wrought ironwork galleries at the Victoria & Albert Museum. When we went for country walks in the Mendips, where he had his first forge, he deplored the understandable tendency of farmers to go for cheap cast-iron gates instead of properly forged blacksmith's ones. Increasingly, his business came from artisan pieces for interior design rather than agricultural use: fire-tool implements, club fenders and wrought-iron brackets.

One thing Fred did have going for him was the perfect name for a blacksmith: Fred Brodnax. You could see the sparks flying off that surname as if it was hammered from the hearth.

Now he needed a bigger forge, so we were visiting some

north-country smiths, who had maintained standards and a robust tradition of independence. At one of them, near Castle Barnard, a small boy called Ivan was being washed in the kitchen sink; none of this soft southern nonsense about a bath.

Fred found what he wanted at a blacksmith's place near Thirlmere. Loading a whole forge into a van back then proved to be much harder work than getting Jethro into one today. In helping, I felt both noble and altruistic, unaccustomed emotions for me – and that I thoroughly deserved the pint of Theakston's 'Old Peculier' he bought me at this same pub. But I was also envious of him for tapping into such an old tradition, with real tangible products.

This was the 1980s, not long after the end of the miners' strike, so such work was becoming rarer. We were moving inexorably towards a service-driven economy.

It had been noticeable driving through County Durham, as we passed from one blacksmith's workshop to another, how polarised the area was becoming – and that this polarisation often ran along old mine seams. Some villages had big, stone-built detached houses around the long wide village greens so characteristic of the North – houses much in demand from commuters to the big cities which lay within reach. Others had narrow, terraced houses lined right up against the main road; these communities were still recovering from the long attrition of the strike, and the heart had been ripped right out of them.

I had seen the same pattern emerging in a less extreme manner in counties further south, between 'pretty', desirable villages and more down-to-earth agricultural ones. It was a divide that has grown even wider over my lifetime, but one that has been little noticed.

The wave of affluence that began in the eighties has carried a large property-owning middle class into a comfortable lifestyle of shopping at Waitrose and holidaying abroad. It has left behind, meanwhile, a significant proportion of the population who that middle class rarely see, screened out in separate, undesirable villages and the sink estates at the back-end of decaying market towns: a benefits culture which they deplore, but seldom witness.

Britain's service-based economy inevitably means cultural fragmentation; people working in small offices, or at home from computers. The internet has accelerated that process. It has become ever easier not to see how the other half lives: all of us with our heads down, on mobile phones or tablets; the couple with the second home in the country who have no idea what is happening in a village they may have adopted, but which has not adopted them.

Back in the eighties, this was still merely a glimmer, lost in the sparkle of what seemed like an entrepreneurial revolution – in the same way that politicians, with a wave of the hand, assumed the miners would all get new jobs in a world of bingo and silicon chips. One of the best British films of the 1980s, *The Ploughman's Lunch* – so called because the dish is a marketing invention that has never been near any self-respecting ploughman, with either red or yellow cheese – brilliantly dissected the low dishonesty of that particular decade. There is a telling if didactic moment in Ian McEwan's script when one of the characters remarks, 'If we leave the remembering to historians then the struggle is already lost. Everyone must have a memory, everyone needs to be a historian. In this country, for example, we're in danger of losing hard-won freedoms by dozing off into a perpetual present.'

While Fred drove back down south with the forge in his van, I headed over to Manchester to see friends who were, like me, trying to get careers going in film, in the buzz of the media. I found Manchester all sharp, padded-shoulder suits and attitude: 'My Filofax is bigger than yours'; far more so than the slacker vibe of the laidback Bristol to which I was accustomed, or even London. Perhaps it was the brisk cold air that funnelled down the wide streets; the mercantile energies that have always fuelled Manchester. The old warehouse blocks had been scrubbed clean and colonised by post-production houses, and by the designer retail shops which we are now so used to, but back then were still as exotic as the bananas on the first ships in after the war.

The sales were on. I felt underdressed and found myself trying on a suit for the first time in years, persuading myself that I might need one for a job interview. This was pure self-deception. I had already learned enough about film to know that any work that came along would never come through such formal channels.

High-street retailers had just started experimenting with commissions for sales staff. Used to the bored inattention char-acteristic of the 1970s, when you almost had to take a ticket and wait before being served, I was an easy mark. Sharp Mancunian shop assistants were all over me with flattery and advice.

'I've this one left in your size. Double-breasted. Italian. Perfect for you. Why don't you try on the jacket first?'

A Cerruti suit, with soft blue and purple lines against the grey and made from linen. I knew it was crumpling already as soon as I looked at it; that the padded shoulders would qualify me for a role in *Dallas* or *Dynasty*; that it was as hopelessly impractical as the faux leopard-skin jacket I had bought in the heyday of punk.

But clothes can have a siren call. For years, the suit hung in my wardrobe as a reproach. Unworn, unloved. A blacksmith would never have bought it.

✵

We stayed that night with Jeff at the house he shared with his partner Fiona in the Northern Fells. Fiona had several horses, so Jethro felt at home. In fact, like us, very comfortably at home, as Jeff and Fiona had lavished care and attention on accommodation for both humans and horses. Jethro had a comfortable pasture to himself, within sight of Fiona's small herd, while Jasper and I enjoyed en-suite guest bedrooms in the beautifully converted farmhouse. Large picture windows gave sweeping views out to the fells.

This wasn't quite the spartan lifestyle of tents and youth hostels I had originally envisaged for the trip, but I wasn't complaining. There were plenty of hostels ahead anyway. Although would readers feel short-changed that we were not bivouacking on the open hillside? Any such readers could put up and shut up – while Jeff opened a bottle of his finest vintage.

Fiona was away on business; a shame, especially as everyone kept reminding us that she was one of the best cooks in the Lake District. Jeff was unable to boil an egg. Jasper took a muleteer's view of food ('anything will do'). He had already burned a pizza to a cinder: 'Must be something funny with the oven.' So cooking duties fell to me, happily, as I enjoyed both food and the kitchen.

While I concentrated on what Jasper and our mutual friend Chris Stewart described as 'man food' – in this case, sausages, mash and treacle pudding – Jeff spread his maps out on the kitchen table to get in my way. Having done the 214 Wainwrights several times, quite enough for one lifetime, he was now attempting all the mountains over 2,000 feet in Ireland, so needed Jasper's local knowledge.

Jasper made the mistake of asking Jeff if he could see his collection of mountaineering books – mistake only in that I knew sausages would be burned and much wine consumed by the time we'd seen the entire collection. Jeff had been building it up for years, with one novel twist. Whereas most collectors wanted a copy signed by the author, Jeff tried to get his mountaineering books signed by every single member of an expedition. Given those members could live continents apart, this was a considerable undertaking. But the resulting 'association copy', as it was known in the book-dealing trade, had financial as well as memorabilia value – particularly if one of the mountaineers then died, on or off a mountain.

After dinner, we visited his local pub, the Old Crown in Hesket Newmarket. I suspected most of the regulars had signed books for Jeff. I've rarely seen such an assembly of mountaineering talent. Because the Northern Fells are less visited – and so cheaper – than the rest of the Lakes, many climbers have chosen to live there, including Chris Bonington and members of his various expeditions. Within short order of arriving, I found myself discussing Changabang, the remote 'Shining Mountain' I had seen near Nanda Devi. A white granite icicle along the Himalayan skyline, it is often described as one of the most beautiful peaks in the world. Few people in Britain have been there, and most of them seemed to be in the Old Crown that night.

Along with many of his neighbours, Jeff owned the pub – one reason, perhaps, why it was so full. There's nothing like buying your own beer. In 2003, the Old Crown became Britain's first co-operatively owned pub, with 150 supporters: the prototype for many others across the country as villages saw the brewery axe falling. I wondered if the initiative had something to do with the mountaineering ethos of teamwork. That, along with the mountaineering ethos of consuming unfeasibly large amounts of alcohol.

They had taken the self-supporting philosophy further by brewing their own beers – all named, as one might expect, after local summits. Ten thousand pints of the various Hesket Newmarket beers were sold a week, both in the Old Crown itself and to other outlets, an extremely respectable amount. One of the locals, Keith Bridges, gave me a tour of the brewery behind the pub so I could taste my way across the hilltops.

'Black Sail' was a dark stout made from chocolate malt, with 'complex flavours of coffee and liquorice' – a bit like the treacle pudding we had eaten for dinner. Whereas 'Haystacks' was a pale-coloured, zesty ale, 'late hopped to give a hint of grapefruit'. I didn't like to ask if the slight residue I noticed was to remind the drinker of Wainwright's ashes.

Keith took me round 'Blencathra', 'Skiddaw', 'Helvellyn Gold' and 'Great Cock-Up', the provocatively named mountain outside Jeff's window. The last beer I sampled was 'Doris' – which even I knew was not one of the Wainwrights. Apparently, she had been the mother-in-law of an earlier publican. It was their biggest seller.

Late that night when we got back, Jeff announced with a sheepish look that he had started collecting something else as well as mountaineering books, not entirely to Fiona's pleasure. He led us out to what was not so much a shed as an air-conditioned storage facility. Behind a set of racing bicycles were rack upon rack of ice axes, from early wooden ones to modern aluminium models.

We murmured admiringly, as you should with any collection, and Jeff let us handle a few. They were easy things to fetishise. The older axes had long shafts, as their primary purpose, before the advent of crampons, was to cut steps into the ice. Modern ones were shorter and lighter, made from metal and with aggressively curved picks and adzes. Even the shafts were bent. A compromise had to be made with the pick as to whether you wanted to be good at 'self-arresting' – digging into the ice if you fell down a slope – or at climbing a steep ice wall.

'You can easily tell the ones which are hot forged,' said Jeff. I hadn't a clue which ones were hot forged. Nor, I suspected, had Jasper. But we both nodded in agreement.

'That way the manufacturers get a thinner, more accurate pick.'

Some of them had been signed by mountaineers for Jeff, just like his books; several were autographed by the great Joe

Brown, one of the first men to set foot on the summit of Kanchenjunga.

'You can pick them up on eBay,' said Jeff. 'Lots of antique ice axes going. Although they won't be signed of course. Or as nice as some of the ones here. I've got a rival in Japan who keeps buying them. Pushes the prices up.'

I had not started off the evening needing an antique ice axe in my life. But sampling the entire range of the Hesket Newmarket Old Crown Brewery had impaired my judgement. Ten minutes in front of a laptop later and I was the proud owner of a vintage wooden Stubai ice axe from the Tyrol. I was only sorry I wouldn't be at home to see my wife's face when it was delivered.

*

Radio Cumbria rang me up first thing in the morning. This was not unexpected. But neither, after a night at the Old Crown, was it welcome.

They had arranged the interview some time before. 'We hear you're taking a mule across the country. Would you mind talking to us on our breakfast show? And will your tent have mobile reception?'

Jeff injected some much-needed black coffee to get me ready.

'That was "Mule Train" by Bo Diddley. And there's a reason for playing it, because on the line we have Hugh Thomson, who has taken it upon himself to cross Cumbria with a mule. And then Yorkshire as well, but we're not so interested in that, are we?

'So Hugh, how does it work? Are you riding the mule?'

I was practised at this particular answer by now. 'No, he's just a pack animal. And his name's Jethro.' I bridled at him being referred to as 'the mule'. Jethro was a name, not a number.

'OK. So Jethro carries everything, does he? Your tent and everything – your *supplies*.'

As has already been duly recorded, Jethro carried so little it was embarrassing. Our standard muleteers' lunch. Perhaps some water. And the symbolic three pebbles for each of us that Jasper had loaded on the beach at St Bees. But it felt disloyal to let him down in public.

'Well, that's the idea . . . '

'And where do you sleep at nights?'

In luxurious accommodation courtesy of Mr Jeff Ford, who was even now getting my second espresso of the morning ready.

'With friends sometimes. We've got a tent, and there are hostels along the way.'

'So what gave you the idea for this? I mean, it seems a very odd thing to do, doesn't it?'

'Maybe. But I've travelled a lot in Peru, where they use mules a great deal. I really enjoyed walking with them. So I thought, why not do it back home, and explore some of the old pack-animal routes that cross the north of England?'

'Best of luck, Hugh. I hope listeners will carry a carrot in their pockets, just in case they meet you. And let me ask something that everyone else will – have you bonded with Jethro yet?'

This was a good question. And also the last. I replied as well as I could ('It's early days' or something equally vague) but realised I needed to answer it for myself.

Jasper was still in bed. He had drunk even more than I had. I wandered out to see Jethro, who did his usual trick of standing sideways in the field so he could keep me in vision without having to acknowledge that he was doing so.

In some ways, looking after Jethro was like having a teenager – and given I had three teenage children of my own and two teenage step-daughters, I felt well qualified on this subject. You can spend weeks with a teenager and get no response, love or thanks; but precisely because of that, when you do, it's so unexpected, it can feel like an almost sublime moment of transfiguration.

I knew Jethro had lived through a troubled past. Although the RSPCA were circumspect, I had learned that in his original home, before they rescued him, he was unloved and misunderstood – enough to make any teenager rebellious. As so often, it sounded as if he had been the unwanted consequence of leaving a donkey in a field with a mare. Just as the English had such startling levels of teenage pregnancies due to lack of sex education, so they seemed blithely unaware that donkeys could procreate with horses. And the result would be a mule. Given all the ignorance and prejudice about mules – that they were stubborn and hard to deal with – it was not surprising that Jethro could be difficult at times. It was more surprising that at times he wasn't.

Jasper had been patiently teaching me the business of mul-eteering: from setting up the electric fence at each place we stopped to how to box him into the horse lorry. But one thing I didn't enjoy was having to catch Jethro, which is what needed to happen now. Despite weeks of training at home and on the road, this wasn't getting any easier.

Usually I was the sous-chef in this particular operation. Jasper would hold out a bucket of pony nuts and make peculiar noises that sounded like Mongolian throat singing. We would then both close on Jethro until he consented to let Jasper attach the lead rope.

Today, however, he got bored of the usual procedure and trotted over to me meekly to present his neck. It was one of those rare moments when we had indeed bonded.

✻

I was doing a correspondence course in handling mules.

An old girlfriend of mine called Annis had decided, with some justification, that I needed instruction if I was going to have any hope of getting Jethro across the country in one piece.

She had started to send long, detailed emails – 10,000 words in all by the time we had finished – with advice that was as frank and direct as only an English horsewoman's can be.

One of her first missives had set the tone: 'So who is going to look after the mule – You? – I don't think so!!'

She had continued, perhaps to soften the blow a little, 'The thing is, you aren't an experienced horse person but you aren't totally stupid.' (I knew from long experience with sisters, wives and girlfriends that this was about as close to a compliment as I was ever likely to get in the English equine world.)

'You can learn if someone tells you what to do. There is a right way to do all this stuff. If you do it wrong, the mule will get nervous that you're inexperienced. Quite apart from picking up on your "I'm not entirely sure I know what I'm doing" pheromones.'

Annis had several horses herself and lived in the middle of Exmoor with her partner Jeremy. As she reminded me, she had been around horses all her life: 'I was off the leading rein at three years old and I don't really remember ever being on it.' Her own pheromones were so horsey, wild Exmoor ponies probably camped outside her rambling farmhouse to be near her.

She had once bred Doberman Pinschers, along with four children and plenty of other livestock. With a frankness that only an old romantic attachment could bring – we had dated when we were teenagers for some years – she proceeded to get down to business, adding some bare-knuckle jabs at my lack of suitability for the enterprise at hand.

**From:**   Annis Sokol
**To:**      Hugh Thomson
**Subject:** Grooming Jethro

I think you don't know enough about equines to look after Jethro properly – so here is a crash course in grooming and pony care. This email is all about grooming a small pony and I imagine that small mules are much the same.

This needs to be done every morning.

If he is in a stable, go to the door and say, 'Hello Jethro'. I always say, 'Good Morning Ponies', and they all neigh back.

Jethro and I had yet to build up a call-and-response routine; nor was it that sort of relationship. More like men arriving at the same workplace and briefly acknowledging they were in the same room before getting on with it. But I could see what Annis was driving at.

Make sure you have the head collar in your hand, open the door a bit, slip in and then bolt the door behind you. Some ponies think it's funny to push you out of the way and vanish. Put the head collar on (he DOESN'T sleep in it) and tie him up using a pony knot. DON'T tuck the end of the rope in, so you can untie him quickly if you have to.

The capitalisation hurt. It became more and more prevalent as

the letters continued. Along with the assumption that I was start-
ing at ground zero, and that Annis needed to make sure I really did
work through each job step-by-step, or in some cases, hoof-by-hoof.

> Find the hoof-pick and pick out his feet, starting with the
> near fore, then the near hind, then the off fore and last the
> off hind. Put the pick BACK in the box.

Annis's need to include this sort of detail stung. What did she
think I was going to do with the hoof-pick? Throw it away?

> Next use the Dandy brush all over his body, starting at the
> nearside head end of his neck and sweeping backwards and
> ending at his tail.
> If he's in the paddock, bring him in to do the grooming.
> You should take a bucket with about 4 oz of sliced carrots
> as a present for being good and coming. You may have to
> walk up to him to catch him. Unless you are very sure that
> he's fine about catching [which Jethro absolutely wasn't], use
> a VERY SMALL paddock like a quarter of an acre at first.

This, like much of Annis's advice, was all good and useful.
Although I wasn't about to start weighing my carrots.

> REMEMBER you use the body brush on his mane and
> tail – NOT the Dandy brush, which is to get mud off. Do
> it gently from the side so he doesn't get annoyed and kick
> you. You separate the long hairs and brush them. It is
> soothing and he'll like having a cuddle. If you love him, he
> will love you back. You don't have to wash his bottom or
> for that matter his penis – that is ok left on its own.

Well, thank God for small mercies. She ended this particular
email with a little note about what to do if, for any reason, Jethro

lived up to a mule's reputation and refused to budge when we were hiking across country.

Don't turn round and stare at him – ponies hate that and mules aren't likely to be different. If he stops, check to see that there isn't something wrong first, e.g. someone hiding in the hedge or a nasty dustbin. If not, then just say nicely, 'What's the matter Jethro? Walk on, Jethro. Walk on.'
If he still doesn't go, then look again and say, 'Is there anybody there? You're upsetting my mule, so come out please.'
The wretched person will usually emerge.
If not, get out your supply of carrots and try again. Hopefully Jethro will then carry on. He might have stood on something, so if his ears are back, have a look at his feet and make sure he's not lame. He'll be doing a lot of walking, so he may get sore feet. He doesn't have shoes, does he?

Annis, with her usual perspicacity, had pinpointed a problem that was going to be of growing concern to Jasper and me over the coming weeks. Jethro was unshod when I took charge of him and at his age, the RSPCA thought it best he should remain so. As they were still his legal custodians, I needed to respect that decision. But the bridleways of the wild parts of England were not all grassy verges. Some were rocky enough to present a potential problem. As many commentators have remarked before, the geography of the Lake District does not lend itself to straight and easy routes.

*

I know not how to give the reader a distinct image of this [the main demarcation of the country] more readily, than by requesting him to place himself with me, in imagination, upon some given point; let it be the top of either of the mountains, Great Gavel, or Scawfell; or, rather, let us suppose our station to be a cloud hanging midway between those two mountains, at not more than half a mile's distance from the summit of each, and but a few yards above their highest elevation, he will then see stretched at his feet a number of Vallies, not fewer than nine, diverging from the point, on which he is supposed to stand, like spokes from the nave of a wheel.

> William Wordsworth, *Select Views in Cumberland, Westmoreland, and Lancashire* (1810)

How Wordsworth came to write a guide to the Lake District I found endlessly fascinating and revealing. For many years he refused to do so, on the grounds that 1) he wrote poetry, not prose, and 2) as he said in a letter of 1808, after ten years in the Lakes, he now knew them too well 'to know where to begin, and where to end'.

But only a year or so later he changed his mind, partly out of financial necessity – the poems weren't selling – and because an opportunity fell into his lap. A painter called Joseph Wilkinson had been a neighbour of the Wordsworths before moving to Norfolk. The flat landscape made him nostalgic for the Lakes, so he embarked on a book of *Select Views in Cumberland, Westmoreland, and Lancashire*. He asked Wordsworth to write the accompanying text.

As the art-book was being sold by subscription, at a hefty price – £6 6s, so over £200 today in real terms – this was a good commission. When it came out in 1810, the publishers declared the paper so luxuriously thick 'it would admit of tinting', should subscribers want to add their own colour to the engravings.

A few years ago I contributed the text to a monstrously large illustrated tome called *50 Wonders of the World*: a book so big, I liked to say, that if you attached legs to each corner it could have become a coffee table in itself. One unforeseen result was that bookshops refused to stock any copies because they took up too much space. Commercially, it was a disaster. Yet while my initial reasons for doing it were, like Wordsworth's, both financial and opportunistic, I found the project engaging once I had begun.

An unexpected commission can be liberating for a writer: to lay aside the imaginative necessity – or burden – of creating your own work *ex nihilo*, and instead craft to order. W. H. Auden enjoyed his time in film cutting-rooms because editors would force him to re-write the verse commentary 'to picture'.

I can't also help thinking Wordsworth was liberated by knowing that what he was doing would be accompanied by illustrations. Or rather, the illustrations, which were very much the main event, were accompanied by his text; when the book was advertised, it hardly mentioned his name. The words didn't have to work so hard.

Necessity forced Wordsworth to find a way of writing about the Lakes. And his way of doing so was what today we might call psychogeographical: by dividing the district into a wheel, with each valley one of the spokes, giving unity but also variety, he could isolate the tone and character of each valley, and suffuse them with personal experience. As a contemporary critic put it in the *Monthly Review*, the strategy was 'as topographically useful as it is *poetically picturesque*'.

Moreover, Wordsworth tried to address the Lake District as a holistic experience. Previous guides – and there had been many of these in the eighteenth century – broke down the Lakes into a series of views, like a modern tour that only lets you off the coach at designated moments. They even recommended travelling with a special viewing instrument, called a Claude's Glass, a convex fold-up mirror. Named after Claude Lorrain, whose paintings of Arcadia had done so much to shape British theories of the picturesque, these devices framed and tinted the landscape. To use one, the viewer had to turn their back to the natural scene and hold up the mirror – much like a modern tourist taking a selfie.

Wordsworth provided the interstices: the people and incidental detail along the way that could make the journey a more lived experience. Although that didn't stop him, like any good poet, from getting bored at writing so much prose. Close to the end, he persuaded his sister Dorothy to 'compose a description or two for the finishing of his work for Wilkinson' as, she recorded, he had started to find it 'irksome'. And there is a fine bohemian swagger to the way he disdains the 'humble and tedious task' of providing any directions; and the way, familiar to today's sensitive travel writers, that he resists all attempts to call it 'a guidebook'.

Nor is he above a little helpful cross-promotion. When moved to quote verse by the sublimity of any scene, the poetry he most often remembers is invariably his own.

Only in 1822 did Wordsworth finally issue the guide as a stand-alone volume: *A Description of the Scenery in the North of England*, with a map that folded out and a new section of 'Directions and Information for the Tourist'. Dorothy added an account of climbing Scafell, then the most tantalising of Lake peaks for the visitor, being remote and not easy to summit. The many editions that followed were a steady earner throughout Wordsworth's long life. Given he had done so much to attract tourists to the Lake District, it seemed only fair he should profit from them.

On one particular point, Wordsworth was absolutely right: trying to negotiate the Lake District was exactly like crossing the spokes of a wheel — awkward to do at the best of times, let alone with a mule. I needed all my not-very-well-honed navigational skills to find the appropriate bridleways that would weave us across.

I had a current incarnation of the guide with me as we drove to the start of the next stage of our walk from Borrowdale, one of the most beautiful of all the valleys. The view of it over Ashness Bridge is a favourite picture postcard, and would often have been framed by a Claude's Glass in the past. It had been much hymned by Wordsworth's predecessors — so perhaps he was too intimidated to write much about it. Instead he came up with a magnificent cop-out:

It would be an endless task to attempt, by verbal descriptions, to guide the traveller among the infinite variety of beautiful or interesting objects which are found in the different reaches of the broad Valley itself, nor less so to attempt to lead him through its little recesses, its nooks, and tributary glens. I must content myself with saying, that this Valley surpasses all the others in variety.

Thank God, his first publisher must have thought, for the illustrations.

*

At the Rosthwaite hotel in Borrowdale, our large old horse lorry looked incongruous beside the walkers' cars: as if a small suburban mock-Tudor house had dropped into the car park.

We attracted a modest crowd of fleece- and anorak-covered spectators as we tried to get Jethro out of the horsebox. 'Be careful,' said one. 'I'd hate to see what he'd do to my wing mirror.'

Although startled at emerging to such a large audience, Jethro behaved impeccably as he strolled down the ramp, frisky and ready for another day in the hills.

I was not sure I could say the same. The night before I'd had two pints of the fearsome Sneck Lifter, spot-checked a range of Hesket Newmarket beers for quality control and shared a bottle of red wine with Jasper and Jeff over dinner, so my head was a little clouded. I also felt annoyed with myself. Surely Robert Macfarlane never set off on one of his walks with a hangover? He would have been up at six and writing a lyrical description of the dawn. As would Wordsworth. Where was my professionalism? At least Jasper looked equally the worse for wear.

We joined forces for the day with Jannicke Wallace, a Norwegian woman Jasper had met in the pub the previous night. Jannicke had lived in the Lakes for the past thirty years, so most of her adult life. She told me they reminded her of Norway, because of the landscape and the Viking heritage – the names like Threlkeld and Thwaites.

'But it's so crowded now. And you can't stop people coming here. That does spoil it for me. Also, I think the parking charges are just ridiculous. Seven pounds to park for the day!'

Like everybody else we'd met in the Old Crown, she was an experienced fell-walker and we set off at a brisk kill-or-cure pace from Rosthwaite. The bridleway was initially good and grassy, and Jethro had his ears alert as he powered forward with Jasper while I chatted to Jannicke. (Readers may notice a curious tendency for every other person – and mule – in this story to have a name beginning with 'J'; this is purely accidental and what happens in a non-fiction book where characters cannot be corralled.)

Even if car parking was not on his agenda, many of the local issues that concerned Jannicke had also preoccupied Wordsworth back in the nineteenth century. His suggestion that the Lake District be seen as 'a sort of national property, in which every man has a right and interest who has an eye to perceive and a heart to enjoy', was the first clarion call for the creation of a national park. That decision has brought in its wake all sorts of issues as to whether to conserve or develop. Wordsworth was already huffing and puffing about insensitive new buildings near Ullswater and what he described as a 'spirit of tasteless and capricious innovation'. He would not have approved of the zip-wire on the Honister Pass.

He also made the subtle and interesting point that builders of new houses in the Lake District were too conscious of the beauty of the landscape; they tried too hard, and were ill-equipped to do so. Rather than settling for modest conventional houses, there was 'a constraint or warping of the natural mind arising out of a sense that, this country being an object of general admiration, every new house would be looked at and commented upon either for approbation or censure. Hence all the deformity. . .'

And instead of building in the sensible valley, they positioned their houses on exposed positions, 'the summits of naked hills', from which they could enjoy the view but also reveal more starkly any failure of architectural ambition. Mr Pocklington of Nottinghamshire felt the full wrath of the poet for 'playing strange pranks by his buildings and plantations'; while a Mr English had the temerity to build a high garden wall on Windermere Island, 'as exclusive as it was ugly'. Wordsworth could have a surprisingly sharp and satirical tongue when he got going.

In 1844, now Poet Laureate and a figure of some weight, Wordsworth wrote a long letter to the *Morning Post*: a letter for which the editor would have needed half the paper. He complained about a proposed new railway between Kendal and Windermere to let in yet more tourists – many attracted, it must be said, precisely by the view of the Lake District he had done so much to promote. Just in case this swinging right-hander didn't work, he followed up with a second letter for the knockout punch. Taken together, they form a magnificent piece of invective. He conjures up the spectre of a railway line being built right through Furness Abbey and thunders that the Sabbath day will be disrupted; he also quotes from no fewer than three of his own poems in supporting evidence. The railway was never built.

The two letters were signed from 'Rydal Mount'. Wordsworth was speaking on behalf of those who lived in the Lake District. The title page of his guide's definitive fifth edition advertised a work 'for the use of Tourists and Residents'; and he anticipated the current concern for the balance between 'incomers' with their second homes and the more permanent inhabitants.

'Yes,' said Jannicke, 'I hope it's not going to become a chocolate box, tied up with a ribbon. We need to see the people who actually work the land get consulted. There are sheep farmers whose families have been here for centuries. That's what I'm worried about. Look at all this bracken we're walking through. They want to take the sheep off the fells, so they can go back to being wild, like this. But that has consequences.'

The bracken looked beautiful up the hillside in the autumnal sun. Yet that was from afar. Walking through it was less enjoyable.

In some ways, what I found remarkable was that the Lake District had stayed so relatively unspoiled. You might not want to be in Grasmere during the height of the summer coach season, but plenty of those 214 Wainwright summits would be deserted. On this October walk from Borrowdale over to Grasmere, a central thoroughfare of the Lakes, we met no one for hours.

We did, however, run into trouble. Jasper had been trying to keep Jethro on the grass, but once past the magnificent buttress of Eagle Crag, our own path started to climb, and became one of flint and stone. It began to be difficult to avoid punishing rocks, which were doing Jethro's feet no good. Although traditionally a bridleway, and marked as such on the map, we suspected few horses – let alone mules – had come here for many a year.

At Lining Crag, we realised it would be impossible to get Jethro any further. The crag jutted out from the side of Greenup Edge; to get over the pass, you had to climb over its shoulder. The path up was not only steep, but had been broken down by the boots of walkers into a precipitate jumble of stone.

It would be stupid to end up with a lame mule at this stage of the journey, argued Jasper forcibly, scratching his head under his beret. He was short-tempered about it, perhaps because, like me, he was suffering the effects of our partying the night before. It was frustrating. This was a key section of our walk across the Lakes. Just over Lining Crag lay the descent to Grasmere.

We agreed that Jasper and Jannicke would head back with Jethro towards Rosthwaite and find him pasture, while I headed over the pass to prospect and at least see what lay on the other side.

I recognised that this was part of the point of travelling with an animal. You had to listen to their needs and adapt. And it was good to do some walking on my own. It cleared my head. This was a path I had never taken before – one reason I had not realised it would be a bridleway in name only.

Once over Lining Crag, a stride over boggy country that Wainwright complained had 'too many cairns' to guide the walker – although in mist, I'm sure no one would object – brought me to Greenup Edge. As visibility was good, I could see a tantalisingly easy descent ahead of me rolling down Easedale Gill to Grasmere. Jethro would have cantered down.

A short detour to the nearby summit of High Raise brought the sweep of the southern lakes around Langdale into focus; an enticing sight as, while I knew the Western Fells, the Southern Fells were new to me.

I am not someone who wears frustrations for long, and my mood quickly changed from irritation to elation. To the north-west, from where we had come, a shaft of light was picking out the distinctive profile of Fleetwith Pike in splendid isolation. 'My mountain', as I liked to think of it proprietorially. The mountain I had run off once with the hounds chasing behind me.

There is something about mountains that encourages a brief moment of Nietzschean excess in the heart of the mildest man. The illusion, however false, that for a brief moment you have at least conquered something on a summit.

But over the years, I realise I've come to value crossing a pass more than 'conquering' a peak. I love the feeling that there is a new valley to explore; for entering a whole new world is surely what mountains and life and literature are about. And Grasmere had plenty of all those waiting for us.

*

## Chapter 4

# A Tintinnabular Clatter

Mules are particularly free kickers, often shy with strangers, and touchy about the head and ears.

The War Office, *Animal Management* (London, 1923)

To get over to Grasmere, we now had to retrace our steps cumbersomely and take Jethro around in the horse lorry: a considerable drive, as you have to head north to Keswick and then down past the murky depths of Thirlmere. At least we had arranged some excellent grazing for him: a large field at Knott House Farm, the home of Peter and Joanne Bland.

Peter was another member of the Bland fell-running dynasty. We had found his number in the *Lakeland Shepherd's Guide*. These guides have been in publication since 1817 and record the smit marks – the daubs of dyed colour on the fleece – and ear tags of every fell sheep. They are produced every ten years to enable every animal to be identified, usually so they can be returned when they've wandered off-piste. And for the same reason, they give the contact details of every farm.

With great generosity, given they didn't know us from Adam and Jethro didn't even have a smit mark, Peter and Joanne offered us a field for the night. As fields went, it was perfect for Jethro: a few non-toxic trees to give shade; plenty of grass; and best of all, a gate where he could stand to survey the world. Mules, like farmers, enjoy looking over gates.

Peter and Joanne lived a little to the north of Grasmere, and there was a youth hostel nearby. Our accommodation was more spartan than Jethro's. The man who opened the reception hatch to sign us in looked like the last resident of Middle Earth: bearded beyond beardiness. There was a long list of rules and regulations which included being shut out of the place during daylight hours. Our room was clean, but had a series of security locks to get inside.

At breakfast the next day, a young man asked if he could have an extra teabag for his Thermos. The staff reacted as if he had suggested burning the place down. In much the same way, in fact, as when I had asked on the phone if they had anywhere we could tie up a mule for the night – which was why we were sleeping apart.

When we arrived to collect Jethro, he was happily rolling on the grass. Peter Bland was amused by having a mule in the field, although he did say it would wreck it for the sheep if, as Joanne and their daughter wanted, they had a more permanent horse.

Peter was in his early forties, athletic and with a light layer of what would have been called designer stubble in London, but here was more like a farmer's 'I'm not bloody bothering to shave when I get up at four o'clock in the morning'.

Sitting out by his front door step, with six or seven dogs, we talked about the recent controversy over Grasmere Common, on which small farmers like Peter had traditionally held grazing rights. The owners of the common, the Lowther Estate, had been blocking applications for increased sheep production because of pressure to 're-wild' the Lake District. They wanted some areas of the fell to be fenced off and revert to nature.

Peter claimed the Lowther Estate's decision could cost him thousands of pounds.

'I'm a tenant farmer here. Have to pay my rent. They shouldn't be allowed to take a decision which effectively puts my livelihood at risk.'

He got me a cup of tea. We could see Jethro from where we were sitting.

'I was expecting a big black mule, but this is a nicely coloured, pretty thing. He's not nearly as big as I thought he'd be. But I guess a bigger animal would take more feeding.

'If we had a horse in that field – which is what, about two and a half acres? – by spring it would be jiggered. Probably would be with that small mule as well. There wouldn't be any grass left. Completely jiggered. So, farmers and horses are not the best of friends.

'I mean years ago, of course, you had to have horses. You'd have so many cows and a horse, maybe two horses for a farm like this. And big horses: cobbs. Then when tractors came along, farmers could keep an extra cow or two instead. A swap – more cows for the horses that were no longer needed.

'When we were growing up, we was told that in the old days, if you found someone else's sheep from another valley, you'd send them a postcard. And they would ride over on a horse to bring them back. Might take a couple of days. Now we get on the telephone and say, "we've got ten sheep of yours", and they come round in the pickup by lunchtime!

'We still do some distances though. We walk our sheep round from the Grisedale valley, over towards Patterdale.'

'So that's a fair way.' I knew it was, because it was our stage for the following day.

'It's not too bad. But the only reason we can do it is because we've got Herdwicks. You wouldn't do it with these low-country sheep or Swaledales. They don't have the energy or the stamina. They'd go soft and lie down and that would be that. But we can walk our sheep back from near Patterdale in four hours. It's not that steep and it's a well-trodden path. Isn't that the route you're going to take with your mule?'

'Yes, it is, but you're fell-runners. I bet even the sheep are in training. You probably do it a bit faster than anybody else.' I couldn't see Jethro doing it in four hours. Or us, for that matter.

I asked Peter the question I had earlier asked Jeff: why was his family so passionate about fell-running when they spent all day on the hills anyway?

'It was always something done from a young age. Junior fell-runners would get involved and then you'd come up through the age group until you ran in the adult races. My father would run when he was a busy shepherd but he never used to train. He always said he had done his training during the week. So come the weekend he could go off and enjoy a race. It was social. But he would never train.

'Whereas his brother Billy Bland, my uncle, who was a stone-mason in Borrowdale . . . Now Billy, he did use to train. A lot. At five o'clock, when he finished work, he would get on the fells to get proper fit. Two hours every night. And Billy was superbly fit – he was British champion and that.

'We Blands are good at getting down mountains. The rougher and steeper, the more we like it. Because we're sure-footed. We pride ourselves on that. Some of the fell-runners who come over from Lancashire and Yorkshire – they aren't used to it, so we make up ground on them.

'So your question: why would you want to do it when you've worked on them all day? I suppose it's just a challenge, isn't it?'

'And in the old days,' I asked, 'would there have been any messing around about not having a drink afterwards? How *austere* was the training regime?'

'My uncle Billy wouldn't drink much. Not when he was winning races every weekend. He wouldn't be a big drinker at all. Sometimes he would have a Mackeson's milk stout. "It does you double good!" as they used to say in the ads. I can remember

Early training session with Jethro. He's still wearing the special Monty Roberts Dually halter which his carers at the RSPCA had needed to control him.

Checking the route.

*'I looked back down on the small town of St Bees. It had the simple clarity of all good beginnings: the breakwaters dividing the beach into neat segments; the buildings clustered in radial lines; the coastline extending away to the south with lucidity and enticement.'*

'The spectacular ring of mountains of the Western Fells, centred on the domed anvil of Great Gable.' Jethro with Haystacks in the distance behind him.

'Isn't this what that donkey keeps doing in *Shrek*?' Jethro playing to camera. Note the size of the saddlebags he was prepared to carry.

The three of us at the start of the Old Moses Trod track. *'He's decided we're his herd. Not a very pleasant herd, and decidedly lacking in intelligence, with terrible ears, but about as good as he's going to get, so he's making the best of it.'*

Jeff Ford telling us about the Bob Graham race: *'The sad thing is, Hugh, that compared to us, they stay fresh.'*

The 5½ ton Dodge van. *'"The thing you have to remember about this van, Hugh," said Steve, who had clearly rehearsed this line for any prospective purchaser — I was the first — "is that it is reassuringly old."'*

One of the old muleteer tracks across the Lake District
described by Wordsworth.

Walking through the Howgills with Jason's dog, Toby: *'Manageable hills of fell and dale, of a soft and fecund green. Jason found them a continuous source of artistic stimulation.'*

Jason Gathorne-Hardy.

The way Jason drew with such a fast and kinetic line matched his conversational style.

'The sort of meandering walk followed in which three men are more interested in the conversation than in where they are going.'

Fox's pulpit: 'A remote stone in a field where he preached to an audience of a thousand people in the safety of the open air, far from persecution.'

The long Bowderdale valley: *'We were walking in a mist, although such a light one that it merely softened the views a touch, like a graduated filter on a lens.'*

Jasper in quintessential muleteer's attitude. *'He was about as near to a professional muleteer as the British Isles would allow.'*

when I was doing the Bob Graham, I'd often have a tin of Mackeson's to give myself a rest before setting off on the next section.

'Uncle Billy used to do the whole race during daylight hours. He would set off at six in the morning. And then as a boy, I'd see him run into the market square in Keswick at eight the same evening. You had pacers for each leg to make sure you did your tops, and the lads that were with him, his pacers, even they couldn't keep up with him! He made it look easy. Even though it wasn't.

'Every valley in the Lake District still has a race, where you run up to a watershed and back. Borrowdale, Ennerdale, Langdale. They're all well supported.'

What was it, I wondered, about the Bland family that had produced so many great runners? What had their mother put in the porridge?'

'Stamina's got a lot to do with it. And my top tip? Take small steps when you're going uphill. A lady's steps. Small, dainty steps like a dancer.' He demonstrated on his porch, going up and down the ledge. The dogs looked on impassively, but Jethro started staring at us over the gate.

'What about downhill?'

'Ah, the downhill. Just close your eyes and run as hard as you can.'

Peter's father arrived from his own nearby farm. He was a larger, more solid version of Peter.

'I've got a big jar of pickle for you in the van,' he told his son, in a broad Cumbrian accent.

Peter explained what Jasper and I were trying to do with Jethro – 'He's got a mule, Dad' – but his father looked blank; at first, I thought, from incomprehension of what might have seemed a daft scheme to transport a mule across the country.

'I can't hear a word you're saying, son,' he said with a poker face. 'I've been at altitude. When you're working all day on the fells, like I have, at 3,000 feet, your ears start to go. When you come down, you can't hear a thing.'

*

There is a tendency to decry Grasmere for its bustling High Street, full of outdoor gear stores – the nearest the Lake District comes to bling – and, well, just for being so popular. But I thought it injected some much-needed vulgarity into proceedings. The large Co-op also had a better (and cheaper) selection of pies than anything in the more genteel villages we had passed.

The young guy serving us espressos in the small takeaway coffee-shop said that, while local himself, most of his friends had left town; much of the workforce was made up of young Europeans, who came for a long summer.

As we left Grasmere, I thought of Wordsworth striding from one valley to another, whether to meet Coleridge or, as he once did along this route, to say goodbye to his brother John for the last time; John was drowned at sea a few years later. He was always a great supporter of what he called 'the old muleteer tracks with their primitive simplicities' which ran through the Lakes.

'If we had a book of his poetry, it would be a gazetteer of almost the whole of the Lake District,' said Jasper.

This was true. Yet I felt strongly that following the Romantic poets through the Lake District was not just a heritage trail. Once you peeled off the layers of varnish that have encrusted Keats, Coleridge and particularly Wordsworth, you came face-to-face with an ambitious project that is as radical today as it was then.

The attempt to examine the human heart – one's own heart – and trace its evolution from the child to the man is as bold as ever. And it is one that is curiously out of favour with British literary culture. In poetry, particularly, the shadow of modernism lies heavy on the land: the idea, attributed to T. S. Eliot, that the poet should be impersonal and the lyric impulse suppressed; that one should speak in other voices, and that to speak in one's own is to 'grandstand'. The work of many a modern poet shows a studied and polished impersonality: one reason why they like translating so much, where the technique is their own but the lives are someone else's.

Of course, Wordsworth can be frustrating. There are times in *The Prelude* when the reader – or certainly this one – wants to throttle him. Just get on with it, man.

'Imagine you're doing the pitch, William. You have three minutes in front of the panel. Don't keep telling us about the thing we *might* need to know before you tell us another thing we *do* need to know, before getting to the whole point of what it's all really about. With a flashback to your earliest memories. It's not a Terrence Malick movie.'

But for all its unwieldiness and slowness, *The Prelude* is still a magnificent manifesto for the humanist project. We all matter as individuals and have our own consciousnesses that crawl towards the light. There are moments when we lose our way, and for that reason those moments when the clouds part and we reconnect – those moments which Wordsworth is so good at isolating – matter even more. And a close encounter with landscape, with nature however red in tooth and claw, can help those moments of self-recognition.

Wordsworth was like the old relative who you feel duty-bound to have a conversation with, only suddenly to be surprised by a flash of unexpected acuity in the midst of a familiar anecdote.

The decision by Wordsworth and then Coleridge to come and live here – and to do so from 1800 as a joint project, together with Wordsworth's sister Dorothy – was a bold one. Daniel Defoe, writing in the 1720s, had famously claimed that the region was 'eminent only for being the wildest, most barren and frightful of any that I have passed over in England'.

But the idea that Wordsworth and Coleridge 'discovered' the Lake District is as absurd as the idea that Elvis invented rock 'n' roll. Thirty years before, Thomas Gray had already put it on the map. His description of Grasmere in his published journal equals anything Wordsworth wrote: ' ... to see Helm-Crag distinguish'd from its rugged neighbours not so much by its height, as by the strange broken outline of its top, like some gigantic building demolish'd, & the stones that composed it, flung cross each other in wild confusion'.

No wonder that most historians of British travel date the birth of modern tourism to roughly 1750 – precisely the moment when Lake District literature emerged, marking the first stirrings of what would become the cult of the picturesque. By the Romantic period, conditions were firmly in place for tourism to flourish on a large scale.

Wordsworth chose to settle in the heart of the Lake District not just because it was his childhood home and the repository of personal memories, but because it had become a prominent aesthetic territory.

We had risen high enough with Jethro to be able to look back and see Grasmere in its valley, with the distinctive silhouette of Helm Crag off to one side – the only 'Wainwright' that the great man himself didn't reach due to the brief scramble involved to get to the top of what Gray described as its 'strange broken outline'. A. W. didn't like climbing.

'What I like about this landscape,' mused Jasper, 'is that you can go from the micro to the macro. So, you can follow this

stone-built wall with your eye from where it leaves us here ...
down to the beck where it opens out to the valley below ... and
of course then I'm lost, as I've never been here before, but it recedes
away into this Narnia-like landscape of woodlands and peaks.'

'And with so many hidden valleys between the larger ones,' I
added. 'Which is why you can spend a lifetime exploring and
mapping it, as Wainwright did.'

I wondered if the Lake District reminded Jasper of Ireland at
all. 'Or was Ireland just an altogether different green?'

Jasper lifted his tanned face towards the hills as he considered
this. 'There are bits of it that do, of course; and probably vice
versa, there are bits of Ireland that remind me of here. But this
is very much its own landscape.'

We started walking on with Jethro. 'There's something about
the scale of the Lake District,' I suggested, 'which is so perfectly
in miniature. Although it's got the highest mountain in England,
Scafell Pike — so not that miniature, I suppose — but compared
to the Andes or the Atlas Mountains, we're still talking about
hills that are very small.'

'Small but perfectly formed. This place is like a cabbage leaf —
lots of intricate indents and folds. But one thing that has caught
my lack of attention, so to speak — and surprised me — is that
there's not a lot of wildlife. Over the last few days, I've seen two
ravens when we were higher, a male kestrel quarter-flying and some
sort of finch skulking in the grass. That's about it. There are plenty
of places for birdlife to go down into, valleys with woodland, but
I guess these higher reaches just don't hold much attraction.'

Jasper was the quintessential muleteer: hard-drinking, a roamer
and given to music and song. He also had a fine eye for the
natural world, and was proving to be the perfect companion. As

a young man, he had taken his guitar and harp around the bars of Cork for sessions in which he played from a high stool by the fire. When I could prevail upon him, he would get his guitar out of the horse van and play us something at night, usually with a few muso mutterings about how he was aiming for Keith Richards' five-string open tuning.

As we travelled, I learned some of his more unusual quirks. He liked to listen to Norwegian long-distance weather forecasts, as he said they were more accurate than British ones; and he consumed prodigious quantities of Cadbury's Fruit and Nut bars to go with the vats of black coffee.

Jasper's advice about mules was usually terse and to the point. 'A mule is not stupid . . . ' was how one of his homilies might begin.

Muleteers have always been one-of-a-kind. For my night-time reading on our travels, I had brought *On the Road with Wellington: The Diary of a War Commissary* by August Schaumann, a classic account of the Peninsular War which the Duke had waged against Napoleon. Schaumann was a commissary whose duties included providing the many mules needed for the campaign.

> The Spanish muleteers form a large and hardy class of men. They seldom change their clothes or sleep under shelter throughout the year; they are always on the road and are very merry and constantly singing. When their mules are hired out for riding, they run alongside them at a trot for ten miles at a stretch in the greatest heat without getting tired. While running along in this way they fling their arms about and this seems to give them great relief. They wear large black felt hats with tassels, short jackets, a blanket with a hole in the middle for their heads, blue plush breeches and spats or sandals.
>
> On arriving at an inn, they are very smart in finding accommodation for themselves and their beasts. Eggs cooked in oil,

codfish, garlic, sardines, bread and a measure of wine are then prepared, and round this meal they sit, to the accompaniment of much noise and smacking of lips.

Schaumann's account of the mule train was also charming, and he himself was so taken by the animals that he chose to ride one rather than a horse:

My foreman had some magnificent mules which I rode by preference. When they are on the road they are decked with numbers of bells which tinkle melodiously in the distance ... Their endurance, strength, unexacting wants and gentle pace, and the fine manners and certainty with which they climb up and down the impracticable mountain roads in which the country [Spain] abounds, are incredible. I have often travelled as many as forty-five miles in one day, and they carry the largest loads day after day on long marches, and patiently and unwearyingly subsist on the most exiguous supplies of food and water.

Jethro still had a little way to go before he could match that sort of stamina. Years of standing around in an RSPCA field watching the world go by had not done his fitness any good, through no fault of his own. The batteries would often run out during a day's walking, so we would have to stop for him to recharge. But I did like the idea of putting some bells around his neck, or perhaps the copper cylinder that another fine nineteenth-century commentator on Spanish mules, Richard Ford, once described as 'having a wooden clapper called a *cencerro zumbón*', which hung down so the mule would gently knock against it, creating a 'tintinnabular clatter'.

Ford also described – in a way that even by nineteenth-century standards was not terribly PC – how mules were pimped up by their owners.

The mules in Spain, as in the East, have their coats closely shorn or clipped; part of the hair is usually left on it striped like a zebra, or cut into fanciful patterns, like the tattooings of an Indian chief. This process of shearing is found to keep the beast cooler and free from cutaneous disorders. The operation is performed in the southern provinces by gypsies, *gitanos*, who are the same tinkers, horse dealers and vagrants in Spain as elsewhere. In the northern provinces all this is done by Arroganese, who, in costume, good for nothingness, and most respects are no better than the worst real gypsies. The mule clippers are called *esquiladores*; they may be known by the formidable shears which they carry in their sashes. They are very particular in clipping the pastern and heels, which they say ought to be as free from hair as the palm of a lady's hand.

Richard Ford, *A Handbook for Travellers in Spain* (1845)

I was tempted to get out the clippers; but it might not go down well with the RSPCA if we returned Jethro looking like he had spent a drunken night at the tattooist's. However, I did like the idea of those bells. The thought of Jethro proceeding ahead of us and tinkling gently with a 'tintinnabular clatter' was immensely appealing.

*

The bridleway led up from High Broadrayne and then divided around the tongue of land that fell from Hause Riggs, with the footpath going one way and the bridleway the other.

Beyond was a small stream in a ravine, a ghyll, of the sort that make the Lake District such a delight. It was banked by ash and rowan. The rushing, forceful noise was a spur for all of us, Jethro included, who always picked up his pace when he was near water. A running stream has a compulsive noise that makes you somehow want to walk faster and further.

Over the watershed was Grisedale Tarn, one of the most emblematic of the mountain lakes, ringed by peaks. A path circled the water and led on to Helvellyn beyond. While Jasper and Jethro had some lunch, I quickly shimmied up a small peak called Seat Sandal which I had never climbed before.

Was I, like Jethro, getting fitter? My wife had made some acerbic comments as I set off on this mission about how a journey of 200 miles on foot might produce a svelter, more streamlined figure, if I kept off the pies and pints along the way. I had patiently explained that it was a necessary part of muleteering practice to subsist heartily; that not to do so would lead to historical inaccuracy; and that moreover, it might disappoint Jasper, who would expect me to follow the strict apprentice rules of that long and honourable tradition. What did she expect me to live on? Salads? I would probably be thrown out of the guild before I'd even begun. Would any of those fine Spanish muleteers who helped Wellington reconquer Spain have ever ordered a salad? Unless it was a chorizo one.

No, a disciplined approach to diet and exercise was already working wonders. Jasper had put it to me well: if you walked twenty miles a day, you could drink and eat as much as you liked, and still get fitter. Seat Sandal was a short but steep climb, and I felt I had done it in overdrive.

Just when I was sitting on the top and feeling pleased with myself, three men came by, at considerably greater speed than I had achieved. They were fell-runners reconnoitring the route for a later attempt – but they still didn't stop for a moment, or even a tin of Mackeson's milk stout. You can always tell a fell-runner because they never look at the view when they get to the summit of anything: only at their feet.

But I was certainly taking in the view, which was a special one for me, even though much of it was swathed in mist. In the foreground stood Grisedale Tarn, an oval fringed by sedge and moorland, with a drop-off at one end where the water cascaded away over the lip. Small pockets of a darker, lusher green marked the hanging valleys that extended down towards Ullswater. And on either side of those valleys, the familiar profiles of some of Lakeland's finest mountains were a guard of honour for the route that lay ahead.

For I knew Grisedale Tarn well, along with the approach to Helvellyn and the dramatic exit down Striding Edge, as I had come here twenty-five years ago, shortly before my first wedding.

✻

The idea of having a stag party in the mountains had initially been a good one. Why go off to some overpriced club with bad drinks and a strippergram, organised by the best man to comply with expectations? When instead we could have a day or two in the mountains and round it off with a final sybaritic meal at one of Ullswater's Michelin-starred hotels?

I invited a heterodox group of friends from different periods of my life: school, college and the buccaneering period in my twenties when I had tried to get going as a filmmaker (with limited success, but considerable enjoyment).

In my enthusiasm, I had forgotten one essential element of the male psyche. If ten young men arrive at a hotel, some of whom know each other extremely well and some of whom don't, and they have come for a weekend's celebration, they are not going to wait for the final evening to get started. They will hit the ground running. Or falling.

It was all over by the end of the Friday night, after we had congregated from different ends of the kingdom. The barman was still handing out malts at midnight. There was a pool table. Some of the London crew had brought cocaine. Saturday saw a distinctly jaundiced group trying to negotiate first Helvellyn and then Striding Edge in the spring sunshine.

Striding Edge is still the postcard ridge walk in the Lake District – a serrated knife that slices brutally down from one of its highest peaks. The fact that, in good weather at least, it is far easier to traverse than it looks is an added bonus. Although a clear head helps.

Coleridge passed it at nightfall, and left one of the first descriptions of its perils when he saw it from Helvellyn:

> That precipice fine on this side was but its ridge, sharp as a jagged knife, level so long, and then ascending so boldly – what a frightful bulgy precipice I stand on, and to my right how the crag which corresponds to the other, how it plunges down, like a waterfall, reaches a level steepness, and again plunges!

Now there's a man who would have been a quite excellent member of our stag party. Coleridge was used to walking with a hangover; indeed, was used to walking when still drunk.

> Many a walk in the clouds on the mountains did I take; but all would not do – till one day I dined at the house of the neighbouring clergyman, and somehow or other drank so much wine, that I found myself on the hither edge of sobriety.

It is the engaging 'somehow or other' I like so much – that and his choice of a clergyman's house to take him to the 'hither edge of sobriety'. Coleridge was then the same age as us, in his late twenties. I can imagine him as wonderful company, holding forth on wild schemes, expostulating as he walked, taking in both the view and the universe with an expansive sweep of the hand.

The revelatory biography of him by Richard Holmes had come out a few months before the stag party, and I had been reading it. The book portrayed a man who was – like many at that age – full of ambitious projects he might never be able to realise.

As Holmes put it: 'His real professional difficulties lay within himself . . . A lack of concentration of his efforts, a thousand brilliant projects without the corresponding energy to execute them. Yet when he did execute, it was still with astonishing speed, power and assurance. Just as physically he was a lazy, easy-going man, yet capable of tremendous feats of walking and climbing; so mentally, he was a drifter and dreamer, yet capable of sudden, short bursts of extremely imaginative intensity.'

The truth is, I have never really thought of the Lake District as Wordsworth country – which anyway is the polite southern bit around Grasmere. I think of it as Coleridge country, and its epicentre for me is Greta Hall near Keswick in the north, a far less cosy place. I have a vision of Coleridge standing in his study at Greta Hall with its big windows, looking out at a vista of mountains and space in which all seemed possible, but nothing was quite within reach.

The two men, although united for a time when they first proposed a radical new poetics, had such different outcomes. Coleridge is a lesson in heroic failure; Wordsworth is a lesson in what happens when you succeed too well.

Coleridge joined Wordsworth in the lakes in 1800, shortly after they had published their first edition of *Lyrical Ballads*. Aged twenty-seven, he was at the peak of his imaginative powers, before opium addiction took hold. 'Kubla Khan' and 'The Rime of the Ancient Mariner' had already been written. He was getting prestigious commissions and recognition as a journalist from the London papers.

For Coleridge, this partnership with Wordsworth was round two. His first poetic affair had been with Southey in Bristol – Coleridge referred to them as 'bedfellows'. Intense and idealistic as this had been, it had not lasted, even though they had married two sisters in the process. The wild ramblings of 'Pantisocracy' and anarchy – thoughts even of founding a new idealistic settlement in America – had blown away into the dust.

Now came the Lake District and a new bromance – with Wordsworth. Coleridge even followed the same pattern by falling in love with Wordsworth's sister-in-law; although, as he was still married to Southey's sister-in-law, this was both inconvenient and complicated.

But then Coleridge never took the easy route: the unpublished poems – almost incredible that 'Kubla Khan' took twenty years to get into print – the opium, the years of despair and failure; and all this set against a prodigal talent. One of his students noted Coleridge's constant habit of looking at himself in the mirror. I doubt this was vanity: more surprise at who he might be that particular day.

There is a rock-star quality to Coleridge that he shares with the young Tolstoy and, more obviously, the young Byron: the wild hair; the full, Jagger-style lips. Contemporaries commentated on the charisma of his presence.

But Coleridge had a signal disadvantage compared to those two aristocrats. He had no money.

When looking at the lives of artists, not enough time is spent examining their finances. Coleridge had young children and debts; his borrowing from friends like Wordsworth often caused embarrassment in what was an already-complicated relationship.

The hills of the Lake District were an escape from everything for Coleridge: his financial problems, his complicated and frustrated love life, his creative impasses and, as time went on, even Wordsworth, when the relationship soured. No wonder he poured himself so fervently into the landscape, going for long marathon walks that would have qualified him for the Bob Graham; yet noting each blade of fern and each cascade of a waterfall with the intensity of an opium addict.

From the moment he arrived, he devised ever-more-epic walks, often at night – both for the drama of it, and because he just set off so late. These walks are detailed in his notebooks, which, far more than the poems, show his senses almost deranged by the beauty and the wildness of the Lake District.

> My spirit courses, drives, and eddies like a leaf in autumn: a wild activity, of thoughts, imaginations, feelings, and impulses of motion, rises up from within me – a sort of *bottom-wind*, that blows to no point of the compass, and comes from I know not whence, but agitates the whole of me.

Wordsworth walked in the Lakes to give himself a poetic constitutional. Coleridge to give himself utterly up to the moment. To get lost.

In 1802, when the relationship with Wordsworth was already deteriorating – the intensity of Coleridge's poetic friendships was short-lived – he left Greta Hall to tramp a huge circuit of the Western and Southern Fells. You have to warm to a man who sets off with a converted broom for a walking stick (although in the conversion, he left most of the broom-brush scattered on the kitchen floor, to the annoyance of the long-suffering Mrs Coleridge). He had special Welsh walking boots, which included a back strap for pulling them on. In his knapsack, along with paper twists of tea and sugar, he carried a portable inkwell, which he put to good use on mountain summits, writing to Wordsworth's sister-in-law Sara Hutchinson, with whom he was still besotted.

One recurring feature of Coleridge's writing in his letters and journals when describing these walks was his obsession with clouds. Here he is, when taking much the same drovers' path past Skiddaw that we had taken Jethro along with Jeff Ford:

> We see a moving pillar of clouds, flame and smoke, rising, bending, arching, and in swift motion. From what God's

chimney does it issue? I scarcely ever saw in the sky such variety of shapes and colours, and colours floating over colours.

If the classical version of pastoral was one of an upland Arcadia fixed in time, the Romantics wanted constant movement. The landscape was only interesting for them if it was changing – was in a state of flux, like the onlooker's mind. No wonder that if Coleridge was not looking at clouds passing, he was staring transfixed at the movement of a waterfall – or, as he preferred to call them, a 'force'. Like the one at Newlands, in whose waters he saw 'an infinity of pearls and glass bulbs, the continual change of the matter ... an awful image and shadow of God and the world'.

Nor was he alone in this. Shelley was prone to lie on his back for hours, watching clouds pass overhead. Meteorology has affected British poetry as much as it has, more famously, affected its art. The turbulent Atlantic brings such changing weather to the Lake District – hence the high rainfall count at the Honister Pass – that there was constant variety and stimulus for the Romantic poets.

Coleridge's favourite analogy for the Lake District was of a sea, forever on the move. When he walked up the Helvellyn ridge, like us, to see Striding Edge, he thought himself on the 'last surge of that enormous ocean formed by the mountains of Ennerdale, Butterdale, Wasdale, and Borrowdale'.

The last thing Coleridge wanted was a Claude's Glass to fix the landscape in a particular view. What he needed was a kaleidoscope to shake it up. A century later he would have been a futurist, enthusing over the speed of trains and aeroplanes. How he would have loved the coming of the movies.

Coleridge our contemporary. My contemporary. Perhaps I empathised so much with the Coleridge of 1800 when I was younger – and still do – because my own life had only started to come together in my late twenties. When I walked here with those ten friends, after years of trying fruitlessly to break into the fortress of the BBC, I had finally succeeded, and was getting married, to a fellow filmmaker. The interesting film commissions were coming. I was already dreaming of being a travel writer. I loved the mountains.

And Coleridge was fascinated by travel writing. It was tremendously influential on his own work. Both 'Kubla Khan' and 'The Rime of the Ancient Mariner' are in some ways pieces of fan-fiction: tributes to the travel books he consumed with the prodigious appetite he applied to every enthusiasm or vice.

Just before coming to the Lakes, when he was supposed to be earning a living as a journalist, he had lost himself in the *Narrative of a Five-Year Expedition in Guiana, on the Wild Coast of South America,* by J. G. Stedman. In some ways, it was lucky for Coleridge's imagination – and for posterity – that he lacked the means to travel abroad. Instead, he recreated exotic locations in his head and in his poetry.

Twenty-seven, the age at which Coleridge arrived in the Lakes, is a far more pivotal age than twenty-one, for both men and women: much more an age of majority. At twenty-one, most people are still trying to make sense of the adult world. By twenty-seven, they should be up on the board and surfing. Or be left floundering in the shallows.

Looking back, I find it interesting to reflect on what has happened to the group of about that age who I invited on the 'stag walk'. Unlike our fathers' generation, few of us have kept to one profession for life. The only one who has is Fred, my blacksmith friend. For both those in finance and the arts, there has been serial insecurity. Many of those friends, like me, have wives who earn more than they do (but then, as my own wife is prone to point out, it's hard to earn less than a writer). Though none of them, unlike Coleridge, have gone on to develop a heavy opium habit.

It had been a happy moment at the end of the day when we

rolled down the hills back towards Ullswater. We had just about walked off our hangovers enough to start incurring another one, with the elated feeling of exhaustion that a true walk brings on – the sort of mood Coleridge was in when he arrived in those early days of their partnership at the Wordsworths' house in Grasmere. Coming by moonlight and staying up with Dorothy until three in the morning; talking about poetry and life; putting the world to rights.

I still have a note of the menu we ate on that final stag party night in Ullswater. This was the end of the eighties, so an age of excess; even so, it reads like something as remote as the banquet served up at a Tudor court. First, smoked duck wrapped in guineafowl; then smoked trout mousse wrapped in smoked salmon; a cleansing sorbet; turbot in cream with lavish trimmings; sirloin steaks in Chateaubriand sauce; blackberry mousse; champagne; cheese and coffee. Port and other fine liqueurs.

No Michelin-starred restaurant would dream of plating that up for customers these days. They would be prosecuted under the Public Health Act. And anyway, for better or worse, we live in an age of measured taste. A few line-caught scallops and locally sourced lamb. A dessert with a Zorro's mark of raspberry coulis etched over some low-sugar confection.

Not that Jasper and I were having any of that. We might be staying that night in a youth hostel rather than a tent, but dinner, when we wearily rolled down at the end of the day, was chicken and chips at the local pub.

＊

We studied the maps to see how best to get around the next obstacle, or spoke in the wheel, which was driving over the Kirkstone Pass with Jethro.

The problem was the old Dodge van. While in time, it might make beautifully converted accommodation for any barmaid, writer or itinerant musician, as a vehicle to get across the high places of England it had considerable limitations. It was a heavy van with a relatively small engine. Jasper did most of the driving while I navigated, as I was supposed to know the route. Getting from second into third was more of a leap of faith than a mechanical manoeuvre. Each time we went over a steep pass, we wondered if we would end up as a sad note in the local newspapers about how traffic had been blocked for hours by a broken-down lorry; it happened so regularly at Sutton Bank, the papers had stopped bothering to run the story.

I had bought the van at speed from a Jehovah's Witness called Steve. He lived in a city in the Midlands that didn't see many horses cantering the streets, even though, according to the amiable and talkative Steve, there was a blacksmith who lived nearby.

He showed me the lorry parked outside some lock-up garages around the back. With its half-timbered, mock-Tudor finish, it was so big it looked like a garage itself.

'The thing you have to remember about this van, Hugh,' said Steve, who had clearly rehearsed this line for any prospective purchaser – I was the first – 'is that it is reassuringly old.'

I wasn't sure how to take this.

'No, you see, what I mean is, it's old. So there's much less to go wrong with it. No electronics. No power steering. No electric windows. It's all *manual*. You know what I mean.'

He showed me the 'Luton compartment' over the driver's seat, with a mattress ('it'll take two'), so that you could sleep in the van, and a simple stove running off a gas canister. The cupboards were hanging off their hinges and tied together with string. 'I'm not sure if the stove works – we've never tried to light it.'

The one owner of the horse lorry previous to Steve had used it to potter between point-to-points, so the Dodge had done less than 1,000 miles each year. The travelling compartment for Jethro was spacious and high, with a 'jockey's door' through to the front. And as Steve said, it did at least start each time.

He was intrigued by my plan to take Jethro across the north of England. 'Well, that might give the Dodge a bit of a work-out.' It would indeed. Perhaps too much of one.

Sold, to the man who knows nothing about horseboxes. The next day, Steve delivered the Dodge and I drove him home: a journey long enough for him to tell me about what had been a complicated life.

There are conversations you have when driving which would be different were you to be looking someone in the eyes. After the conversational preliminaries, Steve told me his parents had separated when he was young. He had left school early to go into the building trade, despite some early talent for professional football, and developed a gambling habit.

Then things got more extreme. To fuel his gambling habit, he had started to rob betting shops with a few other young friends, wearing balaclavas.

'No guns, though, nothing like that,' he said quickly, to reassure me. 'Just baseball bats.'

I felt like saying, 'Oh, OK, so that's all right, then.'

As we navigated the multiple roundabouts of his hometown, Steve quickly came to the denouement of the story.

'But the thing is . . . I got caught.'

This happened on their second outing as an armed band. Steve, in a way he found suspicious – 'I think I was set up' – was the only one of his friends to feel the firm hand of the law on his shoulder. He refused to divulge the names of his accomplices and so got a much longer sentence.

During his five years in prison, 'which were really, really tough', he became a Jehovah's Witness. This helped him give up the gambling which had led him astray in the first place. For the last thirty years, he had led a prosperous and blameless family life. And he had another passion.

'It was football used to help me get rid of all my aggression when I was young,' he told me. 'And I was quite good. If things had turned out differently, I might have gone professional.'

He still looked solidly built. I suspected that if you had been tackled by Steve — and he played in defence — you would have known about it. That he had, as they used to say of Gary Neville, sharp elbows.

The last thing Steve did when I dropped him back off at his house was to tell me how the immobilising cut-off switch worked.

'Worth leaving it disabled. I realise a horsebox is an unlikely thing to steal. But they could break in and nick stuff. You can't be too careful. You never know who might be about.'

*

As it turned out, the Dodge coped with the Kirkstone Pass with aplomb — far better than a modern Winnebago ahead of us, which was clearly following a satnav and hadn't realised the gradients involved.

We parked the van up by the old Cow Bridge near Brothers Water. I wanted to get Jethro out as fast as possible after the journey, so that he could sniff the air of a new valley.

I always took pleasure in getting Jethro out of the Dodge, partly because it was the one time he never gave any trouble whatsoever. As instructed by Annis in my correspondence course, I had tied a large haynet to the ring to which he was secured by baler twine, and put daily fresh straw on the floor of the truck; 'have plenty of shavings on the floor to absorb pee and poo,' as Annis had put it. 'It's not called mucking out for nothing.' The Dodge was designed for at least three animals, so Jethro was enjoying the equine equivalent of a presidential suite. No wonder he was both frisky and pleased with himself after travelling in it. Even Jasper, who had firm views on Jethro's more truculent ways, particularly when it came to catching him in the morning, felt that he was superb at getting off and back on the Dodge. It was like one of those Hollywood movies where the difficult teenager turns out to have a secret talent after all.

We fitted him up with his Colorado riding blanket and elegant packsaddle.

'Excuse me. What's in the saddlebags?' asked a young girl of about nine politely, who was watching with her parents as we positioned them.

'Sandwiches. Water. A knife. Chorizo. Cheese. And a map.'

'Oh,' she said. 'They look almost empty. And your backpacks look quite full.'

Jethro did not have the grace to blush.

Our intrepid party set off through the pretty village of Hartsop and started climbing towards High Raise and the peaks of the Eastern Fells. The bridleway was wide enough for a couple of jeeps to come charging down at us from the small lake that lay above. For once, we were more surprised by them than the occupants were by Jethro.

Inside the two jeeps, rows of business managers wearing yellow safety jackets over their suits were sitting very stiffly in their seats. They had to stop as our mule team blocked the path, so I asked what they were doing.

'We've just had a team meeting before we start installing the pipe for the new hydroelectric scheme up there,' replied the man in the front passenger seat, who seemed to be their leader.

'Hydroelectric scheme?'

'The new National Trust one. It'll generate about 250 kilowatts for the grid — and 200 litres per second of water.'

The leader rattled off the figures with practised ease. Then he took another look at Jethro.

'Never seen a mule here before. Be careful when you get up on the fells towards High Raise. There are wild horses that might attack him. Always trying to eat our sandwiches. And the red deer are rutting now.' His voice took on a darker tone. 'Well into rut.'

We headed on, taking our chances. These hills had long been harvested for water. The lake the engineers were working at was relatively small, but over the brow of the hills we came to Haweswater. This provided the setting and title for Sarah Hall's precociously gifted first novel, published in 2002 when she was twenty-eight — and a far more contentious site for a water project.

*Haweswater* is based on historical events in the 1930s when a dam was built and the valley of Mardale flooded. For the young heroine Janet, and her family and friends, this means not just a dislocation of home, but of the spirit. The whole novel is about a void created at the heart of life; as 20,000 million gallons of water fill the valley, death follows, if by a drowning of the soul rather than the body.

The characters react in different ways when they first hear of the proposed flooding. Janet's father, Sam Lightburn, is a stoic and pragmatic character who will always walk behind a sheep wall if he can avoid the wind. He tries in his own way to accommodate and understand the changes that are to come and the loss of his family inheritance.

Janet is more passionate – likely to advance into the wind, hair and clothes streaming behind her, and declare, 'Blow winds and crack your cheeks!' She responds as characters often do in Sarah Hall's subsequent novels: by both losing and finding herself through sex, in her case a passionate affair with Jack Liggett, the young representative of the Manchester waterworks company sent to implement the dam. Hall has talked elsewhere of the strange telluric attraction between characters, which gives great energy to the scenes of physical love. This is the meeting not of like minds but of strange bodies drawn to each other for reasons that can seem inexplicable to both themselves and others.

The writing in the novel also invokes and caresses the landscape. Janet, we are told, could see her way around the fells blindfold and, so, I suspect, could Sarah Hall, who set two more of her novels in this part of the world. Not since John Cowper Powys has a novelist drawn such an intimate connection between the British landscape and the people who live there; nor in the Lakes themselves, perhaps, since her fellow Cumbrian Wordsworth, who was equally disturbed by changes wrought by technology. Although Sarah Hall, in her own words, 'is more interested in bracken than daffodils'.

She was brought up in a cottage three miles from the reservoir. Some of the locals had once lived in the village of Mardale Green and there was an annual memorial service for its loss. The reservoir is so huge it inverts the usual balance of water and valley. 'There's a sense,' Hall has said of her birthplace, 'that the mountains are inverted in the water and it's slightly discombobulating; you can't quite see where the mountains end and the waters begin.'

I had met Sarah on a writers' course and been impressed by her determination to create strong heroines to appeal as much to male as to female readers. In her novel, 'the yawning blue void of the valley, her family and the past' has a devastating effect on Janet and her family. A series of deaths ensue. It is a haunting, fatalistic tale that leaves the reader, as with some of Thomas Hardy's work, wanting to intervene to create better outcomes: to make sure Tess gets the letter from Angel; to help Hall's lovers from losing each other.

Haweswater is still an unnatural place – there are no seiches for a start, the internal waves one might expect on a normal lake. It is less visited than other lakes of the Eastern Fells, like Ullswater or Windermere, both because there is less road access and also perhaps due to this odd, artificial quality.

One road does travel past it: the old Roman one that runs for twelve miles over the mountain ridges from Galava (modern Ambleside) heading east. We joined it now by climbing up to the Straits of Riggindale, high crags that were famous once for hosting a pair of golden eagles – eagles that play a significant role in Sarah Hall's novel. We did see some raptors circling above but as Jasper said, 'however much you want those to be eagles, they are almost certainly going to be just buzzards'. Not least because the last golden eagle was thought to have died sometime before.

The light fell on the mountainside in such a way that looking back along the ridge, I could see where the modern path had diverged from the old: the ghost of the Roman road was a shadow on the grass falling away below High Street – a natural if disconcerting name for a mountain that lies on the route of an ancient thoroughfare.

But for most of its length, the old Roman road was still used: an extraordinary achievement for both its engineering and its ambition – especially because the Roman camp it served at Ambleside was not a major one, so this was only a spur; a classical

B-road. The broad track rolled ahead along the ridge above Haweswater in a fluid and enticing line for mile after mile. Walking it was like taking one of those motorised conveyor belts at airports where your own pace is artificially accelerated.

I remembered Hardy's lines: 'The Roman Road runs straight and bare / as the pale parting line in hair'. Glancing up at one point, I saw a red deer silhouetted against a ridge and thought it possible a Roman legionary might have done the same two millennia ago (and yes, before any pedant raises objections, there would have been red deer then).

Alfred Wainwright loved this road. He devoted one of his last works to it, a small pamphlet called *Old Roads of Eastern Lakeland* which can be difficult to find. He wrote it when his eyesight was failing and the handwritten text is, movingly, less sure than it once was.

He described the road as 'a monument to the topographical knowledge of its surveyors, who planned the route across virgin terrain and to the skill of the engineers who gave it a firm foundation in mossy and peaty ground'. He also felt it 'a testimony to the endurance of the legions of soldiers who, often in mist and cloud, tramped this long march'. By including part of it in his Coast-to-Coast walk, Wainwright has increased its modern use and appreciation substantially.

He was less enthusiastic about the flooding of the valley below.

> If we can accept as absolutely necessary the conversion of Haweswater [to a reservoir], then it must be conceded that Manchester have done the job as unobtrusively as possible. Mardale is still a noble valley. But man works with such clumsy hands! Gone forever are the quiet wooded bays and shingly shores that nature had fashioned so sweetly in the Haweswater of old; how aggressively ugly is the tidemark of the new Haweswater!

The experience of visiting the already-deserted village of Mardale Green in the 1930s shortly before it was flooded prompted an elegiac and emotional reaction from a man not given to loose sentiment. In later life, Wainwright would often tell of how he walked down the lanes past the church to the empty pub, the Dun Bull; of the eerie absence of humans even though birds were still singing in hedgerows fragrant with wild roses; of the intimation of death and doom with which the village had left him.

Haweswater supplies the north-west with a quarter of all its water. Manchester needed the reservoir. Mardale Green and nearby Measand were small villages. There was a clear rational argument for their destruction and the creation of the dam. But it has left ghosts in its wake.

For many years, I sailed Chew Valley Lake in the shadow of the Mendips near Bristol, another reservoir created by flooding a beautiful valley. There are tales told by the sailors there of how, on certain days when the water level is low and the sun hits the water at the right angle, you can just make out the tops of an old church.

Similar stories are told of Haweswater when it dried up in the drought of 1979: of the glimpses of the buildings beneath. But usually the lake is full to the meniscus brim, like a bath about to overflow, controlled by a series of sluice gates.

The last ridge-point the Roman road traversed was called High Raise. As we swung along in cheerful and good order, Jethro making the odd grunt of approval, I felt pleased that we had successfully passed through the Lakes, our first big hurdle. The bulk of our journey lay in front of us; you could say we had now climbed the mountain before making the ski jump.

The dramatically steep buttresses of Kidsty Pike fell off to one side of the ridge, towards Haweswater, but from High Raise I could also see ahead for the first time, to the edge of the Lake

District and to the plains leading to the Howgills and the York-shire Dales.

After days of walking a circuitous route through the mountains, of feeling encircled by them, the sight of the flat land before us came as a shock, as if I was about to enter another country. Which in some ways I was.

✻

# Chapter 5

# The House in the Howgills

When unsaddled, mules should be allowed to roll, a procedure they thoroughly enjoy and one which rapidly dries the heated back.

The War Office, *Animal Management* (London, 1923)

Sunlight was still falling aslant the lane, but there were dark storm clouds ahead over the cliff scars that edged Crosby Ravensworth Fell, and the air had turned humid with the anticipation of rain. I was walking down the rough, unmade surface of Knott Lane, near the village of Orton, a day's journey to the east. And I had come to see a place of great talismanic importance in the landscape. A detour from the bridleway – so I had left Jethro and Jasper for a while – but a necessary one.

I had no wet-weather gear with me. Instead I was wearing just an old white shirt with blue stripes. It occurred to me that this was one of the few shirts that crossed every boundary in a Britain that was still heavily demarcated: a shirt worn by gypsies, farmers and city businessman alike, over weather-beaten necks and those made pale by a lifetime of air-conditioned offices; perhaps because the thin blue vertical stripes have the universal effect of making the wearer look slimmer. Mine had a looser, more flattering cut – the time was long gone when I could get away with a tailored, fitted shirt – and let in a welcome breeze to combat the humidity.

The stones revealed themselves suddenly as I passed a wall. They were grouped in a field, looking not so much mysterious as a bit lost and forlorn after 5,000 years of existence. The Orton Stone Circle comprised thirty-three stones of different sizes, set in a wide ring of more than a hundred yards in circumference.

The grandeur of the original conception had been lessened by a stone wall built right up against one end of the circle – although nothing as intrusive as at its contemporary, Stonehenge, where roads have made the monument a virtual traffic island. But whereas Stonehenge received a million visitors a year, the only other audience at these stones were sheep. It felt like a forgotten place.

Yet the stones had presence. The grain and the soft pink of the granite glowed in the last of the sun before the rain clouds arrived. I remembered Robert Louis Stevenson's lines:

Grey recumbent tombs of the dead in desert places,
Standing stones on the vacant wine-red moor,
Hills of sheep, and the howes of the silent vanished races,
And winds, austere and pure.
                    'To S. R. Crockett', from *Songs of Travel* (1895)

A 'howe' is an old Scots word for a tumulus. While a stone circle can bring out the best in poets, I've often thought that something about them inhibits guide writers – as if they were such prehistoric oddities that all anyone can do is mention them and pass on briskly. The only extraneous detail about the Orton Stone Circle that commentators like Wainwright love to include, because it's factual so they feel safe, is that these stones are 'erratic boulders brought to this area by glaciers'.

The glacial action on the surrounding landscape is irrelevant, and not something of which prehistoric man would have been conscious. But what does matter is that these stones were so different from the local limestone. Were exotic. And there was nothing Neolithic men appreciated more than a wild bit of stone.

It has long been known that the Stonehenge bluestones were

brought all the way from the Preseli Mountains on the western coast of Wales, a distance of 240 miles. The precise quarry they came from has now even been identified. Recent discoveries have shown that the vast interior of Silbury Hill, the man-made monument in Wiltshire, contains many stones that had equally travelled a very long way. And the previous summer I had made a pilgrimage up to the Outer Hebrides to see the stones of Callanish, shards of unusual Lewisian gneiss stabbing the sky in a cruciform pattern.

The provenance of stones had immense power for prehistoric man, and not just in Britain: I knew from my travels how strong an element it was in the archaeology of Peru, where stones were transported from great distances to other sites. No stone would ever be considered, to use our pejorative and dull term, just a boulder. If you lived that vulnerably and close to the ground, the landscape had far more meaning.

The Orton Stone Circle has been much reduced over the millennia. In 1862, the whole site was ploughed, with the irretrievable loss of archaeological evidence. Some stones were blasted into fragments. Much of the embankment on which the stones originally stood has been flattened. Even a century ago, there were forty rather than thirty stones. They have all fallen, so none now stand over a metre high.

This part of the country was particularly attractive to Bronze Age man. The map of prehistoric sites in Britain makes Cumbria look like a metropolitan area. Castlerigg, near Keswick, and the wonderfully named Long Meg and Her Daughters are two of the better-known stone circles in the Lake District. But even closer to Orton lay a whole nexus of prehistoric sites: including Kemp Howe, which once had an impressive avenue of stones leading to a wide ring until the Victorians built the West Coast Main Line railway right through it. Sensitivity to prehistoric – and therefore pre-Christian – culture was not high on the Victorian agenda.

Outside of a few new-age commentators like Julian Cope, and

his eccentric almanac of prehistoric sites, the smaller stone circles around Britain attract little interest. There was a time when they were more admired. In the late eighteenth century, there was even a fashion for recreating them. The same Mr Pocklington who attracted Wordsworth's ire for building a terrible house on his island in the Lake District also fashioned a mock stone circle. History does not record, sadly, Wordsworth's reaction to this; one imagines it to have been apoplectic. Unlike Stonehenge, it never made it into *The Prelude*.

When Wainwright was taking his Coast-to-Coast route, he complained that such prehistoric monuments can only really be appreciated by aerial photographs. This seems a specious objection when it comes to the stone circle at Orton; a short walk up the steep slopes of nearby Great Asby Scar disturbed the local rabbits and gave me a fine overhead view; one that allowed me to see that strictly speaking it was not a 'stone circle' at all, but a 'stone oval'. The long end of that oval pointed towards the north-west, along the alignment common to many other such rings, as the scholar Aubrey Burl has pointed out – for that is the alignment of sunset on 1 May, the ancient Celtic festival of Beltane, whose roots go very deep indeed.

From above, the stones were also set in their context, with the Howgills beyond – the hills where George Fox gave his tremendous seventeenth-century speech, which launched the Quaker movement, to an audience in the open air.

I wondered if it was something to do with the nature of the Howgills. They are not grand imposing mountains of the sort that dominate the Lake District, but manageable hills of fell and dale, of a soft and fecund green. Human in scale. A landscape that was farmed by prehistoric man just as much as by the shepherds who listened so much later to George Fox. A landscape that could be seen as sacred and full of potential for the human spirit. A green and pleasant land indeed: England at its best.

The scramble up Great Asby Scar had made me grateful again

for my loose white shirt and I rested on the top, looking out at the view and the stone ring below. I took it all in for a while. There was a cairn of stones left by people who had taken this journey over the years and I sheltered beside it, as the wind started up. The same wind that was bringing the storm clouds across. Then the heavens opened and I let the rain drench me to the skin.

*

The rain was still falling as we travelled deeper into the Howgills, almost the first we had seen on our journey so far. Jethro's coat acquired a glistening sheen; Jasper wrapped his cloak tighter around him. When we sheltered in the horse van to make cups of tea on the beaten-up old stove, the rain brushed along the corrugated roof like an artist painting it with watercolours.

The Howgills are the welcoming hills just to the east of the Lake District: a gentler land, outside of the national park boundaries, so less well- (or over-) preserved. They were not a part of the country I knew – so it was doubly welcome that we had a house to shelter in, with the artist Jason Gathorne-Hardy.

I had met Jason in a providential and satisfying way. His drawings of birds and sheep had become well known and sought after. Several of my friends had bought one of them over the years. I became acquisitive, a rare thing for me; but I see very little art I ever like enough to want to buy. Or for that matter, can afford. I rang him up at his gallery and home in Suffolk.

Jason, in a way I soon learned to be typical, was both welcoming and curious. He discovered I was a writer – and as, among other things, he ran an art and literature festival, I was signed up to perform. He asked about my next and future projects.

When I told him I was trying to get a mule across the north

of England, he offered the use of an old farmhouse his family shared as a holiday base in the Howgills.

'I think it could be perfect for a mule,' he enthused. 'There's an old stable. We don't have fields of our own any more but we could borrow a bit of pasture from the local farmer. Or our walled orchard may be big enough.'

Jason met us now when we arrived, wearing an old brown overcoat that covered many woollen layers, and with a cloth cap perched on his head from which a jaunty feather protruded. The flowery shirt that poked out from under his woollen sweater was the only clue that 'you're not from round here'.

Banks Farm was a little way up the lane from Ravenstonedale – a handsome village, large enough to have its own pub. Not that Banks Farm was unwelcoming in its own right, or lacked alcohol. A red front door in the white wall led through to a snug: a living room small enough for three men and Jason's dog to sit round the table and put the world to rights. There was no central heating, but there was a wood-burning stove.

Jason had driven from Suffolk to greet us, a substantial journey made longer because he had, in an eccentric way, come via Wales in order to collect some Dexter beef steaks ('I hadn't realised it was so far, but they were giving them to me'), which he now proceeded to cook. He served them with vintage wine he had bought in a job lot at an auction for a knock-down price but never opened. The cork crumbled when extracted – a bad omen – and the wine tasted like cider vinegar.

'Ah, well,' he said with a shrug, 'you can never know with these things.' Jason was not a man to let anything trip him up.

Every room in the farmhouse had acquired a deep layer of family life. Jason's grandfather had bought it at auction during the agricultural depression of the 1930s (by accident – he had wanted another farm but got this one by default) and the family had been coming here ever since. But while Jason shared the house with other members of that family, it felt imbued with his own artistic presence.

Just as with Edward Piper's studio in Somerset and those of other artists I have known, there was a sense of place (and grace) that extended throughout the house: not only the paintings and prints scattered throughout, as one would expect, but everything from plates to old books to the sheepskin rugs.

The Bloomsbury project, of living the art as well as creating it, still seems a desirable quest. Jason avoided the self-indulgence that often attends this, with a scrupulous attention to the authenticity of place, the roots of the landscape (about which he knew much), and the authenticity of his own work.

And the farmhouse had an austerity to it. This was not Charleston, let alone Sissinghurst, in their comfortable South Downs settings. With only forty acres – which these days the family contracted out – the farmland would not have given much of a living, and the house was in an exposed position at the top of a hill. One previous farmer had hung himself.

Jason showed me the old cow-byres at the end of the farm which had been left unchanged: dark, damp rooms from which the cattle would have emerged blinking after many months in the winter dark. We retired to more commodious accommodation: deep, wide beds surrounded by dark wood furniture, while Jethro had the small orchard to roam.

The next day, Jason took us for a walk across the fields at the back of the farm where he and his siblings used to play when they were small. We crossed a stream tumbling down through the farm from the open fell. He told us that his family often came here on holiday from their own farm in the flatlands of Suffolk, so as a child these hills were a constant revelation and a surprise.

The Howgills sit discreetly and modestly between the Yorkshire Dales and the North Pennines. They are not well known. I would wager that a large proportion of the population of Britain has no idea where they are and, if asked, would guess Scotland. Or Australia.

Jason clearly found them a continuous source of artistic stimulation. He had his sketchbooks with him now as we walked, in an angular canvas knapsack. I could see how the long, lean undulating hills could give a satisfying horizon-line for a painter; mountains, by contrast, with their jagged edges, are notoriously difficult to fit into a frame. Even Turner struggled with the Alps.

To me, this landscape felt empty, and in a good way: the farms that we could see were few and far between. I asked Jason why.

'Yes, the pattern has always been that you get the enclosed land with the farmhouses along the valley bottoms, which has the richer soil, and then as you get up into the Howgills themselves, the hills, you get large areas of open land like Ravenstonedale Common here. So you would climb from richer pastures out onto the fell, the heath.

'And as you walk up the hill, you can almost hear the grass change underfoot. The fell grass often creaks, so it sounds like you're walking over leather – whereas the richer, lower grass we're on now, of the pastures, is soft and silent.'

We went quiet to put this to the test. I liked the idea of listening to grass – very Brian Eno – and the ground was lovely going after the stone and flint of the Lake District; sedge and a little bit of sphagnum moss were underfoot, as the flanks of the hills were often waterlogged, so the peat had a gentle bit of give. Small clouds of midges were rising from the sphagnum. Under normal circumstances this might have been foreboding, but the midges were content just to look picturesque silhouetted against the sun, forming a double helix that spiralled upwards.

Jethro was in his element. I suspected that if asked – loath as I was to ventriloquise – he would have been happy to stay in Howgills for the duration. And Jason would have been equally happy to host him. He had already been making acquisitive enquiries.

'How much hay does Jethro eat? And do you think the RSPCA would let someone adopt him permanently?'

The RSPCA were desperate for someone to adopt Jethro on a long-term basis; I was just fostering him for the duration of the walk. But, quite rightly, they wanted a person who had other horses and mules as companions for him.

We could see sheep up above us on the fells. 'That will be a hefted flock,' said Jason. 'They know their patch and won't stray far.'

The idea of sheep being hefted, drawn back to a particular part of the land, is an attractive one. In a way, we speculated, many of us are hefted ourselves to a piece of land, although we perhaps may not realise it.

Jason told a story of two agricultural labourers in Suffolk who during the depression of the 1930s decided to chance their luck and emigrate to Canada. They sold all their possessions to get the tickets over to Liverpool and the boats. On the slow train across the East Anglian prairie, however, as they saw what they were leaving, they became homesick and abandoned the plan by jumping off the train and walking home instead.

History – or at least Jason – didn't record whether they felt later this had been a good decision; although given the hardship other emigrants experienced in Canada, despite the enticing offer of free land, perhaps this change of heart was providential.

'It would be interesting,' I suggested, 'and even appropriate if we were all marked with a stripe or a smit mark to show where we were hefted. Perhaps a discreet tattoo below the waterline.

Jasper, I think you should be hefted. Although I don't think Jethro would take to it. A mule has a right to roam, after all.'

'I wouldn't mind having a couple of clips taken out of my ears,' said Jasper. 'If it was under anaesthetic.'

He stopped to pick up some sheep's wool that had got carded into the grass.

'This is fantastic stuff to have in your pocket in case you get blisters. Full of natural lanolin. Not that I'm anticipating any blisters on this trip. But as they always say, better to be looking at it than looking for it.'

He added it to the mysterious depths of the poacher's pocket in his jacket. Like a magician's hat, I had seen many things disappear into this; but nothing ever seemed to re-emerge.

We headed up with Jason's dog Toby clipping at our heels – although Toby sensibly gave Jethro a wide berth. There was no path, so the sort of meandering walk followed in which three men are more interested in the conversation than in where they are going; we were aiming for the top of nearby Harter Fell.

Jason explained how his family's small farm here was part of a land stewardship conservation scheme, so some areas had been left for set-aside, with pastures gone to wild meadow and the old stone walls maintained. All admirable stuff, even if, he said, the farmer in him itched to see all available land used well.

We were learning more about Jason's eccentricities. One of them stopped us in our tracks when he mentioned that he had been building a 200-metre-long picnic table back at his main farm in Suffolk.

'Two hundred metres,' both Jasper and I squealed. 'Or do you mean feet? Or inches?'

I did the maths: 200 metres was about 660 feet. Which would mean a picnic table that was too big for most fields, even though in East Anglia they made them large.

'Yes,' said Jason, as if it was a natural ambition, 'it may get into the *Guinness World Records*. Although to do so we need enough people actually having a picnic at the table at the same time – which would be a lot to cater for, let alone arrange.

'At least you haven't asked me, as some people do, whether it was all cut from the same tree! To which I always reply that, wherever you were in the world, you would probably have seen that tree growing.'

We asked how people sat.

'Sawn tree trunks. Or they bring their own chairs. The planks we use for the table are bloody heavy. I'm always getting a bad knee or back from moving them around the farm.

'I had an embarrassing injury two or three years ago when I was walking along at dusk, carrying my drawing bags, so my weight was off-balance. And I saw one of the planks had come loose from the table, knocked by a sheep, so I jumped up onto it to do some repairs. Which was all right. But when I jumped off again, I landed at an awkward angle and ruptured the knee ligaments.

'And I had been conscious at the time there were a lot of things in my life I wasn't really facing up to, which I needed to, because I had been too busy. It was as if God had said, "You idiot, you have to deal with this." *Flick.* And my first thought was, "This is really painful, something has really gone wrong with my knee." And the next was, "OK, this has got to stop now, I need to face up to some decisions." And the third was, again, "This hurts like fuck!"'

We reached Harter Fell to see the ancient woods of Murthwaite below. I wondered if Tolkien had based his Mirkwood on this

Viking name – the sort that would have appealed to him. It is a remnant of the original forest that once covered most of Britain, broadleaved and with orchids growing between its deep, dark glades.

A cold wind started up, so we sheltered under a scrape a little below the summit and had tea from a Thermos. It was a clear October day and we could see a long way in every direction. The big stone farmhouses across the valley were noticeably substantial.

'Several hundred years ago, in the seventeenth and eighteenth century,' said Jason, 'the sheep industry was very profitable here. So they built these farms – and you can tell the stone has been dressed, so they're not just dry-stone walls. The buildings have been assembled with a lot of care.'

To me, it didn't have the 'preserved in aspic' feel of the Lake District – or for that matter, any tourists. Apart from the odd walker who goes to see the famous waterfall at Cautley Spout, few people venture this way. I liked the looser feel, with small communities and farmsteads placed higgledy-piggledy over a beautiful set of hills.

Jason had been here for the hay harvest a few months before. He told us he had sat on a ridge above the River Lune and seen the hay being gathered from the half-a-dozen farms all around; and how it had reminded him that this was still a working farm landscape. And how rare that was these days – how few places were left where agriculture still dominated absolutely.

'What I like,' said Jasper, 'is that it's a softer landscape than we saw in the Lake District. All those rocks we had to clatter across with Jethro. This is more undulating, more forgiving – although of course it would still be harsh in winter.

'The architecture is comfortable. Good stonework. No draughts going through the walls. In Ireland, we would call these people "strong farmers": farmers who are in charge of themselves.'

We could see handsome stone barns backing on to Wild Boar Fell, more common land where sheep could graze. The wool crop must once have been very valuable to sustain such investment. But the agricultural depressions first at the end of the nineteenth century and then in the 1930s had knocked the stuffing out of the prosperous local pillows. Some farmhouses in the distance had been abandoned.

More recently, the foot-and-mouth epidemic of 2001 had been savage in Cumbria, with a share of almost half of the national reported cases and the consequent widespread slaughter of live-stock. To rebuild the flocks of sheep that had always been hefted to one part of the landscape would take patience and time.

'It feels as though there are fewer sheep here up on the common now than when I was a child,' said Jason. 'So many were slaugh-tered during the foot-and-mouth, and so much damage and destruction was done to the flocks.

'Outsiders think you can just purchase a whole new herd with the compensation money and off you go. But it's not as simple as that. The Howgills must have had twenty to thirty flocks beforehand, each hefted to a particular place, and once one of those disappears, it's like losing a piece of the jigsaw. The bound-aries start to fall apart. The sheep stray.'

The burning of sheep and cattle carcasses that took place at the time of foot and mouth – some 10 million animals slaugh-tered, when many could have been vaccinated – was in some ways like the burning of a library, Jason felt. The loss of an inherited hefted knowledge that could not be replaced overnight, of herds that had built up for generations.

Not that sheep were an unmixed blessing. There are precious

few trees in the Howgills. Jason had pointed out a rare covert of them as we passed a steep gorge – birch, rowan and ash, covered in honeysuckle – which had been preserved only because it was too difficult for sheep to graze. 'Land,' as Jason put it, 'wants to be woodland – that is its natural energy and tendency – and sheep nibble that future out.' The uniform green sward they create is not entirely welcome.

The environmental campaigner George Monbiot has been at the vocal forefront of this criticism:

> We pay billions to service a national obsession with sheep, in return for which the woolly maggots kindly trash the countryside. The white plague has done more extensive environmental damage than all the building that has ever taken place here, but to identify it as an agent of destruction is little short of blasphemy. Britain is being shagged by sheep, but hardly anyone dares say so.
>
> 'Sheepwrecked', the *Spectator* (May 2013)

In reply, sheep farmers like James Rebanks, author of *The Shepherd's Life*, would argue that a mixed, balanced economy was perfectly possible, while admitting there has been overgrazing in the past; and that, moreover, a Lake District without sheep farming would become an empty heritage centre. I had heard James lecture and agreed strongly with his concern that there was a current 'disconnect' from farming; that the long tradition of keeping sheep on shared common fells, without fences, was an important reminder of a time when the whole of England had yet to be enclosed.

It was a good example of how the ideological concept of a 'natural England', a state to which we could and should return, was fraught with contradictions. I asked Jason about the controversy George Monbiot's criticism of sheep had caused here as well as in the Lake District.

'The local sheep farmers all hated him for it. But what we perhaps need is some new balance between the open fells for sheep, with all the history they bring with them, and letting some land revert to woodland. And I mean revert – not planted. Just let the natural trees come back, which may take longer than planting up, but will be more in keeping.'

We could see the faint line of paths riding high over the ridges of the hills, slip-sliding between them.

'There are bridleways,' said Jason, 'which go right across the top of the Howgills, some of them very ancient. A lot were abandoned at the end of the nineteenth century with the decline in farming. And sometimes over the years when I've been walking across them, I can imagine the faintest echo of the Roman legions tramping towards Hadrian's Wall and the northern outposts.'

Jason knew how to entice his listeners. I immediately wanted to take one such drovers' road with Jethro along Bowderdale, which would have been the old route for pack horses travelling south to Sedbergh, home of the Quakers.

✢

We drove over to the beginning of the route in the horse van – a van which I noticed Jason was beginning to covet, perhaps because Jasper was talking it up: 'Usually I hate driving, although I've ended up driving a lot on this trip. And I find I really like driving this lorry. It's such a zen experience. It's too loud to listen to the radio, and it's a very difficult, physical thing to steer, so it's a real retro experience. There's no synchromesh.

'You're going along in a sort of time capsule with the rest of the world rushing past. It's quite wide, and you have to be particularly careful in these lanes. It's an instant mindfulness trip. You really can't think of anything else except driving. And you've got the mule in the back, so there's always that constant thought that you must be careful not to jolt or go around corners too sharply.

'In a way, driving is one of the few forms of meditation that Westerners understand – you have to concentrate without thinking.'

I gave Jasper some mints from the stash in the glove compartment to help the concentration. My job was to navigate, listen to Jasper's mule stories and provide occasional sustenance.

Jason hunched forward from the jockey's compartment to put his head between us. 'I always wonder if it should not be so much "I think therefore I am", but rather more "I do therefore I am".'

It was the first time we had had a philosophical conversation in the van. Usually while Jasper talked about mules, I talked about football. Jason's presence had lifted the tone.

Jasper mused. 'Yes, words are powerful creative forces in life but when it comes down to it, one judges situations and people by what gets done. The attraction of so-called "simple people", the ones I work with on horses, is that they say what they're doing and do what they say. It may not make them great conversationalists, but it doesn't half cut to the chase. They're quite often the people I go to for advice. They don't faff around. They will give it to you direct. Whatever you are attempting, they might just say, "That's stupid – you should do it like this. And get on with it!"'

As a writer, I was – like Jasper – all too aware of the truth of this. Words can be a displacement activity; so much easier to talk about things than to do them. In a way, the whole mule trip had come about with a loose way of words. I had talked myself into doing something I then had to fulfil.

When we reached the roadhead, Jethro came bucketing out of the van at tremendous speed, as if itching to get back on to the fells. Jason had already made admiring noises about Jethro's fine mule accoutrements: the Iranian saddle lashed around his girth with my mother's long leather belt from an ancient trunk in the attic; the elegant, if small, saddlebags; the striped saddle blanket. This was an equine starlet who could easily have made the cover of *American Mule*, the *Bulletin of the British Mule Society* or some other such fine publication. He fidgeted impatiently as we made our own small adjustments to boots and rucksacks.

And then we were off, up the long Bowderdale valley ('a noble valley indeed' as Wainwright called it) which heads south past the Calf: an unusual name for a mountain, given that, as the highest in the Howgills, it has no corresponding mother.

The bridleway had once been well trodden, when open-cast coal was taken by pack animals from Galloway Gate to distribution points like Sedbergh. Only in 1840 had such open-cast coal stopped being profitable, when the coming of canals and railways allowed the deep mining of pits in South Yorkshire to begin.

But now it had a faded, ghostly quality. The wide track curved satisfyingly up the long valley. For the first time, we were walking in a mist, although such a light one that it merely softened the views a touch, like a graduated filter on a lens.

This was how I had always imagined a pack-horse route: a green road across the landscape. And I felt man and mule were much more in harmony than we had been through the Lake District. I could walk with only a lead rope held loosely over my shoulder and Jethro following – not at all the regulation way I had done for the RSPCA, but how I was used to travelling in South America. And Jethro was responding at a good pace, ambling along behind me. True, he had playfully headbutted me in the chest when we had stopped for Jasper to take a picture; but a mule must have his fun.

Jasper was enjoying it as well. 'Now, this is one of the first real pack-horse routes we have come across so far. Not just something people have managed to get pack horses over, with complicated chicanes and steep rock faces where Jethro's been struggling to haul himself up – with great aplomb, it must be said, as he is a mule after all, and nimble of foot and strong of heart. But you can tell he's got a real tempo under his hooves here, so it's much more pleasant for him and also much more pleasant for us. It takes away the worry of what's under your feet, or more to the point, what's under your animal's feet.'

We set off up the long gentle valley at a good clip of some four miles an hour; 'song pace' as Jasper called it. He sang us a few bars of folk songs he thought must have been written on the hoof: about marching off to war or of jolly packmen taking their wares up to a high village and courting fair maids. A musical tradition based on long walks and moving from one place to another, with all the accompanying joys and illicit pleasures – drinking and wooing and carousing; making a bit of money and moving on to see new things.

By the time we got back to the old horse van, we were in fine spirits. Jason announced that rather than ride back with us in the van, he would walk over the fells with his dog Toby. Jasper and I looked at each other. It was nearing dusk and the late autumn day was closing in. There were black clouds on the horizon. But Jason was our host and knew these hills well. He had also told us how much he liked to go out in the wind and the rain, and then draw the landscape – letting the water run down the marks he was making on the thick cartridge paper. It would have been churlish to question his decision.

So we drove back without him and enjoyed the warm house and the chicken I cooked, and the supply of beers we had brought. We put the world to rights. The hours went by. Even though neither Jasper nor I would qualify as responsible – we were, after all, both writers – the time came when even we started to be alarmed. It was past midnight and Jason had still not put in an appearance. A wild storm had started up outside. The farm had intermittent mobile reception and it was unlikely Jason's phone would work across the Howgills as he made his way back home.

We both started up as one from our comfortable armchairs. Jasper headed out across the pitch black of one field to look for him, while I went up the hill on the small lane which led to the remote community of Adamthwaite. The moon coming through the clouds gave just enough illumination on the tarmac. There was a howling wind. I had a small torch to flash, hoping that might help Jason if he was out there.

The situation was becoming dreamlike. I could not quite believe that Jason was in serious trouble. But on the other hand, things can go wrong in the hills even for people who know them well – and Jason was on his own, or at least only had his dog.

I came to a small country crossroads right on top of the fells. By now I was soaked from head to toe. The rain was coming in horizontally. It was the sort of place where, in the legend of old blues songs, the devil would appear to make a pact – but then, I thought, surely the devil can only make a pact with a young man? I had little left to bargain with.

Still, it was a wild moment; an elemental one. It had been good to be tucked up beside the fire. But it was also good to be out on the wild heath in the middle of a storm with the elements raging. And if Jason was still out there, he needed all the help he could get.

I trudged back down the lane to the farm. Jasper had already returned. He too had found nothing. We consulted. Should we ring the emergency services? We would need to drive down to the village and use the pub phone. And we would look very stupid if it was a false alarm.

Just then Jason appeared, walking up the road, with Toby trotting at his heels. He looked insouciant and relaxed, if a little sheepish, as only a man can who has spent his life drawing them.

'I realised I was heading into the storm pretty quickly, so I turned back down to the road instead and got a lift to Raven-stonedale. I've been in the pub for the last couple of hours warming up and drinking whisky. But don't worry, before that I got some wonderful sketches.'

*

Because we were staying several days at Jason's farm, I had the luxury of writing by daylight, rather than trying to keep a journal at the end of each long day. The night after the storm, I was able to sit in the sunny orchard, with my legs up in the crook of a tree, watching Jethro as he wandered around working out which gate or low wall gave him the best view. The sun was filtering through the sycamore trees from the east and lighting up the grass.

I was once shown Wilfred Thesiger's journals in his personal archive. They were of a large foolscap size and must have been bulky to travel with, although Thesiger usually had plenty of native porters.

In immaculate copperplate handwriting, he detailed how he 'rose at dawn, as is my habit, and circled the lake as the ibis were feeding in the shallows. Then I returned to the camp to write this journal before breakfast.' Like Trollope knocking off thousands of words before beginning a day's shift at the Post Office.

I was not made of such stern stuff. But I did try to get everything down straight away – often stopping to record thoughts in the middle of a walk, to the occasional frustration of travelling companions. To be able to write with a mug of coffee in my hand, sitting in the sun, was a rare treat. Although, as ever, there were displacement activities happening all around to distract me.

Two rams were getting frisky over in the next field. It was a curious dance of rivalry. They went alongside each other not head-to-head but head-to-tail – 'measuring each other', as Jason described it to me later – so that each was rubbing the other's flank. Then they rubbed each other violently to see which would give way.

It's remarkable how vague the great British public are about sheep, given that we live alongside 20 million of them. Some walkers get hysterical at the thought of walking through a field with cattle, let alone a bull; but assume all sheep are, well, sheepish by disposition. A ram can still have plenty of testosterone, some of it misplaced, and the advice I was once given by a shepherd – 'never turn your back on a ram' – still holds true.

This is easier to remember with the Texel rams that have been brought over from Holland in the last twenty years to toughen and 'beef up' our own breeds, as they look half bulldog anyway; sheep that have worked out in the gym, with impressive and alarming musculature. The time when young men in tough urban areas have a Texel on a lead when they make the rounds between off-licence, betting shop and drug dealer cannot be far off.

The orchard had a swing in it – another distraction. I amused myself by swinging low beside Jethro, so that his head loomed high above me as I passed. He looked puzzled at the sight I presented: puzzled but intrigued.

Jason arrived in his beaten-up old Mercedes; he had gone to the station to collect a friend, Gwennie von Einsiedel, a talented actress and musician who also had a radio show of her own.

We showed her both Jethro and the Dodge horse van, which was parked in front of the farm – indeed, was more than filling the entrance way, so hard to miss. I expanded on my theory as to how, once our journey was done, it could convert into a wonderful writer's shed on wheels.

Jason's eyes lit up. 'So do you think it might make a good mobile artist's studio? Which would make even more sense. You could just drive up to wherever you wanted to paint and flap down the back. And I've plenty of space to keep it at the farm in Suffolk. Only when you've finished the trip with Jethro, of course.'

There were some men for whom the idea of a challenge, of taking an old beaten-up van and lavishing time and enthusiasm to turn it into a cherished and loved object, was tremendously attractive.

I was not one of them. But I could tell that Jason was.

I considered further. I was not sure whether my wife would appreciate having a five-and-a-half-ton mobile writer's studio permanently parked outside our house, even if I could always go and sleep there after any domestic altercation. As a bachelor, Jason didn't have to worry about such considerations. The Dodge would be going to a good home. And I could still see the van in its new incarnation as a roving arts centre whenever I visited him. Moreover, the next time Jason decided to head out into the wild and the wet in the middle of the night to do some sketching, he would at least have a place to lay his head.

'Well, the thing you have to remember about this van, Jason,' I began, 'is that it is reassuringly old . . . '

*

That night we lit a fire and gathered around it for the evening. Jasper played guitar and Gwennie sang; Jasper fetched his harmonica and they taught each other tunes as they played: folk songs from the north country, or a fragment Jasper had heard around the gaucho fires of Argentina.

Then Jason began to sing songs on his own – surprising plain-song that he had improvised about Suffolk rivers like the Stour, the Orwell and the one that ran through his farm, the Alde:

> Beneath a half moon
> the quiet waters rise
> and the rushes they do move
> as the hawthorn bows her leaves

He sang them almost as if they were psalms, with simple occasional changes of the note rather than a melody. I read some of my poems, which I rarely share.

I felt a great happiness envelop me. This was something that all my life I had sensed could happen, but rarely did: a coming together of people bound to each other by imagination and art. A fellowship. What writers in particular, in their natural condition of solitude, have often sought. I had come home to a vision I had always wanted: of being with friends in a warm house, reading and playing music, and brewing up a quiet storm of our own. A community of like-minded and creative souls, which happens rarely.

Jasper began to play his open-tuned guitar and harmonica at the same time, with Gwennie singing some old songs, including the strange and lovely one of how:

> If all the young men were hares on the mountain,
> how many young girls would take guns and go hunting?
> If all the young men were fish in the water,
> how many young girls would undress and go under?

It was similar to the feeling I had experienced in the beech grove near Avebury when staying with the Rainbow Circle, when I took the long walk across southern England described in *The Green Road into the Trees*. When the circle had taken me inside, and offered me music and food and storytelling. When we had sky-danced half naked with the sun sending out its shadows, and for a brief moment I could let go, of prejudice and self. Of that tendency the American poet Tony Hoagland described so honestly about his own character, of 'persistent selfishness— / one of my hands offering the gift, the other / trying to take something back': a tendency that is so easy to have in everyday life.

Loneliness is the Anglo-Saxon way. *Beowulf* is many things, but amongst them it is a study in early individualism. The hero must leave the community of the King's Hall and go off on his own to battle Grendel: the loneliness of the long-distance axe warrior.

Arthurian knights spend very little time at the Round Table in Malory's epic – an ideal which soon dissipates anyway into warfare and discord. They leave on individual quests to find the damsel or grail. And that was before the Protestant Reformation placed even more emphasis on a lonely pilgrimage to salvation. The northern European culture of rugged self-improvement is so ingrained in us that those rare moments when we can let go – in a choir or a team or a coming together, as now, of like-minded spirits – are as different and strange as when you dive deep underwater.

We talked around the fire late into the night. Of travels and of music. Of where we had been and where we wanted to go. But I was feeling too happy to write it all down, and next morning found the conversations hard to remember, not least because it had taken us around the world. I knew that at one point Jasper had produced a Berber cloak which he had used when taking a mule across Morocco, and Jason had tried it on; that Jasper had also told us how he had played at the desert music festival in Mali; and that it was apparently good to travel with reindeer because they radiate natural warmth. Campfire conversation of the best sort, but difficult to join up the dots.

I've noticed before that it is one of the tricks of memory for some of one's happiest moments to be forgotten – as if it needs grains of resistant sand to stick to the paper. Is it because the brain is too busy in its own happiness, too satisfied, to bother with the usual bureaucratic procedure of filing those sensations to memory?

However, I woke next day with an unusual spring in my step to cook bacon for them all, well sourced from the local butchers, and enough coffee for even Jasper to be satiated; I reckoned he could get through about half a pack of ground coffee a day, a black powder habit that even a Colorado cowboy would find impressive.

Although the farm lay somewhere up the hill from Ravenstonedale, I had been down to the village a few times to get supplies and been impressed by its handsome streets and air of independence.

Usually, the history of these remote villages has been lost – but this was a rare exception, as an enterprising nineteenth-century vicar, Rev. W. Nicholls, had spent a great deal of time chasing down old court records in Ravenstonedale. In Elizabethan times, according to Nicholls, the local court at first sat in the old church. However, proceedings were so argumentative, it was considered unseemly, so the court was moved to an inn where liquid refreshment could aid those making judgements.

The jurors had considerable power and could sentence prisoners to death (there is still a Gallows Hill near Ravenstonedale), but they expended more energy on punishing slander within the parish. Those who spoke 'unlawful words against their neighbours' had to apologise in church and pay a hefty fine to the Lord of the Manor. Equal punishment was given to eavesdroppers, 'who lie or hearken in any man's doors or windows'.

Other fines were meted out to any woman pregnant out of wedlock – a harsh and cruel punishment given, as Nicholls points out with compassion, that there was no such punishment for her seducer; to anyone who cut timber without express permission from the Lord of the Manor; to anyone who played dice or cards; and most bizarrely, to anyone who played football.

More understandable was the requirement that every single parishioner teach their children and servants to use a longbow. This was border country, and had long been used to incursions from Scotland.

Those not born within the parish were considered 'foreigners'. They could not come within the parish boundary to cut peat or buy property; but most importantly of all, they could not marry any of the inhabitants. Nicholls remarks that, 'A young man could not commit a greater offence against the general feeling of society than to marry a lass from another parish,' and goes on to quote the most extraordinary letter.

Whereas we ladies of Ravenstonedale have for many years past been much injured and abused by the illegal practice of our neighbouring parishioners, we are no longer able to contain and bear the sufferings of this insupportable damage:-

Notice is hereby given — To all gentlemen bachelors of the said parish of Ravenstonedale, who attempt to contract the bands of marriage, or try any experiment instrumental to the same, and not with a lady of their own parish, shall immediately pay the sum of £20, to be distributed amongst the poor of the said parish; and if any such offenders shall refuse to pay the said sum justly liable for their offence, shall be imprisoned during the first ten months after their marriage. Given under our hands this fifth day of September, 1776. — Majority of females.

Rev. W. Nicholls,
*History and Traditions of Ravenstonedale* (1877)

The turn of phrase 'or try any experiment instrumental to the same' is a delightful bit of casuistry; and the letter can, and perhaps should, be read tongue-in-cheek. But even so, the overall picture is of a closed and close society. One in which, like Hamlet's Polonius, men hid behind the arras to hear secrets; where you were expected to marry within the community. One in which the Lord of the Manor had remarkable power, right up until the end of the eighteenth century. But one, also, of considerable autonomy.

And it is that independence which allowed the Quaker movement to begin and flourish here.

They came from a mercantile community of an independent bent, which to me was a familiar proposition. I have always been drawn to the revisionist view that the fishermen of Galilee from whom Jesus drew his initial support were not the 'simple folk' of popular imagining. They were relatively wealthy and sufficiently remote from Jerusalem to have both the resources and freedom to develop a new way of thinking – which Christianity clearly represented.

The Quaker movement began in Sedbergh and this part of Westmorland for a reason. So remote that, unlike Yorkshire, it was not even included in the Domesday Book, but with the independence that the wool trade later provided, this was receptive ground for a new and unconventional approach to religion.

I have always been intrigued by the Quakers – the lack of an authority figure like the priest, the communal way of taking services, the pacifism – without knowing much about them. And a little to the south of us, on the road between Ravenstonedale and Sedbergh, Jason told me there was a Quaker stronghold, the last surviving temperance inn in the country.

✷

# Chapter 6

# In a Silent Way

Mules are usually cheerful, intelligent animals, appreciate proper handling, and resent violence.

The War Office, *Animal Management* (London, 1923)

The sixteenth-century building stood proudly by the side of the road, whitewashed and with a sign saying 'ham and eggs'. What the sign didn't say was that, while to all intents and purposes this looked like any other pub, it didn't serve alcohol. The Cross Keys was a temperance inn and its name had been carefully chosen: the keys are those which Saint Peter holds to the gates of heaven.

Jasper had not been enthusiastic about coming, but became more interested when he read out the unusual list of drinks displayed in the dining room.

'Dandelion and burdock, sarsaparilla, although they warn you should "be alert to the fact that sarsaparilla contains chemicals that aid the production of testosterone in the body". There's also a ginger slammer. And a concoction made from nettles, which apparently has "the aroma of a Sauvignon Blanc". Hmm. They've definitely tried to give the botanicals a bit of a lift.'

The young waitress took our order. Jasper went for the sarsaparilla, to my amusement. We asked if she ever got disappointed customers who hadn't checked in advance about the availability of alcohol.

'Yes, we do. And they just go away.'

It felt not so much like a bar as a tea-room, with low beams, old ticking clocks and wooden dressers, together with the odd eccentric touch, like a policeman's helmet hanging from a wall. Built in 1619, updated and extended in 1732, the Cross Keys had been turned into a temperance inn in the late nineteenth century when the movement was at its height.

The owner appeared, a cheerful, rumpled man in a green sweater, a Quaker himself. His name was Alan Clowes. He told us the property had originally been owned by one of the first Quakers, a man called Gervase Benson, who had been a colonel in the Civil War and a man of considerable influence. Like most temperance inns, by the end of the twentieth century it had fallen into disuse, and Alan and his wife had done a great deal of work to restore it, supported by the National Trust.

'We have a lady buried under the floorboards in the dining room,' he told us. 'She was buried there when it was the garden. Now, let me take your order for food.'

But I wasn't letting Alan get away with that; and it was too early in the morning for food. I got him to tell the story. The woman had been Gervase Benson's wife Dorothy, like him first a Westmorland Seeker and then, when the movement began, a Quaker. As such, she had been prosecuted for her beliefs.

'Dorothy was a very staunch and steadfast person. She would walk for miles if she had to. She once walked all the way to Carlisle gaol to see George Fox when he was in prison – but they wouldn't let her in, so she had to walk all the way back again.

'When she lived here, she was always disrupting church services and after many warnings was finally imprisoned – hauled off to York when she was seven months pregnant. She was told she would be released if she gave an undertaking not to disrupt church services in the future. But she wouldn't. So she died in prison four years later. And her husband asked that her body be brought back and buried here, rather than in an Anglican churchyard.

'It's not a well-known story. The Quakers never talked much about themselves. Still don't. But there was a lot of hardship in those early days.'

I asked Alan why conditions had been so propitious in what was once the county of Westmorland for the Quaker movement to begin. Was it because of the self-reliant nature of those who lived here?

'Well, I tell you what: we need more independence all over again. And we need to get our county back. It's ridiculous that they abolished Westmorland and put it inside Cumbria, which is a different place altogether.

'By the way,' added Alan, 'you do know this wasn't turned into a temperance inn for religious reasons?'

I didn't. Given the house's long association with the Quaker movement, I had assumed precisely that.

'It's because the landlord died and his widow couldn't afford to keep up the licence. For most of the nineteenth century they served alcohol here.'

I sipped my dandelion and burdock. To be honest, I thought it was the sort of drink that Jethro would appreciate more than me. The principle of a teetotal pub was an interesting one; I just wasn't sure if I could welcome it in practice.

Jasper made a complimentary remark about his sarsaparilla.

'Ah,' said Alan, 'I can tell from your accent that you hail from across the water. Did you know it was an Irish family, the Fitzpatricks, who did more than anybody else to set up the temperance inns here? They came over to Lancashire in the 1880s. Like a lot of Irish, they had signed the pledge, and they brought their recipes for herbal drinks with them. By the time they'd finished, they had over twenty temperance bars. It used to be a really big movement, in the North particularly.

'We had a man from CAMRA come here once,' Alan continued. 'Had a fit. Said he wanted to sue us under the Trade Descriptions Act – that we weren't an inn at all. Only came because a Sunday magazine included us in a list of the best pubs in the country. He obviously hadn't read the small print. Some people are just so *sad*.'

I asked if Alan came from a long family of Quakers.

'No, not at all. In fact, none of my family were Quakers. I was very fond of my dad, he was a bus driver. And when he died I went into the local church, an Anglican one, and I thought, "I'm getting nothing out of this place, it's cold and it's miserable." But then I went and sat in Brigflatts, the meeting house at Sedbergh. And at once I felt at home. The lad who was the warden at the time was an American, whose day-job was over at Durham Prison. He was working with prisoners who were serving life, and he was trying to give them a reason to keep on living. And I thought that must be a hell of a job. I liked him.

'For many of the first meetings I went to, nobody ever spoke at all. Then a lady started speaking. She'd been on a Women's Institute outing to an old country house where they'd recently found a doorway that had been blocked up and led to a room. And that was it. That was the story. Nothing more. And I could see everybody thinking. And somebody else got up and said, yes, we all had these rooms that were blocked away inside of us.'

I enjoyed Alan's calm and deliberate way of telling a story. One of the most attractive qualities of Quakers must be that, unlike most religious movements, they do not proselytise; they let others see by quiet example. If you are moved to do so, they will always make you welcome at a meeting house, but they won't be knocking on your door with a Bible in their hand.

We made our goodbyes. Jasper decided to head back to the farm and check that Jethro was all right; he probably needed a walk to work off all the excess testosterone in his sarsaparilla.

Meanwhile, I headed on to nearby Sedbergh, inspired by Alan's stories and wanting to find out more about the birthplace of the Quaker movement.

*

Coming down from the Howgills into the valley where Sedbergh lies, I was struck by the beautiful setting. More lush and green than the high fells I had been travelling across, the last waves of the Lake District rolled down to meet the western Yorkshire Dales and gave the best of both worlds: roads that wound and curled to reveal a storybook landscape, where every lane seemed to peel off a small hill and the fields were a patchwork in shades of green.

As a place to ignite a movement – a place to inspire hope in a new beginning for England – it would be hard to beat. And of course, for the Quakers, this part of Westmorland had one great advantage: it was remote from the religious authorities, not just in London, but also York.

At the bookshop in Sedbergh, all was not well. I looked in to ask for a book on the early Quaker movement. Oddly, they didn't have any, given the local relevance. But an argument was going on and they may have been distracted. It was a large shop arranged over two floors and there were books scattered all over the entranceway.

'We've *got to rehouse these orphans!*' exclaimed an older man, who I guessed was the owner. 'The situation's out of control. They're all over the place. And somebody's mixed them in with the table books . . . I can hardly believe it! I just can't find anything.' He sounded at the end of his rag. The two women helping him made soothing suggestions in unnaturally slow voices. 'It's all right. I'm sure we can rehouse all the orphans,' said one. 'Yes, we just need to do it *systematically*,' said the other.

They didn't have the book I wanted on the start of the Quakers – and I noticed throughout my visit that it was a curiously unheralded movement, perhaps because Quakers are so inherently modest. Instead, I found row upon row of old county histories: the literary equivalent of sporting prints, designed to line a wall rather than ever be read.

Only one second-hand volume caught my fancy – by that old rogue Robert Gibbings, whose path I had crossed in my previous book when crossing a stretch of the Thames, which he had once floated down in a glass-bottomed punt. His popular wartime account of that journey, *Sweet Thames Run Softly*, had inspired a sequel, *Floating down the Seine*, which I had not come across before. I flicked open the pages at random, not least to be able to talk about it with Jasper later, as he was a great Gibbings fan.

Gibbings had reached Paris. He was telling a tall story about how Montparnasse models were so used to posing nude for artists that they would drop all their clothes on entering any studio, with predictably embarrassing consequences. But I suspect if I had opened just about any page there would have been a story involving a naked girl and an artist; Gibbings was of that bohemian Augustus John generation for whom the two inevitably went together.

However, this was a distraction from my purer quest to discover more about the origins of Quakerism. For like Buddhism, it was one of those religious movements which everyone broadly approved of but few understood – indeed, knew little about other than the headlines: Pacifists – Quiet – Independent Thinking. All qualities that were difficult to disagree with, if harder to practise.

Sedbergh was a small and appealing market town at the foot of the Howgills. It did not have one of the big cobbled market squares of its Yorkshire equivalents; more self-effacing, the quiet high street was filled with old-fashioned greengrocers and charity shops.

A little past Sedbergh, I came to the quiet hamlet of Brigflatts where one of the first Quaker meeting houses was built. It was here that a charismatic preacher called George Fox arrived in June of 1652 from the south, from Leicestershire, and found such a receptive audience for his radical message that the whole movement was born. The owner of Brigflatts at the time was a man called Richard Robinson, who Fox had heard might be sympathetic to his way of thinking.

> And from Major Bousfield's I came to Richard Robinson's; and as I was passing along the way, I asked a man, 'which was Richard Robinson's?', and he asked me from whence I came, and I told him, 'from the Lord'.
>
> And so when I came in to Richard Robinson's, I declared the everlasting truth to him; and then a dark jealousy rose up in him after I was gone to bed, that I might be somebody that was come to rob his house; and he locked all his doors fast.
>
> *The Journal of George Fox*

George Fox's *Journal*, written many years later when he was in prison, gives a vivid and idiosyncratic account of those heady days, which he considered the most important of his life. When I had been at the temperance inn, Alan Clowes suggested that this encounter with a man when Fox was trying to find Robinson's house has an edge of humour to it. The reason the man asked him 'from whence he came' was probably due to Fox's thick Leicestershire accent; in those days, when regional dialects were more pronounced, it must have sounded comical to Westmorland ears. Fox's tart retort, 'from the Lord', may have been because he was tired of people commenting on it.

> And the next day I went to a separate meeting at Justice Benson's, where the people was generally convinced; and this was the place that I had seen a people coming forth in white raiment; and a mighty meeting there was and is to this day near Sedbergh which I gathered in the name of Jesus.

The people 'coming forth in white raiment' were the Westmorland Seekers, and the reason that George Fox's message found such a quick reception. The Seekers had been established in this part of Westmorland for some years and already proposed a radical, puritan form of Christianity. One of their doctrines was that priests should live austerely and not extract tithes from the flock. But Fox went further. He questioned the need for a formal priest, and indeed church, at all. If God was everywhere, then one might as well preach in the open air. 'A church,' said Fox, 'is only a building.' Moreover, the members of a community, both men and women, should all be empowered to debate with each other on matters of faith.

It was a revolutionary message and not surprisingly the Established Church reacted to it with extraordinary hostility. The later persecution of Quakers, at times vicious, often followed from the Church's concern that it would lose its financial support as much as for theological reasons.

So, what did (and do) Quakers actually believe? This is harder to pin down. In some ways, they have always liked to define themselves by rejecting the ideas of others. In the seventeenth

century, this meant they were opposed to the hard-line predesti-
nation views of some puritans who believed they were an elect;
for the Quakers, salvation was possible for everyone, and men
and women were equal in the eyes of the Lord. Moreover, people
were urged to turn to the light of Christ within themselves. Even
the Bible was less important than this inner spirit. As one commentator has put it, for the Quaker believer, 'Heaven was within'.

When I found the Brigflatts meeting house down the end of
a small country lane – with no one querying my strange southern
accent – I found a class in progress: a group of Quakers were
being taught how to scythe grass on the lawn just in front of
the meeting house.

'Why use a strimmer,' asked the young man giving the lesson,
'when you can do this instead? When you can be at peace with
yourself?'

Given that using a full-length scythe clearly needed a great
deal of instruction – the class were advancing cautiously over the
grass to make sure they didn't cut their toes – I could see why
people might keep the strimmer. But the scythes all moving across
the lawn in unison had a quiet grace that was instantly appealing.
It was a lovely thing to watch.

'What you have to do,' the young man told the class, 'is use
your whole body weight and balance to swing the scythe from
side to side, like t'ai chi. The mistake is to do it the way the
Austrians do, the haymaking way, and just use the strength in
your upper arms and shoulders.'

He demonstrated. The class murmured in sympathetic appreciation. They were a gentle, middle-aged group in fleeces. Many
of the men and women had long hair, the men's often in a pony-
tail, the women's loose and frizzy. None of them looked as if

they worked out at the gym to build up Austrian-style upper arm and shoulder strength for haymaking.

'Hold the snath tightly.' The snath was the handle. 'And make sure the snath doesn't swing and bang against your knees. That's not a good look. And it hurts.

'Right,' he carried on briskly, 'we'll do two or three passes across the lawn and then we'll talk about sharpening, which is going to take a while. There's a lot to learn. Remember that when you're scything grass, you need to sharpen your blade almost every five minutes. For the moment, you can leave your whetting stones with your bags.'

The class set off, swinging gently from their hips as the blades swung across a lawn that was already cut, so this was strictly a rehearsal. When I went inside the cool, dark meeting room, with its long benches and wood-panelled walls, where I was the only person, I could hear the voices of the class outside from the sunlit lawn.

I am not a practising Christian, but I enjoy sitting in a quiet church. 'Stone and oak shelter / silence while we ask nothing / but silence', as Basil Bunting put it in one of his poems about Brigflatts. There was something about the democratic layout of the meeting house, which has no pulpit as there is no priest leading the service – all the Friends present contribute thoughts when they are 'moved to do so' – that I found appealing. It was a reminder of the need to be attentive in life; to listen more and talk less.

Modern Quakers are not necessarily theist at all – many say they find the whole notion of a God looking down on the world problematic – and I suspect more people would be drawn to them if they were not so self-deprecating and hidden. In a world which likes to shout from the rooftops, the Quakers are whispering in a corner.

There was a small, rather good library at Brigflatts, with all the books I had been unable to find in the Sedbergh bookshop: many out of print, like Braithwaite's long account of the early Quaker movement in two volumes, an Edwardian doorstopper. What came across from all the accounts of those heady days in 1652 was the excitement of their debates. The name 'Quaker' was a nickname given to Fox and his followers by a judge for their habit of shaking with ecstasy when they talked about religious ideas in the dock. In Fox's memoirs, he often refers to disputations he has with people along the way – theological discussions that could last for hours.

I had noticed in my encounters with Quakers that everyone talks in a soft, low and reasonable voice, which is very attractive for a while, although longer exposure would make me want to go and put on some rock 'n' roll. I suspect that Fox was not a great orator in the rhetorical sense; he did not whip up the crowd. His insistent and patient arguing of the case was what won his audience over.

George Fox had arrived in Sedbergh at a busy time. There was an annual fair taking place at which traditionally servants were hired by the gentry – which meant a lot of young people were looking for work. Fox started holding forth in the steeple-house yard and attracted a large crowd. Local clergymen berated him; one told him he was mad. But Fox stood his ground and found a receptive audience, especially among those already influenced by the Westmorland Seekers.

One of the Seeker preachers, perhaps sensing this was not the place and occasion to pick an argument with the church, invited Fox to speak at Firbank Fell, where the Seekers had a chapel that was discreetly far enough from Sedbergh.

I felt reflective as I walked up the long lane towards Firbank Fell, and what is now locally called 'Fox's pulpit': a remote stone in a field where he preached to an audience of a thousand people in the safety of the open air, far from persecution. For Fox refused to speak in the small Firbank Chapel itself – which given the size of the congregation would anyway have been impractical – but drew his audience out to the open air, speaking for some three hours in what he always judged to be the greatest address he ever gave: 'for the word of the Lord came to me, I must go and sit down upon the rock in the mountain even as Christ had done before.'

If the longevity of a hedge can be told by the variety of species you find within it, then the hedge along that lane to Fox's pulpit was one of the oldest I have ever seen. This was still a very wild and exposed part of the Howgills, on the western flanks. Fox was giving his address in June, which is still late spring this far north, and the hedgerows would have been full of spring flowers, with lambs in the fields.

It took me longer than I expected to walk to Firbank Fell – long enough to be impressed at how many of the people of Sedbergh and the surrounding district had made the effort to come to hear him. So it was around three in the afternoon when I arrived, about the time of day that Fox had given his address.

I was surprised to see how little now marked the spot of what must surely be one of the great moments in English Christianity. There was nothing left of the chapel; just a small graveyard with a few windblown trees, one of them a yew, and a retaining wall. If the stone from which Fox spoke, his pulpit, had not had a small plaque, it would have been easy to miss. Moreover, it was one of those places, increasingly rare in England, where not a single human habitation was visible for miles. Just sheep.

Fox himself had been a shepherd in his Leicestershire days, and his writing is full of references to the simple and sober life of those living in the countryside; he was also alert to the biblical comparisons.

That speech to the faithful in this wild place was perhaps the highlight of his life. He was just twenty-seven. Ahead lay many years of persecution, both for himself and for his companions and disciples, the 'valiant sixty' who spread the word for the Society of Friends, as they called themselves.

George Fox is virtually forgotten by the wider public in Britain. Hardly a portrait of him exists, as a young man at least, although we know he had long hair 'like rats' tails', so the seventeenth-century equivalent of Rasta locks.

At the height of the movement, almost half the population of Westmorland were Quakers; today there are estimated to be no more than 20,000 in the whole of the country. But the Quakers have always punched above their weight – to use a deeply inappropriate metaphor – and not just with their commendable commitment to pacifism, an inheritance from Fox, whose early youth had been spent during the turbulence of the Civil War.

Because of their nonconformism, they were unable to join many of the established professions – not only the clergy, but also the law, Parliament, universities and many more – and therefore applied their considerable energies to business, where their integrity and honesty quickly made them successful. Clarks Shoes, Bryant & May matches, and both Barclays and Lloyds are among the substantial companies founded by Friends.

Their quixotic quest to convert the working-class man from beer to hot chocolate resulted in a lucrative near-monopoly as Rowntree, Cadbury and the oldest Quaker family business of them all, Fry's of Bristol, came to dominate the chocolate trade. I had once lived in a part of Bristol, Redlands, which didn't have a single pub due to the dominance of the Quakers when it was built.

Like nearly any religious movement, the Quakers have at times had a darker side: their insistence at one point that members marry only within the community led to much unhappiness; and people forget that Richard Nixon was a Quaker, which didn't stop him bombing Cambodia.

But the simplicity and directness of Quaker dealings, still echoed in Westmorland, and above all their unabashed habit of 'speaking truth to power', as George Fox did to Cromwell when he was brought before him under armed guard, is a wonderful legacy. The Protector was at the height of his powers and held Fox's life in his hands, but Fox was as direct and honest as ever, exhorting Cromwell 'to keep in the fear of God'. When Fox was leaving, after an intense and long discussion, Cromwell caught him by the hand and was heard to say, with tears in his eyes, 'Come again to my house.'

After Cromwell's death and the return of Charles II, the Quakers were lumped in with all the other millenarian movements that had contributed to his father's execution, and many were imprisoned, including women and children. Fox wrote much of his memoirs in jail and died a broken man in 1691. When he was carried to his grave in London's Bunhill Fields by his fellow Quakers, a bystander remarked that 'for a considerable time there was nothing but deep sighs, groans and tears and roaring to admiration, and, after that all had vented and eased themselves, and grew quiet in their minds.'

I felt humble to have briefly followed in Fox's footsteps and stood on his pulpit; ignorant that I had previously known so little about him; and profoundly lacking in the grace and courage which seems to have sustained him for so many years, and through so many troubles.

\*

On the way back to Jason's farm, I rang my parents. My father David answered the phone. He was surprised that I was travelling across the North with a mule, although we had discussed this many times. I told him where I was in the Howgills and that the next day, Jasper and I would be travelling further east to Kirkby Stephen with Jethro.

For the last ten years, my father, like so many of his contemporaries, had been slowly losing his memory; he was suffering from vascular dementia, more benign than Alzheimer's, but with similar short-term memory loss. While he could remember the events of his childhood and of the Second World War with great clarity, he found more recent events and day-to-day recall increasingly difficult.

My father bore this change with fortitude, as he had some of the other difficult events in his life: the death of his mother when he was a boy, and the disruptions of the war. But it is a cruel disease, both for the sufferer and those close to them, like my mother, who had needed to become his full-time carer.

Such forms of dementia have, of course, become increasingly and distressingly common, although our family has always had a history of such memory loss in older age: both my grandfather and his father suffered from the same thing, while keeping physically fit well into their eighties.

The odds are good – or rather, bad – that I may well suffer in the future from it myself. My father's illness had made me more conscious of the value of memory; and also of its vagaries, its deceptions.

Each time we talked, we needed to start from first principles – as now, when I had to explain why and how I was getting a mule from one side of the country to the other. This often made for fuller and more detailed conversations. With those who are close to us, such chats on the phone can be quick progress updates – where we are, what happened yesterday. With my father, it needed to be the full story and would force me each time I told it to consider exactly what I was doing and why.

Before he became ill, my father would sometimes tell the story of how he had been present in the hospital when his mother had died from tuberculosis. He had been twelve. His brothers and sisters were not with him, as the war had separated the family. Only his father was there.

Because he had been considered so young, no one had told him how gravely ill his mother Kathleen had become. Her death therefore came as an even greater horror of shock and surprise. But in the years of telling the story – and he would do so only during certain intimate moments – it had acquired a patina, a way in the telling, as may happen to us all with any memory, however painful. We make a narrative: in my father's case, much of it exculpatory, first of his own father, who had been forced to divide the family; of the mores of the time, which thought it better for children to be kept in ignorance of their parents' illnesses; and then of the war, which anyway caused so much grief to so many.

When he became ill, much of this fell away. While he could remember his mother's death, he could no longer remember how he had continually told the story. He had to tell it afresh.

One day when we were having coffee and talking, the real, true memory of that moment suddenly came back to him: the moment when he had been in a dark hospital anteroom, left by himself, and someone had come to tell him that his mother had died. The existential pain of that moment.

Telling me that story afresh, he had suddenly burst into tears. A wall in his memory had given way.

And it had made me realise how easy it is to do that: to construct memories that are not so much false as a way of telling the story. Of sometimes making it bearable, or even simply comprehensible.

It is something we do collectively as a country. Dunkirk becomes in retrospect a gallant rescue of the British Expeditionary Force by a fleet of little boats, rather than the squalid endgame of what Churchill described at the time as 'a colossal military disaster'. The Restoration of Charles II is remembered as a festive return to 'royal business as usual', with Nell Gwynne and bucolic licentiousness; not the start of a witch-hunt which saw Quakers and other religious minorities brutally persecuted, leading to the deaths of George Fox and many of his followers.

Nothing beats going back to the source to reveal the inconvenient truths that scatter our history; and being forced to walk slowly across the country with a mule was a great way of making sure you always looked at the ground.

*

My father had asked why I had chosen a mule and whether this had been a good decision.

As Jasper and I loaded Jethro back into the Dodge van back at Jason's place and made our goodbyes — with a promise that he could buy the van after the journey was completed, and a demonstration of the immobilisation lock — I thought more about this.

I was beginning to feel that Jethro had come to trust me. This might have been a delusion, but he was less prone to obstinate behaviour. He would box up into the horse lorry well; could be left loose close to us while we had a picnic; even seemed to look at me with more confidence in his beautiful eyes.

Which was not to say he still didn't want to assert a sturdy independence at all times. But then I was used to that from the women in my life.

Mules were sterile. Nobody had told Jethro. He had kept all the inclinations of a stallion, despite having been gelded. Every time we put him into a field, Jasper and I had to erect a portable electric fence to prevent him bothering any mares. I knew from experiences at my sister's place in Oxfordshire before we had left — where Jethro had behaved with such rock 'n' roll abandon with the female ponies that he was almost thrown out of the hotel — how unpopular this could be.

The problem was that Jethro's feelings were often reciprocated. At one of the places we had berthed, there had been some beautiful white mares. They kept coming to the little stand of trees between the paddocks and flaunting their long white manes at poor Jethro, who had been told firmly by both Jasper and me to be on his best behaviour. They even kept making those soft little 'why are you ignoring us' neighs.

It was the classic appeal of the bad boy. Here was Jethro with his troubled borstal past – the rescue mule from the RSPCA – and unconventional 'interesting ugly' looks, short in height maybe but with attitude and unusual colouring. He was Mick Jagger in an astrakhan coat, or a rapper from East London, arriving in the demure pastures of the Home Counties. Nice middle-class mares had never seen anything quite like Jethro before. There was bound to be trouble.

A mule proper is the offspring of a jack donkey and female horse; the other way round – the offspring of a female donkey and male horse – is, strictly speaking, called a hinny not a mule, and there are far fewer of them.

The height difference between the parents – and let's not get too technical here – is important. A jack donkey can serve a mare up to three hands larger than himself. If the mare's any taller, he's going to need snookers, so to speak. Or the owner of the mare will have to use artificial insemination.

A mule is always said to have the body of a horse with the extremities of a donkey. So the things that stick out in its appearance, literally, are its long ears and short, thin mane. It has the straight legs of a donkey with tough straight-sided hooves that need far less looking after than the troublesome horse's. Unique to the mule, though, are the eyes, which are quite different from those of either a donkey or a horse. Jethro's were deeply soulful.

By contrast, a hinny gets the worst of both worlds. It has the body of a donkey with the extremities of a horse. This is not a good combination. Moreover, they tend to align themselves with donkeys. A test muleteers always use if they are concerned whether an animal is a mule or a hinny is to set them loose in a field with both donkeys and horses present. The mules will always associate with the horses, while the hinnies will associate with the donkeys. And hinnies are more donkey-like in temperament: they are less adventurous and independent than mules, although for some owners this may be a good thing. They are not even as vocal. Whereas Jethro was given to quite a lot of conversational ad libs as we strolled across the country – a mule's bawl has been well described as sounding like 'an asthmatic steamboat in distress' – a hinny was virtually silent. Which I would find disconcerting. There's nothing worse than a travelling companion who never says anything.

Apart from isolated pockets in Europe – like Cyprus and Ireland – there are few hinnies around and the breeding needs considerable ingenuity: it is usually done with wiry pony stallions on strong female donkeys of about the same size. However, only a small proportion of donkey mares will conceive when served by a horse.

Mules are much easier to breed. Ever since the nomads of Nubia discovered in around 1750 BC that if you left a domesticated mare tethered outside your tent for a wild jack donkey to find, you would end up with desirable offspring, mankind has loved the mule. Ancient records show that the Hittites would pay three times as much for a mule as a horse because of their greater staying power. Mule models have been found in Egyptian pyramids. King David rode a mule to enter Jerusalem.

A vase found at Thebes shows a mule-drawn chariot; while Homer celebrated mules in the famous passage when Princess Nausicaa uses them to take her laundry to the seashore with her ladies in waiting, and is surprised by Odysseus. Alexander the Great was carried to his grave by a train of sixty-four mules yoked together in teams of four. Roman senators preferred to take their shopping home from the forum, so to speak, riding a mule not a horse; a mule was steadier and less likely to bolt for the horizon if surprised by a man wearing the wrong sort of toga.

In more recent times, Americans used mules to conquer the Wild West. They were more adaptable than horses to the arid conditions of desert frontier lands, as well as to the humid plantations of the South. Freed slaves were awarded not only a grant of land – forty acres – but a mule to go with them. George Washington was such an aficionado of the mule that he petitioned the Spanish king to send him tall jack donkeys to sire them. American mules still tend to come in larger sizes, like their portion control; their breeding donkeys are called American Mammoth Jacks. So highly are they valued, the United States even celebrates a National Mule Day each year.

When the mujahideen were struggling against the Russians in Afghanistan, the CIA sent 7,000 large mules from Texas. It may well have been on one of these same mules that Osama bin Laden make good his escape after the later Allied invasion; even if in Islamic hagiography he is portrayed as riding the passes on a white stallion.

However, when I said that mankind has always loved the mule, there is one significant and strange exception: the British. Elsewhere in the world, from the Middle East to China, the mule is still used as a universal pack and saddle animal. In Europe, mules have flourished from Ireland to the Balkans. Yet for reasons which seem mysterious, the mule has almost disappeared from this country.

Why? It was a question that puzzled me more and more as I made my journey. They were so obviously well suited to the British climate and even, dare I say it, temperament. We had plenty of donkeys, even if most of them were now in sanctuaries. And plenty of mares.

It took a certain amount of digging in the historical archives to come up with a possible solution. But finally, I came up with the answer – and it was one that surprised me.

It seems mules were still greatly valued in medieval England, especially among the clergy. There had always been a prejudice against the riding of horses by priests, as it was considered too worldly or military. But it was precisely because of this that they may have disappeared.

The Pope was often portrayed riding a mule. Cardinal Wolsey used one to transport his considerable bulk around the country before 'he fell sick suddenly, and grew so ill / he could not sit his mule', as Shakespeare described his death. And so, come the Reformation, the mule was indelibly stamped as being the mark of a Catholic priest.

Records show that they fell sharply out of favour towards the end of the sixteenth century, after Henry VIII's dissolution of the monasteries. If you rode a mule, you might as well have carried rosary beads or worn a T-shirt proclaiming your allegiance to Rome or Spain. Mules were thought of as incorrigibly Latin and Catholic – and to a certain extent still are. That was why it had been so incredibly difficult for me to find a mule for this journey: religious prejudice dating back almost 500 years, pure and simple. If you rode a horse, you supported Glasgow Rangers; if you used a mule, you supported Celtic.

Instead, the English had turned to ponies as pack animals – unless it came to their numerous wars in Europe, when they unapologetically led hundreds of thousands of mules to their slaughter in Spain or in France; foreign mules, not mules they had bred themselves.

I felt like launching a campaign to bring back the mule to Britain. The Act of Emancipation of 1829 seemed to have passed mules by. We had welcomed Catholics back into public life; why not their mules as well?

Jethro had been extraordinarily good company on the journey. Perhaps he was not quite as handsome as a horse. But then the way I had come to feel about it was that while horses can have faces of impossible elegance – like models in a magazine – mules have the sort of faces of people you might meet in a pub. Who have had a couple of drinks. And for a long crossing of the country like this one, I knew which I would prefer.

*

# Chapter 7

# An Auction of Love and Sheep

Owing to the mule's propensity for gnawing everything, any woodwork within reach should be smeared with soft soap.

The War Office, *Animal Management* (London, 1923)

A few hours after leaving Jason's farm, Jethro was looking incongruous hitched up to a railing in the Kirkby Stephen car park. We were outside the livestock auction-rooms. A century ago, every farmer would have come here by horse, with or without the carriage. Now there was an expensive set of new Range Rovers and pickup trucks filling the spaces. Our Dodge van was by some way the oldest thing on wheels.

Farmers like to complain they're not doing well, but a simple audit of their vehicles can tell you otherwise. We had tied Jethro off to one side; if he kicked out at any of the shiny Range Rovers in a fit of pique – or chewed a wing mirror, as mules do like to chomp on anything within reach – there would be a hefty bill to pay.

I could hear the auctioneer's voice echoing out of the concrete pens where the sheep had been herded. It was unclear whether any old member of the public could just wander in, but after a couple of weeks with Jethro, I looked suitably weather-beaten to pass muster; most of the farmers were, anyway, more interested in checking out sheep than people.

Just outside the entrance, a farmer was muttering to himself as he left. I asked what was wrong.

'I've spent too much money, that's what's wrong, boy! Got carried away.'

I hoped he had at least a few beans to take home to his wife.

Inside the auction, a hefty-looking man sat on a bale of hay holding a Swaledale ram by the horns, peering intently into its face, eyeball to eyeball. As I walked down the long alleyway between the sheep pens, many other breeders and buyers were huddled down in corners in a way that strangely matched the sheep they were studying.

A couple leaning over a pen turned and caught my eye, as if they recognised me. But it was because they *hadn't* recognised me.

'Don't worry, you can say you're with us. Where are you from?' asked the woman, who introduced herself as Ruth.

I explained about my journey with Jethro.

'We breed mules as well.'

'Really?' I was both intrigued and puzzled. Nobody else seemed to breed mules in England.

The man laughed. 'Mule sheep. Swaledale crossed with Blue-faced Leicester.' Technically, a mule is the term for any hybrid between species.

'Do you have Texel as well?' I remained fascinated by these tough, bulldog-looking rams. 'Are they as fierce as they look?'

'A few. But they're difficult. The wool's so short, there's not much to grab when you're dealing with them. There's no horns to hold. They're all muscle.'

I asked about the key signs that people were looking for when they checked over the sheep.

'The colouring of the black and white. That's important. A lot of time's spent plucking the grey hairs out using tweezers.'

I had already learned that sheep were 'tonsed', as it was called, their faces plucked of any extraneous strands as scrupulously as with any teenage girl attending to their eyebrows.

'The size and shape as well. And they like the hair to be hard and the face to be hard. But not too much wool. They don't like too much wool on a sheep.'

This seemed counter-intuitive. But long past were the days when anybody made any money from selling the fleece.

'What about height?'

'Tall,' said Ruth. 'Definitely tall. My dad always liked to say he wanted to see the daylight under them.'

'And what about attitude? Particularly with a ram.'

They started chorusing together on this.

'Oh, you can definitely tell if they're a good 'un or not.'
'Right from being born we can tell.'
'Also, we know where they've come from. We know the breeding.'
'We know the yow and the tup. We would never buy a sheep without knowing ... '
' ... Absolutely. Without knowing they were coming from a good breeder.'
'To improve them. That's the whole point. To get the bloodlines

that you need. It's more complicated than you think.' They both nodded.

I asked how far back they went with a sheep's genealogy: with the 'yows and tups', the local words for ewes and rams, of yesteryear.

'Maybe a sire and a dam. And one more generation perhaps. But mostly it's who you buy from in the first place,' said Ruth's husband.

I felt mischievous. 'What about those people in the Lake District who say Swaledales aren't tough enough compared to Herdwicks?'
Ruth bridled. I was lucky she didn't have a Texel to set loose.

'Well, I'm a born and bred Swaledale girl. I'll never leave until I'm carried out in a box. So, I would say they were the better sheep. Not just probably. *Definitely.*'

Her husband – whose name I never learned – came in with a more tempered view. 'It's horses for courses with sheep. They're made for up there, the Herdwicks. It's rough terrain. The Swaledale can be a bigger breed and they're heavier. So, they don't get about as well as the Herdwicks. Better for valleys. They've got shorter legs.'
Now they were warmed up, I asked how much a good breeder could clear in a day's work at the auction.

'Hundreds of thousands sometimes,' said Ruth. 'Last year, the top price for a single tup was £55,000. I know to an ordinary person, they all look the same, but they're far from identical.'

'£55,000? Isn't that like having a Ferrari running around?' I asked. 'Loose on the fells. Scary stuff. Can't a prize sheep get lost or, for that matter, stolen?'

Ruth shrugged. 'We've got 800 to 1,000 sheep. You're going to lose a few. They don't look after themselves. Sheep will die for no reason at all.'

She lowered her voice as if a potential buyer might overhear us.

'They're very good at giving up the ghost, sheep. Very good indeed. You don't notice the symptoms until it's too late. Then they roll over and die. My auntie used to say, "A farmer could live off his losses." And that's a true saying.'

Still, even if most rams went for hundreds rather than thousands of pounds, it sounded as if a farmer could also 'live off his gains'. No wonder those brand-new Range Rovers were parked outside with Jethro. And the pickup trucks were all tax-deductible, I learned, as they were used on the farm.

Throughout my conversation with Ruth and her husband, the auctioneer's voice had been sounding like a metronome, ringing out the changes on the prices. I wandered over to the ring where sheep were being paraded by their anxious owners. It was noticeable how tall the farmers who had gathered round it were, not least because I was trying to see over their heads – perhaps due to the high proportion of Viking blood still swirling around this end of the Dales.

The area around the ring was very loud: the auctioneer's voice over the PA, the clang of metal as gates were swept over concrete floors to move flocks of sheep and the farmers' shouted conversations so they could be heard.

'So how much did you get for that gimmer hogg?' one well-upholstered farmer was bellowing to another, the hint of anxiety in his voice showing that the question was not entirely disinterested. Before he got an answer, the auctioneer introduced a new breeder who had entered the ring with a ram.

'Now this tup,' the auctioneer enthused in a booming voice over the PA, 'is *built* like a proper tup.'

Meaning he was going to get the job done. You could almost smell the testosterone swirling around the room as the farmers started the bidding. They didn't need any extra sarsaparilla drinks.

I left the auction rooms and wandered across the broad, hand-some main street of Kirkby Stephen to the nearest pub, which like the others in town had been open all day for the sheep market. But if I was looking for a bit of peace and quiet after the hurly-burly of the auctioneering ring, I had come to the wrong place.

The Black Bull was full of noise. Men were punch-drunk with the business of buying and selling sheep for large sums of money before they even walked through the swing doors. Pints of beer were going down like water in a field-trough, much of it the appropriately named 'Black Sheep', the brewery founded by a rebellious member of the Theakston dynasty.

Some men were silently drowning their sorrows at the bar. For others, the talk was full of boasts and regrets – of prices paid and sheep mislaid, or at least not bid for hard enough.

I noticed an old man sitting very upright on a battered sofa in the saloon. He was wearing a three-piece suit with a tartan waistcoat, as if dressed for market day in *The Mayor of Casterbridge*; a handsome man with a mane of silver-grey hair. In each of his hands, he held a silver-topped cane, gripped tightly. Beside him was a much younger woman. They were the only people in the pub drinking wine, and by the large goblet.

The old man's voice suddenly rang out over all the others. It was impossible to ignore. Nor was anyone trying. He was speaking in a firm, very deliberate tone, talking to the young woman beside him, but not actually looking at her, as if addressing the room.

'I've spent a lifetime doing the wrong thing. I've had children and been married. I've had arguments with a great many people. But only now that I'm old and I've met you, Carol, do I realise what true love means.'

The rest of the pub went quiet.

'Maybe I'm a foolish old man for falling in love again at my age. But I don't think so.' And he took the hand of the woman beside him.

Carol did not seem the slightest bit embarrassed by this public declaration. I learned from the subsequent conversation, as did the rest of the pub, that she ran a sandwich shop in Burnley and had recently come over to Kirkby Stephen on a visit.

The old man noticed I was listening to him, like everybody else, and that I was a stranger. He beckoned me over.

We talked about my trip across country with Jethro. 'A mule, eh? You don't see many of those around. Unless they're mule sheep.'

He gripped the silver-topped cane in his hand even more tightly.

'You should feel this cane, young man.'

It was made of a curiously light material, similar to the titanium racing bikes in Jeff's shed which you could pick up with a finger.

'That's been crafted from narwhal.' He looked at me with bright blue eyes. 'Impossible to get nowadays. You're not allowed to kill them. This one is over 200 years old.'

He took it from me reverentially, and skittered the tip across the saloon floor in front of us as if the cane was tap-dancing by itself.

Now that I was closer to him, and could see the stretched skin over his still-handsome face, I could see that he was in his eighties at least. There was a bright pin in his lapel and a spring to his step, like an elderly Fred Astaire. He used his pair of canes to steer his way past the respectful men who made way for him as he headed out into the bright street with Carol.

'If I were you, young man,' he called over his shoulder, 'I'd leave the mule behind. Settle down and find yourself a wife.' He laughed.

There wasn't time to tell him I was already married; or that my career as an itinerant muleteer was a brief one. I ordered another pint of Black Sheep instead.

On emerging sometime later, after a man had tried to sell me a surplus ewe ('It will follow along behind your mule and then you can always eat it on the way'), the main street was gleaming as a little light rain had washed the cobbles. Unlike many of the market towns I had visited, the place still had a vibrancy and not only because of the sheep auction. There was a Coast-to-Coast fish and chip shop, a Coast-to-Coast walking-gear shop and a bustling tourist information centre in the old cloisters.

A lot of this was due to one person. By including Kirkby Stephen as a key stopping point for his Coast-to-Coast route, Wainwright had put it on the map.

I discussed him with Mark, the owner of the walking-gear shop.

'I know there's a plaque in the main square, but shouldn't they put up a statue to Wainwright as well?' I asked, imagining a handsome bronze of the man, map in hand, a little stooped like Churchill outside the Houses of Parliament, and equally grumpy.

'I was born in what is now the Coast-to-Coast Fish and Chip Shop,' said Mark, who I guessed was in his fifties. 'Fish and chips was Wainwright's favourite dish. I remember him eating it. And you're right, we wouldn't get any visitors at all without him. Half the businesses in this town would have gone bust. Nobody had ever heard of Kirkby Stephen before Wainwright. These days, the hotels get a bucket-load of people staying right through the season. Something like 150 come by every night.

'I always refer to the walkers as swallows. They start arriving in the spring, mass in the summer and then by autumn they're leaving. It's not just because of the cold. You need long days to manage the stages. By November, the light's fading too early.'

I asked him if the going would be good on Nine Standards Rigg, the next section of our walk east, which was known to be boggy. Or more particularly, if the going would be good for a mule.

'Well, I've never tried taking a mule, to be honest! Or wanted to. But it's been dry for so long, this is probably as good a time as any. Springtime is the worst. That's when people get caught out, because there's sunshine, so they're not expecting the ground still to be so wet from winter.

'There was a fellow sunk in last year. Rescue team had to get him out. He was carrying a big pack. Went down to his waist. Got sucked right in and couldn't get back out again. He came into the shop later and told me the story or I wouldn't have believed it. Apparently, he was stuck for over an hour before the rescue team arrived. And his girlfriend took pictures of him stuck in the bog while they were waiting.'

'That was nice of her.'

'Well, at least he's got something to remember it by, I sup-pose ... I chatted to people afterwards and the problem was he had such a big pack that once he started going into the mud, he kept on going. And he was too heavy for his girlfriend to lift out. But that's a one-off. Usually Nine Standards Rigg is as safe as houses.

'And it's the halfway point on the Coast-to-Coast. The water-shed as well. The old county boundary between Westmorland and Yorkshire. A landmark on the skyline for people to follow.'

This was true. We had seen the iconic stones of Nine Standards Rigg for miles when approaching Kirkby Stephen.

Mark had some thoughts about how the Coast-to-Coast path had changed in character since Wainwright first devised the route in 1973.

'It used to be just British people who walked it. The sort of people who had used his guides in the Lake District and then followed through with this. But now it's much more international. More than half the people who come through are from overseas. And those international travellers usually want their kit carried for them, so there are lots of services that have grown up to help. You know, drive their luggage round to the next destination while they walk. That's been a big change. In the old days, everyone carried it themselves in a big rucksack.'

'They should use a mule,' I suggested.

Mark paused as if unsure I was being serious. 'Well, I suppose they could,' he said, diplomatically. 'Maybe. But certainly, it's now the long-distance walk for which Britain is best-known abroad. People come from all over the world to do it.'

I could see why this had happened. The Coast-to-Coast (or, to use a dreadful abbreviation, the C2C) is a far more attractive walk than, say, the Pennine Way, which as the poet Simon Armitage pointed out in a book is one hell of a slog, and one, moreover, which keeps to the same sort of landscape throughout. Whereas the Coast-to-Coast crosses from the Lake District through the Dales to the Yorkshire Moors on what is almost a heritage trail from Wordsworth to the Brontës, with a bit of James Herriot thrown in for good measure.

However, despite its huge popularity, the Coast-to-Coast is not an official long-distance path. This might appear a purely academic distinction. But official long-distance paths get special funding earmarked for them by Natural England, the body which maintains the National Trails. Whereas the Coast-to-Coast has to look after itself.

Which is why when we had taken Jethro along the sections of the Coast-to-Coast walk that were bridleways, we had often been surprised that they were so little cared for. And for that matter, under-signposted. I had met many walkers who had got lost, particularly in bad weather. A whole BBC television crew had run into trouble crossing the next section past Nine Standards Rigg.

So when I joined up with Jasper again, who had been setting his own world to rights, we led Jethro in some trepidation over the lovely Frank's Bridge that takes you out from Kirkby Stephen towards Nine Standards Rigg. The sound of the sheep market slowly receded in the distance. As the lane took a dip under some trees past a damp little gully and stream, with Jethro clip-clopping along with his usual freshness at the start of a walk, we came to a wonderful bank of ferns hiding in the shade.

Ferns must surely be one of the great unacknowledged pleasures of the English countryside: ferns growing out of dry-stone walls; hart's-tongue ferns; big glaucous-leaved ferns, black and green, some exotic, some familiar. We get them all over the country, from the South Coast to where I was now in the North, and in every shape and size. Wild ferns are one of our natural assets; yet perhaps we don't appreciate them as much as we should.

One attraction is their antiquity – which also means resilience. Young dinosaur hatchlings would have nestled under ferns back in the day. They are one of our oldest plants, the spores remarkable for their ability to disperse so efficiently; much more so than by the seed–plant life cycle with which we are more familiar. In places, this can cause problems, as anyone who has tried to deal with bracken knows. But in the damp, dark places of England, where the spread of ferns tends to be limited, they can come into their own.

Not far above, we passed the big quarry at Hartley, almost completely shielded from sight, save for the one small turn of the lane which revealed it. The path diverged so that instead you

got a beautiful view ahead of the Dales and Standard Nine Riggs.
Yet the whole of the next valley alongside us had been decimated
by the quarry. It was a wasteland of stripped limestone stretching
for some 100 acres, gleaming pink like flayed skin, with a puff
of smoke at the bottom from the last activity in the plant –
although most of that was now coming to an end.

It made me think that we lived in a sort of Potemkin countryside, where all the bad stuff – the mines, the quarries, the
wind-farms – were nicely screened away, while we were marshalled
along a few polite narrow corridors of protected greenery.

Jethro was advancing well up the hill. There was a green
verge alongside the lane which made for good going, which was
lucky, as there was a reasonable haul ahead to Nine Standards
Rigg. There's nothing like walking across the country, particularly
with a mule who, being unshod, is very sensitive to surfaces, to
make you start thinking more about those surfaces. You worry
what might abrade the hooves or make for more comfortable
going. It reminded me of when I was a teenager riding along
country lanes on a motorbike, when you become so aware of
tarmac or the lack of it: the sudden ruts and gravel that could
unseat you.

All went well until we passed a field with some alpaca grazing.
I had a few alpaca of my own back home, so could cast a professional eye over these ones. Jethro, who had probably never seen
a camelid before, was less sanguine. He bolted suddenly and it
was only with some effort – and a few choice muleteer oaths
from Jasper – that we recaptured him. But by now this was something at which we had plenty of practice.

As we climbed higher, Jasper was amazed at how hostile
everything was botanically in the uplands above Kirkby Stephen.
'Wherever I turn, it's thorny and thistly. Look at all this stuff!
I can see numerous stinging nettles, lots of gorse spread out over
the hillside, hawthorn trees and dog roses. Spikes, spikes, spikes.
Thorns, thorns, thorns. Basically anything that's got protection

so it won't get eaten by sheep or fell ponies. Nature red in tooth and thorn.'

The Nine Standards stood out clearly on the horizon. A local wit back at the pub had told me there had originally been ten of the upright cairns, but that one of them had been removed at some stage, 'because Nine Standards Rigg sounds a lot better than Ten Standards Rigg'.

The nine cairns strode across the ridge in a self-confident way. They were shaped like beehives. No one knew how old they were. That's the thing about stone: it doesn't date. They could have been a few centuries old or a few millennia. Up close, the stone was stacked carefully, if without any particular precision. Nor were the cairns of equal size.

They reminded me of the cheap set design you see in old TV shows like *Star Trek* or *Stargate*, of which my wife was an avid fan – a shorthand to signify that the intrepid crew had landed on a different world. The stone beehives would have made perfect cover for a phaser shootout.

It was unfortunate that we had no way of beaming ourselves out, even if Scotty's transportation system could have handled 300 kilos of mule. Ahead was a considerable walk down through the bogs before we could reach Ravenseat.

It was a beautiful clear day and we had reached what was a defining watershed moment on the walk, almost exactly halfway from west to east. I had the momentary illusion I could almost see from coast to coast. Up to the north, the gleam of the metal cars moving along the A66 looked like a flock of geese. They seemed on a different planet to me; indeed, I felt on a different planet myself, moving among these strange cairns on the top of Hartley Fell as if I had just been teleported there by some alien device.

It was an experience I had already had several times on the walk – when we had arrived, for instance, at the desolate Sunbiggin Tarn in the middle of nowhere in the Howgills, or the valley of Smardale with its railway viaduct swinging across a deserted landscape: those lacunae of wilderness which still lay within a country that in others ways had become so tame.

✳

Down across some notoriously waterlogged bog – the area that the unfortunate man had sunk into while his girlfriend documented the occasion – lay the oasis of Ravenseat, at the head of the Yorkshire Dales.

I already knew this tiny hamlet of three or four houses from an earlier visit I had made, to assess the lay of the land and determine whether it would be suitable for a mule. On that trip, I stopped off at Ravenseat because the setting was remote and idyllic, and one of the farmhouses offered a full tea at a reasonable price. A stream came rushing down from the hills past a tumble of stone and slate houses and under a small humpback bridge. Most of the neighbouring fields had a small barn at their centre, perfectly square and looking for all the world like little Monopoly houses that a player had put down to show he owned the property.

A gaggle of other walkers had assembled at the trestle tables on the grass outside the farmhouse with an air of communal anticipation. It was, after all, exactly four o'clock.

'So is the tea here meant to be good?' I asked.

'It is,' said a woman with a Yorkshire accent. 'I mean that's what made her *famous*.'

'Famous?'

'Don't you know? This is where "famous Amanda" lives. Or

does usually. But she's not here at the moment. Somebody else is doing the tea.'

I caught up. This was apparently the home of Amanda Owen, bestselling author of *A Yorkshire Shepherdess*, which, as it said on the cover, was 'the story of a farmer's wife and shepherdess, living alongside her husband Clive and seven children at Ravenseat, a 2,000-acre sheep hill farm at the head of Swaledale in North Yorkshire ... How a rebellious girl from Huddersfield, who always wanted to be a shepherdess, achieved her dreams.' Helped by a TV series, it had made her a local celebrity. And she now had eight children.

Ravenseat boasted a shepherd's hut where you could stay for bed-and-breakfast, so I signed myself up and came back in the early evening after what had been a baking hot day. Harvesting had begun that week and there were neat bales of hay in black plastic lining the fields. Kids were playing in the farmyard. A small boy poked his head out of an upstairs bedroom window and directed me towards the shepherd's hut.

This stood off on its own by an enchanting little ghyll, surrounded by ferns and beautiful tall foxgloves. Swallows and dippers were swooping over the water. The hut was long and rectangular – more like a railway carriage – and 'comfortably appointed', with a log-burning stove and a bed across the far end. The small bookcase was lined with past editions of the *Swaledale Flock Book* in case anyone had problems sleeping. An old Bush radio was still set to the Third Programme on long wave. I turned it on experimentally. It worked. The armchair had a sheep's fleece draped over it. Plain curtains framed the small windows and the tongue-and-groove pine panelling felt warm and inviting. An old wooden shepherd's crook was tucked into the corner.

I was busy taking in this interior detail when there was a knock on the door. One of the children, Reuben, was outside. He was twelve, he told me. Despite the baking temperature, Reuben had been deputised to light the wood-burning stove — indeed, was determined to do so, despite my protestations about the heat.

'It won't take a moment,' he said, as if that might be my concern. And nor did it. Reuben was clearly good with his hands.

He asked me what I did and I explained, self-consciously, what was expected of, but rarely delivered by, anyone describing themselves as a travel writer. Feeling that this might be falling a little flat, I mentioned that my son Owen, who was twenty, had just started to train to be a pilot — a far more impressive occupation.

'I wouldn't want to fly. I don't like the idea. I like home best. I want to be a mechanic. I like fixing things. I've been fixing up a go-kart. I've got a muck-spreader. I fixed that up as well. And I fixed up a tractor for a wedding.'

I looked questioningly at this last remark.

'For the bride to ride to church,' he added.

Reuben was clearly, like his parents, entrepreneurial. Within five minutes, he had persuaded me that he could mend an old strimmer I had lying in a shed hundreds of miles away to the south.

As I had been walking a fair bit that day, and Clive and Amanda themselves were nowhere to be seen, I bedded down for the night, lulled by the sound of the stream outside and the warmth of Reuben's expertly lit stove. I didn't need the *Swaledale Flock Book* to send me to sleep.

Next morning, Clive arrived bearing a large breakfast tray. He was bearded, good-humoured and clearly in a hurry to get on with the harvesting before the weather broke. I only met Amanda for the first time when I wandered up to find the shower, which was in one of the outhouses. She was standing in the farmyard, tall, blonde and striking, with a warm grasp on life. After checking that all had gone well with my sojourn in the shepherd's hut, she wanted to know what I was doing.

'You want to come by this way with a mule? I don't see why not. I don't know anybody who's ever done that, along the Coast-to-Coast. And they all come through here. You'll just have to choose your bridleways carefully when you get down below Keld.'

I told her my theory that the reason there were so few mules around in Britain was that in the past they had been considered a 'Catholic animal'.

'People always think I'm Catholic. Because I've so many kids. But I'm not.'

There was an interruption as Clive came by, herding some sheep that needed clipping. I noticed that Amanda looked a bit fazed, standing in the bright sunshine in the middle of her yard.

'It's all right. It's all seeming a little unreal today. It's just that I had a baby daughter two days ago.'

She must have seen my jaw drop.

'Premature. She was born premature. So she's in the unit at Middlesbrough seventy miles away. She's fine. She's doing well. But everything's strange, as if I'm floating. Nothing quite seems real.'

She invited me into the kitchen for a cup of tea. I needed one to help me recover from this news. None of her children – or for that matter Clive – had mentioned that Amanda had just given birth to another baby. But then with eight kids already, perhaps they had thought it wasn't newsworthy.

A phone with the loudest ringtone I've ever heard went off somewhere in the kitchen. Amanda located it and hesitated before answering – rightly. It was a cross customer for the shepherd's hut, asking in a loud voice — so I could hear every word — why she hadn't heard back about her booking request. Which was 'very inconvenient' as she had to make plans. Amanda gave the woman time to get it all off her chest.

'Well, the thing is, I had a baby two days ago. It was premature, so a bit of a rush. She's at Middlesbrough hospital at the unit, so I can visit every other day. And I'm hauling bales of hay around in between. So, I've been too busy to answer emails.'

I could hear the alarm in the caller's voice as she started backtracking and apologising in the mortified way only the English middle class can do. She sounded like Lynda Snell from *The Archers*.

'Oh, I'm so, so sorry. So, so sorry. I should never have rung. And is she all right? Is the baby OK?'

'She's fine,' said Amanda firmly. 'Life goes on, after all. Now, what were the dates you were asking about?'

I instinctively liked Amanda. She was quick, funny and passionate about farming. And down to earth. If she was famous, she gave no signs of knowing it. I also admired the way her children had untrammelled access to a life of messing around on the land and the farm. 'Beware: free-range children' ran a sign on the drive, although a greater danger to any traffic were the assembled bits of farm machinery and kids' scooters scattered on this remote valley road, all waiting for Reuben's mechanical attention.

'We still make the smaller conventional square bales of hay, rather than the usual big round ones people like these days,' Amanda told me. 'Because we can't get a bigger baler into the fields. And the square ones Clive can lift himself into a barn in the winter if the animals need extra food.

'Though if he can lift them now, when we are making them, he says they're too light.'

She looked at me expectantly. It was lucky I had helped with the odd harvest for local farmers in my youth.

'Because they lose weight as they dry?'

She relaxed. I felt I had passed a test.

'I get a lot of people who come through here who are difficult to talk to about the countryside. They're lovely people, but we've not got much in common.'

I asked how she managed to find time for her writing – given the children, 2,000 acres and a lot of sheep, as well as a husband. Not so much a pram in the hallway as a tractor parked in the bedroom.

'It's impossible in summer. Too much going on. But winter is perfect. It gets dark early. We haven't got TV here. So I can work late into the night.

'I can always tell what mood I'm in when I write. If I'm angry, it comes out in the book. Fifteen minutes when you're in the mood is worth two hours when you're not.'

Her great model was James Herriot and his *It Shouldn't Happen to a Vet* books.

'I love the way he writes about the remote bits of Yorkshire. It's the reason I chose the publishers I'm with. They do James Herriot's books. And they put me out in hardback first, before the paperback, like old-fashioned publishers used to do!' As Amanda's book was a top-ten bestseller, the publishers must also have been pleased with her decision.

After the book's success, she was asked, which gave her considerable pleasure, to write an introduction to the James Herriot classics for a centenary edition. And her own books – for *The Yorkshire Shepherdess* led to a sequel and she had, she told me, recently been commissioned to write another – had brought the realities of life in the Dales to a wide audience.

'In my own writing, what I really enjoy are the details. Like baler twine. No one else ever really writes about baler twine. But it's what holds a farm together. Round gates. Round children, holding clothes up. Round stable doors. I don't know what I'd do in life without baler twine.'

I knew all about baler twine. Annis had given me copious instructions about how to use it to tie Jethro in his horsebox stall.

Before I left, Clive asked me to have a look at his prize rams which were being kept in a barn to pamper them in advance of a big sheep auction later that month. To my surprise, there was an electric fence running around the inside of the barn walls, something I had never seen before.

'Looks high security,' I said to Clive. 'Even Hannibal Lecter didn't need that.'

'It's so they don't try to headbutt or scratch the walls,' he explained, 'which would ruin their colouring.'

Two rams were huddled together in the centre of the barn. One had bigger horns than the other. Like narcissistic male models, they had positioned themselves to show off their best attributes; if able to, they would have draped their arms over each other's shoulders.

I made the appropriate cooing and aahing noises about their fine features and well-tonsed faces. They were being kept in the ovine equivalent of cotton wool — straw bedding. Even so, Clive worried there might be a risk of them getting fluke.

Amanda joined us to lean over the barn door and admire the two charges.

'The thing about sheep auctions,' she said, 'is that you can never know which way it's going to go. Also, you keep looking at the tups so much in the run-up to the auction that you end up believing they're better than they are. But it takes two to make a sale. The worst is when you start off with two rival bidders and then they decide to share the tup, so put in a low joint bid. The best is when you have two rival bidders who hate each other. We once had two bidders and we knew that one of them had stolen the other one's wife! Which was perfect.'

Even for someone with as firm a hold on life as Amanda, having a small baby in a premature unit while trying to carry on normally was a big ask. I was impressed — and also annoyed by the many people I later met along the way, particularly the women, who were suspicious of her.

'Famous Amanda? You know she's not really from Swaledale. Now, *I am* . . .'

So what if she grew up in Huddersfield? It made me respect her even more. Why should it matter that she was not 'to the farm born'? She had always longed for the rural life, and left a job as a bored shop girl in Boots to find one and made it happen. As my grandfather Lawrence, who came from the farming Bragg family at Wigton, used to tell me, 'You should always be careful what you wish for as a child. Because you will surely get it.'

*

# Chapter 8

# The Idea of the North

Their feet generally are strong, the horn tough, thick and quick growing, so that on unmetalled roads mules are frequently worked unshod.

The War Office, *Animal Management* (London, 1923)

Down the road from Ravenseat was an establishment called Swaledale Yurts for those who wanted more luxurious accommodation than a traditional tent could provide. What with the shepherd's hut at Ravenseat, any visiting Lynda Snell would be spoilt for choice.

Five big and brightly coloured yurts stood proudly out in the open. It wasn't something that Jasper, Jethro and I were tempted by – or could afford – but the principle was terrific. Who wants to be in a tent so small your toes stick out? When you can bring your own Mongolian throw-rug and live large, with a roaring fire and perhaps a goat turning on the spit? They even offered a hot tub, although whether Jethro would have fitted in was debatable.

I consoled myself with a simpler pleasure: a toasted cheese and pickle sandwich at the handsome Keld Lodge, which stood proudly by the roadside in isolated splendour. This far end of Swaledale saw only the most determined of walkers or motorists. The sandwich was drowned in pickle, a signal that we had truly arrived in Yorkshire. We had crossed the boundary earlier that day on Nine Standards Rigg.

Ahead lay what was almost the perfect bridle path for Jethro, stretching out wide and green alongside the river; what Wainwright described as 'the royal way to see Swaledale'. Swaledale is a long handsome valley that runs the width of the Yorkshire Dales. As the river descends from Ravenseat and the head of the valley, it widens and the towns become more substantial, as do the farms.

Above Muker, another good Norse name just meaning 'place' – the Vikings liked to keep things simple – there were some fine stone barns and even more substantial longhouses, another part of the Norse heritage of this part of the world. Traditionally, families would have lived at one end of the longhouse and kept animals at the other; although in the larger and more prosperous farms we saw as we descended the valley, farmers would have lived separately in their own houses and put the labourers in the barns.

The history of these labourers was fascinating. Called 'hinds', their status was somewhere between servant and employee. An unusual feature of their employment contract was that they received most of their benefits in kind rather than in cash. While they received accommodation in the longhouses, they would also be paid in grain, beans and potatoes, with perhaps a small bit of pasture to keep their own few personal cattle if they had them. Any additional money payment would be relatively small, and just enough to keep them clothed.

If the hinds came as a family, one of them – usually the wife or daughter – would be specified as a 'bondager' who had to provide labour on request for the farmer. It was a paternalistic arrangement, which of course gave far less freedom to the labouring class than if they received straight wages.

And just to show that 'zero hours' contracts are not a modern innovation for agricultural workers, farmers could often be mean in their contractual arrangements. The young hinds were typically in their early twenties, and hired by the year at the great fairs around the country, particularly in spring (Lady Day) and autumn (Martinmas). It had been at such a fair that George Fox had ignited the Quaker movement, perhaps because of the dissatisfaction felt by those putting themselves out to hire. A small retainer fee would be given, called 'earnest money'; but because if employed for a full year, the servant would then be eligible for local Poor Law payments, farmers often issued contracts for exactly fifty-one weeks to deny them this.

We could always tell a longhouse that was used by the hinds, as it had a chimney at one end and often a separate, higher entrance on the uphill side. The hinds slept directly above the cattle, which at least would have kept them warm in winter, if also making them liable to disease.

Now, though, the longhouses were less used for cattle because sheep had become more dominant; the shape of the longhouses was also incompatible with modern farming techniques for storing hay. As Amanda had said, farmers these days preferred round bales in favour of the old square ones. Whereas in the past a man could lift a square bale, you really needed a machine for a round one, unless a man had the arm-span of a Hercules. You couldn't get a machine into a longhouse, so they had needed to construct more modern farm outhouses in the usual ugly mixture of prefab panels and corrugated iron.

This was why the old stone longhouses of the Yorkshire Dales were falling into disrepair – or rather disuse, as there were some handsome grants to keep the buildings maintained, given the character they added to the landscape. At least, there *had* been landscape grants. Many of those had come from the European Union, so what would happen now we were leaving was anybody's guess. British governments in recent years, both Labour and Conservative, had seen little advantage in promoting the countryside, other than as a potential source of new housing.

As we walked along with Jethro, I had time to take in what an extraordinary landscape this was, with field systems preserved to an unusual degree. The bottom of the valley was a maze of immaculately built stone walls, designed to keep sheep in, with small, narrow 'squeezer' stiles as their only exit. Even if anyone wanted to keep a bridleway open, it would have been difficult to do so. As a result, Jasper and I had to circle up and around above Reeth, skirting high up the hills with Jethro.

But this was no bad thing. The going was good and the heather beautiful. The views each way down the Swaledale Valley were sublime. Our spirits were excellent. When we stopped for a picnic, we let Jethro off the rope so he could graze freely; although by this stage we had bonded with him so well, he preferred to loom above us as we lay on the grass — at one point trying to eat Jasper's hat.

Jasper took this philosophically. 'At least, I've got a buttercup's view up Jethro's nostrils. And he didn't try to eat the chorizo.'

If anything, Jethro preferred nibbling heather, which surprised me, although by now I'd realised he had a far tougher digestive system than a horse's. He disturbed some grouse who started shouting in their tinny way: 'Go back, go back, go back.'

'They sound like cheap children's toys, don't they?' said Jasper.

And it was true. They gave out an odd muffled sound, almost half-hearted. Nor were they terribly clever in the way they displayed themselves so provocatively, as if tempting a gun. But then, like pheasants, there's a reason grouse never live long enough to become terribly clever.

*

Look at the picture-postcard landscape of the Dales — the lush green valleys with stone barns dotted over their neat fields — and you might think this a model for the prosperous countryside.

Of course this brings in the tourists. And of course the sheep pay their way. But in many ways, it's window-dressing, heavily subsidised and not the real engine behind the continued survival of places like Swaledale. For centuries, the real money has not been made here in the fields at all, but in the scraggy moorlands that fringe the tops of the valley.

First it was the lead mining, which has left a strange industrial archaeology of deserted mills and spoil heaps hidden above the ridge-line. But then, after cheaper Spanish lead knocked the bottom out of that market, it has been grouse shooting.

And these were not just any old grouse moors. They were some of the finest in the country. When Earl Peel sold part of his nearby estate to American billionaire Robert Miller in 1995, he received £9 million for the deal. And Robert Miller was thought lucky at the time; the old money that owns the grouse moors rarely needs to sell.

As grouse have become more important to the local farming economy than sheep, rich men have flocked here. Other neighbours of Earl Peel included Lord Bolton and the Duke of Norfolk.

The economics of grouse shooting were mad but compelling. Guns could pay upwards of £150 for the pleasure of shooting two grouse – birds worth only £3.50 a brace from the local game dealer. And they would expect to shoot a great deal of grouse to make sure they were losing money in a satisfactory way. An upmarket grouse shoot could command between £5,000 and £10,000 a day from each of its guns. And that was before they added tips.

But the estates didn't have it all their own way. Grouse liked to eat young heather. Older plants therefore needed to be burned each year, in careful rotation. This could get out of hand. Locals had told me stories of widespread heather fires that often went under-reported in the media. On Earl Peel's estate, a blaze had recently spread across thirty acres, needing fourteen fire engines, water bowsers and slurry tankers to put it out.

Moreover, a troublesome and debilitating gut worm spread easily between grouse if their numbers were not carefully controlled. For this and other reasons, the number of grouse could often go down. The season was a limited one, between the so-called 'Glorious Twelfth' of August and the end of grouse shooting on 10 December. The best – and most expensive – shooting took place early, in August and September. By October, the period when we were travelling through with Jethro, the guns had gone quieter, for which I was grateful; I wasn't sure how Jethro would react under fire.

The owners groused themselves about all this. They claimed their huge revenues 'went back into the estate'; that by the time they paid for the gamekeepers, beaters and maintenance, there was no profit from the twenty-five or so days shooting they might sell a year. These claims needed to be taken with a judicious pinch of snuff. (Eighteenth-century sportsmen liked to leaven their snuff with lead-pellet filings from the guns, as it was said to improve one's aim – although it can't have done much for their health.)

There was a lot of money in grouse shooting, which may be what attracted Robert Miller to buy his enormous 32,000-acre estate in the first place. This was a man who had made his money from building an empire of duty-free shops across the airports of the world.

But talk to the locals, as I had in many a pub up and down Swaledale, and they were clear who was making all the money: the gamekeepers.

I've had many run-ins with gamekeepers over the years, partly from a fondness for trespassing, and partly because game-keepers have a justified reputation for being bloody-minded and difficult individuals. But the days of Richard Jefferies (whose *The Gamekeeper at Home* is still for me his finest, if neglected, work), when the gamekeeper lived off the scraps from the shooting party lunch, are long gone.

Gamekeepers have become the new rural aristocracy. They can make £40,000 a year – and that is before the substantial tips, which come in cash.

Picture the scene: a group of obscenely wealthy self-made men and aristocrats are milling around their Range Rovers at the end of a day's shoot. There is only so much showing off they can do about the quality of their guns – preferably older Purdy twelve-bores that have been in the family rather than anything too nouveau-riche – and the satellite Wi-Fi in their vehicles. Or patronising of any newcomers who have shot the birds that were flying too low. When it comes to a simple bit of flashing the cash to tip the gamekeeper, they can be ostentatious – and by God, they are. Not least because if the gamekeeper has done well, then so, by inference, have they.

'You gave us a tremendous day's shooting, George.' Meaning, 'I did tremendously well, even if nobody else did.' And here's the wonga to prove it. My money's on the table. Hope you all saw it. Now, beat that.

At the pub in Muker, I had heard a story – one I later heard repeated, with variants, elsewhere, so clearly a developing rural myth – about the gamekeeper who turned up at a Range Rover dealership and bought the most exclusive model, for cash. A lot of it. The dealership accepted this happily, but reported the transaction of almost £100,000 to the bank, who duly, as they must, turned over the inquiry to HMRC, Her Majesty's tax inspectors. This, it was discovered, was only the tip of the iceberg. The gamekeeper had been salting away undeclared cash from his tips for many a season.

At this point, the man telling the story pointed out the moral: which was not that the gamekeeper 'got done' for undeclared back tax, although of course that happened; but that the gamekeeper, unbelievably, did not get fired even though convicted – because he was too valuable to the estate. And next time around, should be a little more careful how he spent his cash. 'He could buy a round in here for a start!'

The 'my Range Rover is bigger than yours' world was not one I found appealing. Thousands of grouse being driven by lowly-paid beaters to fly over a ridge and present a phalanx of wealthy men with something to shoot at. The suspicion also persisted – voiced by Chris Packham, among others – that gamekeepers were using devious means to control raptors and other predators who might get their fledgling grouse.

But if it was managed ethically and kept the rural economy going, there was something to be said for it. And having accompanied a shooting party once out of journalistic interest – although not to shoot, as I have no desire to kill any animal – it would be churlish to deny that I enjoyed the consider-able pleasures of the shooting party lunch. Because another thing the very wealthy like to show off about is the quality of their cellars. Nothing quite beats a good vintage claret after you have been walking across the countryside in the crisp autumn sun; accompanied by a freshly grilled grouse on toast with bacon – and perhaps a traditional sprig of heather shoved up its rear vent.

*

As we walked on through the heather – without shooting at any of the grouse that talked to us – I felt a sense of tranquillity descending. Between us, Jasper and I had established a good rhythm for looking after Jethro and as long as the going was good, he fell in with us well. If we really reached an impassable stretch, we could always walk it ourselves and then ship Jethro around in the horse van.

Swaledale was a revelation. Outside of the James Herriot series, which like every other child of my generation I had dutifully watched, I knew nothing about the Dales. The handsome market towns of Keld and of Reeth in particular, with its big, broad square, lined on one side by no fewer than three pubs, came as welcome surprises.

Outside one of those pubs, the Buck, I got talking to a man in his forties who was sitting at the next table. He was lean, dark-haired and, I guessed, a local, because he wasn't wearing trekking gear. From where we sat, there was a magnificent view down from the top of the square over its cobbled expanse. It was a market day and there were stalls set up alongside the road that threaded diagonally across the hill.

'It may look pretty to you, but it's different for those of us who live in the place.' The man leaned closer over towards me, as if wanting to confide a secret. 'I'll tell you something about Reeth.'

I waited. He leaned even closer into me.

'It's full of bitter, disappointed single women who've retired here.'

I wasn't quite sure how to take this; or whether he was going to elaborate further on quite what had led him to this conclusion. But he retreated to his own table, as if he had said too much. The conversation was over.

It was in Reeth that I suffered a galling loss. Somehow between one of the pubs and the small museum, I managed to lose the large notebook I was using as a diary.

Perhaps the lunchtime pint of Black Sheep had lulled me into a false sense of security; or the sense that the most difficult part of our journey was behind us. My guard was down. When travelling in Peru or the Himalaya, I protected my diaries with paranoid levels of security – not from fear that anyone else might read them (friends and family thought my handwriting illegible), but because they were also my principal resource when it came to writing up a trip. I had never lost a diary when travelling abroad; so how come I now had when pottering around a small Yorkshire market town?

I put up notices in the post office and other likely venues; even offered a reward. Nothing. The diary, which of course had my name and address at the front, had vanished into the ether. I had copied all the entries onto my laptop, so at least no information had been lost. But that was not the point. My journals were talismanic objects for me; a row of them at home encompassed my entire life. To mislay one was a tragedy. Although perhaps, like my ancestor Robert Bragg's wedding ring, it will one day re-emerge.

The worst thing about losing something is that you can't stop thinking about it. The loss was nagging away at me as I walked. Was there somewhere that I hadn't looked?

It was a good long walk as we continued across the heather from Reeth. Time for my mind to settle and to get into my stride – up to a point.

✻

Many of my journeys in the past had been taken on my own. I was not used to having company, although lucky to have in Jasper and Jethro companions of such varied and stimulating temperaments.

Although in a way I had never travelled on my own. For if we are honest, we are always accompanied by other voices when we walk: voices of old friends, of family, of the past. We may have moments of 'mindfulness' when we do nothing but take in what is in front of us; but these will be varied by long stretches when the mind is anything but present. When it loops off in long circles, remembering other times and other places. There is nothing wrong with that, of course; indeed, I see it as part of the purpose of a walk to stimulate the memory – to reawaken long-forgotten thoughts.

But you can have too much of a good thing, and spend so much time letting the mind drift that you don't appreciate the landscape in front of you. I had been increasingly conscious of this: that there is so much noise in our lives, from iPhones, iPads, iPods and all the other media which keep us so social that we never have time to reflect. Inevitably, some of it ends up buzzing around inside our heads – worst of all being the repetitive, boring thoughts that can plague us all about plans or unresolved conflicts, within ourselves or with others.

My father's illness had brought the whole question of our attention to the present even more into focus. My mother often commented that while he had lost his short-term memory, his enjoyment of the moment was that much more intense as a consequence.

When we had all gone for a walk through the bluebells in spring earlier that year, he had frequently stopped to exclaim at their beauty. Each turn of the path had brought him a sight he had never seen before.

'This is just so extraordinary. I've never seen bluebells like this.'

Conversations were also more interesting – or could be, if steered in the right direction. Dad was unable to remember short-term plans, so there would be none of the usual discussion of what we were doing today and what we were doing tomorrow. Although naturally, as he could not remember such details, he often became anxious about what he was supposed to be doing.

But if we started to talk about something where clear, rational judgement was involved, his faculties were sharp. And if he asked what you were doing at the moment, this needed a much fuller answer than you might normally give; an answer in which you really had to present your life as it was, on the assumption that he might not know anything about it.

With family members, it is easy never to discuss the most important things. There is often an assumption that somehow they have been shared by osmosis over the years. But I found that these days with my father I needed to give a much fuller and clearer account. And as he would forget what I had said and ask again at some later stage, I got better and better, *Groundhog Day* style, at giving a coherent answer.

I thought of my father now, as we crossed the heather-clad expanse above Reeth; I also allowed myself simply to take in the landscape as well, with not an empty head but a clear one.

✳

This was a landscape that was impossible to look at without remembering W. H. Auden. As a poet, he made this part of Swaledale very much his own, at a time when it did not figure on anybody else's poetic map. He told his friend Geoffrey Grigson that 'my great good place is the part of the Pennines bounded on the south by Swaledale', and he used often to come here.

I liked to think of him now in his scoutmasterly shorts and hiking gear sprawled out in the sunshine beside Upper Kisdon Force which we were passing. The lines he wrote there for his poem 'Streams' were some of the finest of his later career, deliberately using a skaldic, northern meter:

> Lately, in that dale of all Yorkshire's the loveliest,
> Where, off its fell-side helter-skelter, Kisdon Beck
> Jumps into Swale with a boyish shouting,
> Sprawled out on grass, I dozed for a second . . .

When he wakes to the sound of the water again, he finds it

. . . dearer, water, than ever your voice, as if
Glad—though goodness knows why—to run with
                      the human race,
    Wishing, I thought, the least of men their
  Figures of splendour, their holy places.

Around the same time as this poem of 1954, he did a little-known piece for *Vogue*, which had asked some eminent writers to nominate their favourite travel destinations. Most had chosen sunlit spots in the Mediterranean or Caribbean; Auden, with mischievous perversity, proposed Swaledale and the north of England.

Entitled 'Six Unexpected Days in the Pennines', he begins the journey at Keld, extolling the landscape and letting slip the unexpected news that T. S. Eliot had always been very fond of Wensleydale cheese. (There is an interesting or at least unexplored thesis to be done on the relationship between poetry and cheese: Wordsworth and Coleridge regularly demolished whole truckles of Cheddar in the Lake District.)

Auden's love for the area was partly geological. His famous poem, 'In Praise of Limestone', ends with the declaration that:

. . . when I try to imagine a faultless love
Or the life to come, what I hear is the murmur
Of underground streams, what I see is a limestone landscape.

And he makes clear what it is about limestone that he finds so attractive:

If it form the one landscape that we, the inconstant ones,
Are consistently homesick for, this is chiefly
Because it dissolves in water.

The way limestone dissolves gives many of the hills of the North their particular shape – and also created the geological strata and mining that so fascinated Auden. This, after all, was a poet who had read *Mines and Mining in the English Lake District* by John Postlethwaite. His signed copy is in Carlisle City Library.

But more than anything else, Auden loved 'the idea of the North', not least because it was going in a completely different direction from everybody else. After the First World War, writers from D. H. Lawrence to Norman Douglas headed south for the warm embrace of the sun: Capri, Italy, Mexico, the Greek islands. Auden was proud of having been born in York and liked to position himself as a northern outsider.

He went even further north to Iceland not just for its wild beauty but also for its poetry. Auden loved the epics of the Vikings and Anglo-Saxons and built their alliterative jangle back into his own work to disrupt the expectations of the conventional iambic pentameter.

'North is the good direction,' as he once said. I had always liked the North myself, but it was a guilty pleasure: in general, southerners are quietly patronising about the North and northerners more bluntly rude about the South. Would a soft southerner writing about the North be considered, to use a PC term much favoured by North American intellectuals, 'voice appropriation'? Could you only write about the North if you came from there?

There's a good moment in John Steinbeck's *Travels with Charley*, one of my favourite books. Steinbeck is driving with his dog, Charley, and heading out of Chicago through Illinois. He describes it as a noble land of good fields and magnificent trees, neat and white-fenced. But he goes on to make the telling point that this is a subsidised countryside, without 'the thrust of land that supports itself and its owner. Rather, it was like a beautiful woman who requires the support and help of many faceless ones just to keep going.'

I felt the same about the south of England. The counties I knew well – Oxfordshire, Wiltshire, Kent – all had rural identities and areas of such outstanding natural beauty they didn't need a designation to tell us so. But they were kept women. They relied on the money that flowed out of London.

Whereas the North had a starkness to it. This was land that had to work for itself.

✻

The road over from Reeth towards Barnard Castle must be one of the most beautiful in England and was much filmed for the James Herriot vet books: picturesque bridges, the sweep of a narrow lane across the high fells and then the descent out of Arkengarthdale as the sheep scatter; all perfect for negotiating at great speed in an Austin 7.

I made a detour down it because I wanted to see someone I had last visited thirty years ago: Brian Russell, the blacksmith who I had stayed with when Fred and I were trying to collect a forge.

It was a shock when I arrived at Little Newsham, the village where he lived with his wife Hilda — a shock, because so little had changed. The outside of the forge still had the same familiar sign swinging. The village looked exactly as it always had.

Brian greeted me at the door with his large, reassuring presence. 'It hasn't changed much, has it? At least on the outside. Although inside I've expanded a bit.'

He showed me round. The forge fire was burning. There were enough tongs and heavy-duty instruments to satisfy the most industrious team of devils. Most of Brian's commissions were now for large-scale decorative gates, with iron flowers hammered cunningly into intricate patterns, then shot-blasted and galvanised to be weather-proof.

'There's no money left in farm gates. They can just get any

The Yorkshire Dales. *'Most of the neighbouring fields had a small barn at their centre, perfectly square and looking for all the world like little Monopoly houses that a player had put down to show he owned the property.'*

*'The high proportion of Viking blood — and place names — still swirling around this end of the Dales.'*

*'Quick, funny and passionate about farming'* — Amanda Owen looking up at her husband Clive. Because he's on a step.

A Texel ram guarding some wether lambs. *'Brought over from Holland in the last twenty years to toughen and "beef up" our own breeds. They look half bulldog; sheep that have worked out in the gym, with impressive and alarming musculature.'*

The shepherd's hut at Ravenseat. *'Long and rectangular — more like a railway carriage — and "comfortably appointed", with a log-burning stove and a bed across the far end.'*

Stopping for a picnic while roaming down the Dales. *'No, you can't have any.'*
Jasper takes a firm line as he has a buttercup's view up Jethro's nostrils.

Reeth: *'Its big, broad square, lined on one side by no fewer than three pubs.'*
They might not have a statue to Wainwright in the main square, but
at least they had named a beer after him.

'Henry Jenkins, who, it was claimed, died at the fabulous age of 169. The mythology that had grown up around him was as interesting as the historical evidence.'

Hugo Hildyard. '"As a way of life, in some sense this is finished," said Hugo, with a wave of his hand at the small fields.'

Catterick Races. 'A thoroughbred horse would have been useless for crossing England. That was a job for the equine equivalent of a mountain bike, not a Tour de France racer.'

The Yorkshire Moors. *'To swing up and down from summit to summit along the stone-lined Cleveland Way must surely rank as one of the great walking experiences in England.'*

The Animals in War Memorial. *'A rare recognition of the contribution made by mules to British military success — and of the price they paid.'*

Steampunks in Whitby. *'Time travel with attitude. So it can be Victorian but it can also be post-apocalyptic, like Mad Max.'*

Goths in Whitby. *'What happens when you wear black and only come out of your bedroom at night. And listen to darkwave.'*

Still talking after 200 miles. ' "Mule pace" is a bit brisker than a normal human one, like being on an exercise machine.'

At Robin Hood's Bay: *'We led Jethro to the edge of the waves, which were dancing up the launching ramp for the trawlers.'*

Jethro at his new stables after he had been permanently adopted.
*'He always looks at me in the way the English do on such occasions – with a friendly if slightly quizzical expression that leaves the changes in both our circumstances unspoken.'*

old cast ironwork, from the fabricator. We depend on people who want something a little fancy for a house, or maybe a public building. A lot of work comes from local authorities and developers.'

When Brian started in the 1970s – 'and I'm sixty-four now' – he found there weren't any blacksmithing courses he could do at the local colleges. Instead he found some books in a library about German wrought ironwork. Luckily, one of his tutors had worked as a blacksmith, so could give him some help outside class. When he left college, he couldn't find anybody to apprentice himself to either. 'And in those days, there was no internet to give YouTube instructional videos.'

In some ways, he told me, that had been the lowest period for blacksmithing in this country. But since then, there had been a very clear revival.

His young assistant Tom was helping him with what would be a month's work of hammering out a gate. Tom made a good point: that when he told people he was a blacksmith, they all assumed he was part of some nostalgic revival and that, as a trade, it had died out. Whereas in some ways it was flourishing and had been growing strongly in recent years, with more female blacksmiths as well. Discerning customers had come to appreciate the value of wrought ironwork – and I could see why. Fred had once made me a wrought-iron fire guard, as well as wall brackets for a hanging basket. Both had a more robust quality than the moulded mass-market work you could buy off the shelf. And both had lasted well.

'We still have quiet patches,' Brian told me. 'But nothing like as hard as when I started out.'

I reminded him that when we'd first met, not long after he had opened the forge, he had been lucky with an enlightened landlord. He had been given six months' free rent to get going, partly out of the landlord's desire to see the forge occupied again, as it had been empty since the 1890s.

'That same man owned the whole village. It's an estate village. He's dead, but his daughter runs it now.'

I walked with Brian back from the forge to his home; not exactly a long commute, as while when I had first met him he lived a little distance away, he had since rented a cottage in the village with his wife Hilda. We passed a small paddock where they kept a pony, which I eyed up with professional interest.

'You're welcome to bring your mule any time,' said Brian. This was kind, but I had left Jethro in comfortable quarters near Reeth; and unlike me, Jethro hated to make any detours that involved additional distance when he could stay in the same place and look over a gate.

Their garden was filled with roses, peonies and immaculately hoed vegetables, which put my own small allotment back home to shame.

'Hilda loves to weed,' Brian told me.

Hilda herself was at the doorway. A small and alert woman, she kept the books for the business. Her brother was a miner from County Durham, who had been forced to take on a wide variety of other jobs after the pit closures, and we talked over the evening meal about the changes that had taken place in the north-east. The closures at the old steelworks in Redcar had been much in the news – as had the tactless claim by Michael Heseltine that 'if you are going to lose your job, this is as good a time as any. Because the number of new jobs in the economy today is one of the most exciting features of this economy compared with many others.'

'They always say things like that,' said Hilda. 'They said things like that during the pit closures. Look what happened to those communities. The other thing they do is make the claim that people doing courses – retraining, health and safety, IT and stuff like that – have somehow found work. They haven't. They've just been taken off the unemployment register.'

Brian looked through his old record collection to find 'No Mule's Fool' by Family, with the immortal couplet:

> We're sitting here, me and my mule
> We make our own rules, and it's cool.

The late evening sun was coming through the large glass windows they had built onto their dining room, as we listened to Roger Chapman sing about a boy and his mule lazing around at the end of a summer's day. The crops in the field outside came right up to the windows. It was a peaceful setting.

'The only problem with this house,' said Brian, 'is that we couldn't buy it. Because the whole village is owned by the one estate. So, we're still renting, which isn't great. We did try to build our own place, but we couldn't get planning permission. That's a big problem in all these villages. Not enough new houses.'

Their son Ivan arrived home to join us. The last time I had seen him was as that baby in the kitchen sink when I had travelled with Fred. Ivan was now thirty and helped Brian part-time in the forge, but didn't particularly want to take the business over.

Brian got out the whisky and we talked of travels around the world. He had visited the States several times for international blacksmithing 'forge-ins', which were popular in places like Memphis. They questioned me about Peru and Mexico and my previous walk across England for *The Green Road into the Trees*.

'So is there anywhere left that you would really like to see?' Ivan asked.

'Colombia. And also the Orkney Islands. Though it probably takes less time from London to get to Colombia.'

They put me up for the night on a sofa. There was a curious incident when I was bringing in my bag. A young man, who I guessed to be a neighbour, was mowing the grass on the communal verge. He looked at me oddly – in a small village, I realised that strangers must be rare – so I mumbled some explanation about how I was getting things in from the car. He waited, as if for more. So I made a few inconsequential remarks about the weather, in the way the English do, before moving on.

Hilda explained his potential confusion. 'That must be the new neighbour. We haven't seen them yet as they've only just arrived. So I'm pleased to see they're cutting the grass already. But he obviously thought you were living here – and that you must be the blacksmith!'

She was too polite to add that I didn't live up to anyone's image of a blacksmith, given that Brian himself, at sixty-four, was still a tall, imposing presence who looked as if he could bend a ductile bit of iron with his bare hands.

But I was happy to be taken for a blacksmith, if only for a brief moment. There is satisfaction in making things – in being a maker, as Auden used to say ('A poet is a professional maker of verbal objects'). And in some ways, as a writer and filmmaker, I have been one. But words and images are more insubstantial. To be able to hold something in your hand that you have fashioned out of the fire must be a truly primordial feeling.

✻

The countryside started to change as we descended down the Swale River from Reeth. It became softer, more inviting. By the time we got to the village of Marske (pronounced '*Mass-k*' by the locals, with a soft 'a' and no 'r'), there were more trees, for a start. Alder lined the pretty banks of the small Marske Beck, which ran up from the village and the picturesque packhorse bridge that Jethro clattered over with some aplomb, and perhaps even a sense of ownership.

Even more pronounced than the alder were the ash trees. It is estimated that 70 per cent of the trees in the Yorkshire Dales are ash — so if and when ash dieback ever reaches the North, the landscape will change irretrievably, as it has in Denmark, where the disease has almost wiped out the nation's stock of ash.

The Dales are a far more changeable landscape than is often presumed. It is only in the last few centuries that sheep have become so predominant; there would previously have been far more cattle. And the greenness of the valley that we were travelling down was due to generations of farmers improving the soil: first applying lime in earlier centuries when the local lime kilns could provide so much, and then from the nineteenth century using bone-based fertiliser, and even South American guano.

Nor were the most dominant features of the valley — the walls that divided up the fields — as straightforward as they might appear. People who don't live in the country often view dry-stone walls as an almost organic part of the upland landscape. But there are well-made stone walls and badly-made ones. Nowhere could this be seen better than a short way along Marske Beck, near one of the farms which lay on the opposite bank from the bridle path we were taking. We could look across to a patchwork of these dry-stone walls dividing up the hillside.

Some of the walls meandered in eccentric wavy lines like a kid's drawing; but other sections had been completed in rigid rectangles, like city blocks. The meandering walls were, perhaps counter-intuitively, the better-built ones. These walls followed the contours of the landscape, so kept a natural line and were often very ancient.

It was the walls that looked so neat and rectangular that were the shoddy ones. They had been thrown up quickly after the Parliamentary Enclosure Acts of the nineteenth century. Labour gangs from South Yorkshire were brought up to enforce the new division of what had always previously been common land for grazing. These unskilled gangs, who had no background in building dry-stone walls, were shipped in because there was not enough – or particularly willing – local labour. And rather than follow the contours of the land, which kept a wall level and gave it strength, they simply marched the walls in rigid lines over whatever lay in the way.

Dry-stone walling is an attractive and complicated art. It requires great skill to bind together stones without mortar so that they are strong enough to withstand the stresses of weather and livestock. I had already noticed throughout Cumbria and Yorkshire that walls in the North were subtly different from the ones I was used to in the South. In places like Devon, they often incorporated large boulders, while here, the walls were double-skinned, with frequent 'tie stones' right through both skins to bond the wall together. These sometimes protruded far enough out for a walker to rest the edge of their buttocks on while eating lunch, as long as their figure was suitably callipygian.

To select local field stones – which by definition are irregular – and lock them together firmly enough to give stability, so that 'the hearting', as they call it, of the stone can bind, needs a knowledgeable eye as well as strong arms. The stones must be graded on the spot for suitability as either foundation, hearting or capping material.

There are still a dozen or so professional dry-stone wallers working in North Yorkshire; some estimates say there are over 7,000 kilometres of dry-stone wall in the Dales Park alone. It is an important part of managing the land. But I could see they had a sizeable job on their hands. Jethro, Jasper and I often passed walls that had sagged like old washing lines. Some had broken down and collapsed, often to the extent that it would have been easier to build a whole new wall than restore them. Where several courses had come away, we could see a cross-section of what was clearly a wall that had been put up in a hurry: shoddy work brought on by what some would say was a shoddy piece of legislation in the first place, which deprived many people of their livelihoods.

The village of Marske itself also showed some of the changes that had taken place over the centuries: for, even by the standards of English villages, it was an extraordinarily ancient one. While the bleaker upper end of Swaledale near Keld had been Viking, this lower end of the valley had been a Saxon enclave; to the extent that after Lindisfarne was sacked by the Vikings in AD 793 – a pivotal moment in the history of the North – the bones of St Cuthbert were rescued and kept in the church here for safety until they were finally moved to Durham Cathedral. These were revered relics and a measure of Marske's importance, as St Cuthbert was almost the unofficial patron saint of northern England: his cross, with its bowed ends, was a symbol emblazoned everywhere on gravestones and memorials, and on the flag of Northumberland.

As soon as I stepped into the small church, it felt both cold and indescribably old. Small white stalls lined the nave. Although the present church had Norman foundations from 1090, there must have been an even earlier church on the same site to house St Cuthbert's bones. The churchyard outside – 'God's acre', to use the lovely medieval term – was a peaceful place with yews; a local man told me that in winter it was always covered in snowdrops, which grow well in this part of the world.

Across from the church was Marske Hall, the old squire's house and another sign of the times. This had once been an absolutely typical local manor house, whose shadow fell over the village and controlled both the church and estate. Attention is often focussed on the grand aristocratic estates in the North, like those belonging to the Duke of Northumberland or the Marquess of Zetland, for obvious reasons: they have the glamour and the huge landholdings.

But the influence of a local squire could be of much more importance. In this case, one family had owned the estate continuously for many centuries after Matthew Hutton, then Archbishop of York, bought it in Elizabethan times. The church was full of the tombs of his descendants. The Huttons steered the estate through all the changes that took place over the following centuries: the mining, the move from sheep to cattle and back again, the many architectural changes to the church itself. However, after 1900 the family became absentee landlords. In 1960, big country houses were going to the wall because of death duties – the property was sold by the next surviving descendant, who had never even seen it.

Now the village had no resident squire, parson or doctor – or for that matter, publican. Nor was there a shop, although the church sold a few supplies. The bus service was meagre, and the message was clear: like so many smaller villages in England today, unless you could afford a car, you certainly couldn't afford to live in Marske.

✳

## Chapter 9

# Richmond in Wonderland

Mules are not, as a rule, at all fastidious as to the quality of the forage offered to them.

The War Office, *Animal Management* (London, 1923)

Jasper and I started to get excited as we got closer to Richmond. It was a long time since we had been near any metropolitan pleasures. Richmond had a Georgian theatre, a cinema and numerous restaurants. Even Wainwright, not a man for urban delights, had felt a quickening of the pulse on approaching the town. It might have been my imagination, but I thought Jethro picked up his pace as well. He snorted in an appreciative manner. Although the next moment, he tried to nibble at a yew tree; we had to stop him as the leaves would not have done his digestion any good.

We met a farmer in a tractor who complimented Jethro as a 'bonny animal' – although at first he said he didn't know what the hell he was looking at.

'So he's a mule. Don't see many of them.'

He pointed out the effects of a summer hailstorm that had demolished many of the sheds on the nearby slopes and ripped through a lot of the trees.

'Unbelievable, that was. A freak, freak storm. There's a farmer over there who had to pay out over £150,000 and he wasn't even insured. Nobody expected anything like that.'

Just past Applegarth Farm, I started to feel we were leaving Swaledale behind and entering Richmondshire proper. The low evening light was falling from the south-west over the russets and ochres of the woods on the riverbank, while a few striking red ornamental trees from Richmond's outlying houses punctuated the green fields. It was a richer, more lush setting than the Dales had provided.

As we swept around a broad grass bridleway that made perfect walking for Jethro, there were tantalising first glimpses of the towers of Richmond, both the folly of Culloden and the unmistakable profile of the Norman castle. In the foreground, the bracken had browned to a coppery sheen. The Swaleview Caravan Park below us undercut the sublimity of the scene – but overall it was still a pincushion of reds, yellows and greens.

Looking up, I could see the monument for Williance's Leap on the skyline, above the cliffs of Whitcliffe Scar. The story goes that Robert Williance, a local lead miner, was out with a hunting party one day in 1606 when he got lost in thick fog. He and his horse fell over the cliff. The horse was killed but protected his rider from the impact; Williance survived with only a broken leg. Unable to move after the fall, and while waiting for rescue, he slit open the dead horse's stomach and stuck his broken leg inside, a trick later adopted by Leonardo DiCaprio in *The Revenant*.

I wondered whether Jethro would have been equally heroic and tried to break my fall if we had met any precipitous moments – although somehow I doubted it. And anyway, I had to get him back to the RSPCA in one piece. The nearest we had come to danger so far was when Jethro had spooked crossing a stream and shoulder-charged me. Having 300 kilos of mule come at you was like being tackled by two Jonah Lomus at the same time and I had hit the deck hard – though it had left me with little more than a few bruises and some wounded pride.

The wind started to pick up strongly. The trees over the path bent down low towards each other, their branches whipping sideways, stretching out like serpents. The sound as we went through some of the small woods was extraordinary, as if the trees were talking to one another, and doing so in a guttural Viking tongue, all clashing consonants.

Walking into Richmond, we passed people with their heads down against the wind, clutching bags of shopping, focussed on the pavement. No one noticed us. Coming along the street was a determined young woman with walking poles in both hands and a backpack, who was clearly doing the Coast-to-Coast the other way round. For a moment, I felt like asking what lay ahead for us, but she had such a running gait on her that I didn't want to disturb her rhythm — and there was the worry she might spike one of Jethro's hooves with her poles.

We had arranged for Jethro to spend the night in stables out-side Richmond, at Brough Park. This was courtesy of a kind man called John Haslam who I had met on an earlier visit to Richmond. He had asked what I was planning to do next and when I told him about this trip with a mule, John and his wife Jude offered both stabling for Jethro and dinner for Jasper and me. Not only was this extremely kind, but it also kept up the strange alliteration governing our journey, by which so many people we met had names beginning with 'J'.

\*

John Haslam had also invited some friends of his to dinner — Austin Lynch and Tim Culkin, a gay couple who used to teach at John's school and now ran what sounded an upmarket bed-and-breakfast in the centre of Richmond called Millgate House.

I went to see them the next day for coffee. 'Upmarket' didn't do it justice. It was to your average B&B what a Jaguar is to a

Ford Fiesta. There were antique furnishings dripping off the walls, and fine Turkish carpets, in what was a stately Georgian house off Richmond's handsome marketplace. A large Renaissance picture of the Annunciation dominated the dining room, to the amusement of a couple who were staying there. 'I've never had an angel looking down at me over breakfast,' said the woman.

Both Austin and Tim were of pensionable age, but looked in excellent shape: Austin had spiky hair and wore a bright blue sleeveless gilet which showed off tattooed eagles on both arms ('there's another tattoo on my back'); Tim was taller and more relaxed, like a gentle John Le Mesurier. Austin had been Head of Art at Richmond School, Tim the Head of Sixth Form.

'This was an old wool merchant's house,' Tim told me over coffee, which he prepared meticulously – 'exactly twenty-five seconds to brew' – and served in a silver pot. 'It was completely rundown when we bought it thirty-seven years ago. Part of the ceiling had collapsed. It was like a lot of Georgian buildings in the seventies. Undervalued and forgotten.'

'So is that how long you've been together?' I asked. 'Thirty-seven years?'

'No, no, no,' said Austin. 'We've been together much longer than that. We've been together *forty-seven years.*' They looked at each other as if in mutual wonder at this longevity. 'We had places of our own before we bought this jointly.'

'And,' Austin added, 'we were one of the first couples to have a civil partnership. On the very first date you could, 21 December 2005.'

Both of them had originally moved up from London. I wondered how accepting they had found Richmond and North Yorkshire of their homosexuality.

'Well, of course,' said Tim, 'London was and is far more liberal. But really, we've hardly had any problems here at all. People just let us get on with it. When we moved here, we were teaching at what was then the grammar school before it became the big Richmond comprehensive with 1,600 pupils. There was a time in the 1980s when it was very difficult with Clause 28, and the worry we might be criticised for promoting homosexuality in schools. But in general, it's been fine. In fact, at the school they've recently elected an openly gay student as Head Boy. Just shows how far we've come.

'What was more difficult for me,' Tim continued, 'was the period before I came up here. I spent twenty years or so never telling anybody – my family and friends – about who I was. It was terrible. I was brought up a strict Catholic. We both were. When he discovered, my father sent me to a psychiatrist to "cure me".'

Austin joined in. They had the agreeable habit, common to many couples who have been together a long time, of sensing when to pick up each other's baton.

'I knew from the age of three that I was gay. I would keep looking at the pictures of Michelangelo's *David* in a picture book. I'm surprised the pages didn't fall out!

'So, in answer to your earlier question, yes: we are accepted here, and they know us, and we have this beautiful house and have been around a while, so I suppose we have some status – but I think sometimes they treat us as court jesters, outsiders who are tolerated. Not that we push it in people's faces. Some of my more militant gay friends come up from London and say, "Why don't you wander round the marketplace holding hands?" But that's not the point.

'Although it's so beautiful, Richmond has kept its working-class feel. It's down to earth. And we like that. Of course, a lot of Georgian houses have been restored – and the council's given grants for people to do that. But it's not self-conscious. It hasn't got the window boxes. And I think it's really important it's not a commuter place. If we were just fifteen minutes from Newcastle or Leeds, it would be different.'

We were sitting near the windows of one of the reception rooms. There must have been some dozen grandfather clocks against the walls, all ticking with disconcerting asynchronicity; below was their sheltered walled garden, filled with hostas, peonies and roses. A secret garden.

'Did you know that Lewis Carroll came from Richmond?' asked Austin.

I didn't, but I could believe it.

'Charles Dodgson, as he was then. His father was the rector at one of the parishes near here. So he went to Richmond School, the one we taught at. He had a bad stammer.'

I had never thought of the *Alice* books as being written by a Yorkshireman. But it made sense. The bluntness of the Duchess telling off her cook, let alone the various queens. The long tea party. The fondness for nonsense; for telling it like it was, but with a twist.

I wandered out into Richmond with fresh eyes, looking out at the castle on top of the hill. The streets – called 'Wynds' – did indeed wind round the mount, like the stripes of a helter-skelter. It was a topsy-turvy place with an upside-down logic, more like a Tuscan hill-town than the staid Yorkshire municipalities that lay further south on the plains. No wonder James Herriot described it as 'the most romantic and charming town in the country'. And yes, that's country, not county.

How strange it must have been for the young Charles Dodgson to arrive here at twelve and a half as a boarder at Richmond Grammar School. Until then, he had lived with his parents in the rector's house in Croft, seven miles away — far enough to need to be a boarder. The house in Croft had been unusual in that a previous owner had planted exotic species in the garden, like specimen trees from the Himalaya and a cactus that flowered for one night only. It made for a wonderful space for Charles and his ten brothers and sisters to make up their games; to play croquet with imaginary flamingos.

And so when he came to Richmond in 1844, he inevitably suffered a little from loneliness and the strangeness of a new school. The stammer, or 'hesitation', as he called it, can't have helped. Victorian schoolboys were not a forgiving bunch.

In his letters home, the young Charles sounded as anxious as the White Rabbit. He complained on arrival that the headmaster's wife had confiscated half his clothes as being inappropriate. He had three main worries: that he had lost his toothbrush; that his blotting paper had gone missing, perhaps taken by someone else; and that he couldn't find his shoehorn. In one letter he wrote, 'I have *not* got any warm gloves, but must do so soon.' Twenty years afterwards, the White Rabbit was still ordering Alice to fetch him some when he confuses her for the maid.

Moreover, his Tweedledum and Tweedledee schoolfellows in their boater hats were, to say the least, unkind:

> The boys proposed to play at King of the Cobblers and asked me if I would be King, to which I agreed; then they made me sit down and sat (on the ground) in a circle round me, and told me to say 'go to work'. Which I said, and they immediately began kicking me and knocking me on all sides . . . The chief games here are football, wrestling, leap-frog and fighting.

It is interesting that this letter was addressed not to his parents, but to his sisters. He was already adopting that tone of complicit, sardonic intelligence which was to become so characteristic of Alice.

I went to see Swale House where he lived with his schoolfellows, at the bottom of the lane that falls away from the marketplace and now takes most of its traffic: a handsome house, with a large extension at the back that the enlightened Tate family, who were headmasters for several generations, had built for their charges.

James Tate quickly realised that the young Dodgson was something of a prodigy. 'He has,' he wrote in a letter to Charles's parents, 'a very uncommon share of genius.' Moreover, he was 'a gentle, intelligent and well-conducted boy'.

Even though he left to go to Rugby School, Charles Dodgson kept in touch with James Tate and his children for many years and often returned to Richmond as a touchstone. When staying with his own family in Croft, he would walk there and back in a day – some fourteen miles, not bad for a man who is usually thought of as an Oxford aesthete.

How much better to re-imagine him as a Yorkshire writer: to think of *Alice's Adventures in Wonderland* being read, not by some mellifluous received-pronunciation RADA accent, but by Alan Bennett. With the Cheshire Cat voiced in a guest appearance by Geoffrey Boycott. And Yorkshire Tea being poured by the Mad Hatter.

✳

Near the headmaster's house, a small ivy-covered plaque in the church graveyard commemorated the site of Charles Dodgson's original school, which had moved several times over the centuries since Dodgson was there. But what had remained in the same place was the Georgian Theatre Royal, which was still up and running in the last heyday of Regency Richmond, and which Dodgson almost certainly attended. It had been restored and was still a working theatre, lying just off the marketplace.

This again was a miniature world. The stage was tiny and so was the auditorium. There was a fashion for ladies to conceal wooden blocks under their wigs to raise them higher on their heads, particularly when dressing up for a night at the theatre. I liked to think of the schoolboy Dodgson craning over these elaborately coiffured wigs; or peering down through the candelabra from the cheap shilling seats above.

Performances would certainly have been raucous. So-called 'kicking boards' lined the stalls, and were used with vigour if the audience disapproved or got bored. And given that they quite often showed two plays together on the same night as a double bill – a serious Shakespeare play like *Hamlet* might be followed by a lighter Restoration comedy – there would have been plenty of time for buttocks to get restless on the hard wooden seats. Moreover, the army garrison at nearby Catterick provided plenty of rowdy soldiers looking for entertainment.

A lady called Glen kindly showed me round both the theatre and the back of the stage, 'as I've nothing better to do'. She was blonde and buxom, in an agreeable Beryl Cook sort of way, and had a strong Yorkshire accent. We stopped at a portrait of the founding spirit of the theatre, the wonderfully named Tryphosa Brockell. After getting through two husbands who acted with her in the company – 'so you could say she was a bit of a black widow, was Tryphosa,' said Glen – she married her third and final husband, Samuel Butler, who was also in the company. At twenty-six, Samuel was almost twenty years younger than her: 'so really' – no one says 'really' as well as they do in Yorkshire – 'really,' said Glen, 'he was a toy-boy for her.'

Tryphosa and Samuel built up a thriving repertory theatre that toured right across the North and performed at theatres from Whitby to Harrowgate; the theatre at Richmond is the only one that survives. The programme they put on was surprisingly radical. The opening night in Richmond in 1788 had one play about freedom for slaves, some fifty years ahead of its time – and another about giving votes to women, a good 150 years ahead of its time.

Samuel was the actor-manager, and while clearly an able manager who built up a thriving company with Tryphosa, his reputation as an actor was less secure. He inspired widespread ridicule by performing as Hamlet with a strong Yorkshire accent; then, as now, more problematic than it really ought to be.

It is perhaps unfortunate that he chose as the epitaph for his gravestone these lines from *Macbeth*: 'A poor player, that struts and frets his hour upon the stage, and then is heard no more.'

The young Edmund Kean was far more successful. The Marlon Brando of his day, who followed a far more naturalistic style of acting, he cut his teeth at the Richmond Theatre when he was only eighteen. Samuel Butler spotted his talent and sent him on a stagecoach to London.

But not before he had established a rip-roaring reputation in Richmond. As a wide-eyed Glen put it, 'Now, he was an A-lister right from the start. Kept a tame lion in his drawing room. A big drinker. Chased after the ladies. He used to ride his horse up the street straight into the theatre. And you can see, it's not a big lobby.

'Not like the young male actors who come here today. They're more *herbivorous*, if you know what I mean. They all wear those long scarves. More polite these days. I suppose they have to be if they want to get on.'

Old playbills lined the walls. Two things intrigued me. The first was that the entertainment was presented as mainly a musical concert, with plays attached. This, according to Glen, was to get around strict censorship laws which forbade showing plays outside London, in case they were satirical.

But more worrying was that none of the writers of the plays ever got a name-check. Not even Shakespeare. Just the play's title and a long list of actors headed by Samuel Butler were given instead. It was like Hollywood. Writers were way, way down the pecking order when it came to promoting the product. I had no illusions that when coming to sell this book, Jethro as 'the mule' would get a far bigger billing and typeface than I would on the front cover. And would be front of stage in any photo. He had made it quite clear there was only one A-lister on this trip – and it wasn't Jasper or me.

*

I rang my dad again.

'Taking a mule across England? Really? Whatever for? Just one? Or are you taking a whole train of mules?'

For some reason, this last thought amused him. He gave his characteristic rich, warm laugh.

'And when you finish, will you have to do it all over again? You could make a career of it.'

I didn't think there was much of a future in becoming a full-time muleteer. And besides, Britain already had Jasper, if only on loan from Ireland. But Dad's enthusiasm was encouraging.

We spent several days in Richmond to regroup and gather strength, while Jethro enjoyed the fine facilities in his country-house stabling. Jasper and I were staying with a kind friend whose dog needed considerable exercise, so over the many days that followed I had the chance to wander the streets and talk to people.

I soon discovered that, along with its Georgian charm and impossibly picturesque setting of castle and river, as painted by Turner, there was a darker side to Richmond. The lamps along the castle walkway had been vandalised. Locals told me about an epic pub fight involving around thirty people which had taken place outside the Buck the previous Christmas. One of the guys at the petrol-station counter had a black eye after remonstrating with a customer who had tried to do a runner.

In the sandwich shop, Jefferson's, I got chatting to the ebullient owner Gary while he was selling me a sausage roll with black pudding (and giving me an extra one for free, as he could tell I was an enthusiast). He told me that 'although it might seem a contradiction in terms, there's a thriving food bank in Richmond'. Decent jobs were scarce – indeed 'were like hens' teeth'.

Along with the more genteel establishments, the delis, cafés and gift shops, there were tattoo parlours and cheap booze outlets. I could see from some of the clothes people wore they were having to get by on not very much; nor were they helped by the inflated house prices, pushed up by the retirees drawn to such a chocolate box town. Even in Charles Dodgson's time, it had been a fashionable place for widows to eke out their pensions.

To a certain extent, Richmond had often been a little like this. Celia Fiennes, one of our earliest and most astute travel writers, commented back in 1698 that 'it looks like a sad, shattered town and fallen much to decay and like a disregarded place'. Even Turner, when he visited in the 1820s during its Regency heyday, was criticised for including the overflowing tanneries and breweries beside the river in his paintings, along with the more sublime aspects of the scene.

The poorer parts of resort towns are often overlooked. Bath has some noticeably rough areas, while the Blackbird Leys estate on the outskirts of Oxford is a world away from the dreaming spires.

But even if there was a layer of grime under the rim of the silver plate, it was hard not to be seduced by Richmond: by the cobbled street of Newbiggin bestriding the top of the hill with such wide elegance; by the Wynds uncurling around the town; and most of all by the fine cobbled marketplace ('don't ever call it a "square",' Gary had told me, 'because it isn't one'), the largest in England, with its obelisk and church and, of course, towering over proceedings, the handsome Norman castle.

*

Jethro made it quite clear he thought it foolish and misguided for us to continue our journey. He was living in clover. Fine stables at his country house, plenty of pasture, and admiring mares looking at him over the fence, whinnying appreciatively. He had amused himself by sending my wife Irena a postcard: 'Hugh tells me that you can sometimes be a bit grumpy and stubborn like me, but I think he's wrong and we're both misunderstood?'

Now he gave me the enquiring look that I was beginning to know well. It meant, 'I'm more intelligent than you. I just can't always put it into words.' Although when he saw me with the head collar, he knew we were going to move on, come what may. Meanwhile Jasper was doing his own thing elsewhere for this stretch of the journey; as it was, I felt guilty he had been helping me so much.

Not long after Jethro and I headed east from Richmond, we came to the ruined remains of Easby Abbey. Grand and imposing, these large buildings stood as 'bare ruined choirs where once the sweet birds sang'. English Heritage had not imposed the usual apparatus of gift shops, or for that matter charges, so they lay open to travellers like us, with a field nearby in which, to Jethro's pleasure, horses roamed.

We had already passed such desolate reminders of the dissolution of the monasteries before – at Shap, for instance, in the Lake District. And I was well used to the great beached carcasses of monastic life at Tintern Abbey and Malmesbury in the South. Yet there was something peculiarly melancholic about Easby.

I did not feel much sympathy for those monks who had spent centuries living off the fat of the land and whose excesses were well, if zealously, documented by Cromwell and Cranmer. The banqueting hall looked solid and substantial; although of course some monks had also been deeply devout, and deserving of pity when the waves of Henry VIII's wrath and greed had come crashing down.

But I thought more about the parishioners, particularly in the North and here in Richmondshire, who had lost their lives trying to defend monasteries such as this Abbey of St Agatha at Easby. Who had risen in their hundreds of thousands for the Pilgrimage of Grace in 1536.

'Rather than our house in St Agatha should go down, we shall all die,' went the local proclamation.

And it was easy to imagine those parishioners. Because in the parish church of Easby, which stood intact beside the ruined abbey, some remarkable early frescoes had been restored in the chancel only a few years previously. Originally painted directly onto the wet plaster, they had been concealed with whitewash during the Restoration.

The frescoes depicted traditional Christian scenes like the Annunciation and the Nativity vision of the shepherds. However, they did so with a local cast. The shepherds wore the loose medieval smocks and cowls characteristic of Tudor England. And their faces had a startling veracity which suggested they had been drawn from local models. The recent restoration – done as a commendable project for the new millennium by English Heritage – had made those faces sing out again from the usual anonymity of history.

The pilgrims from Richmond and elsewhere in the North were drawn from such people. They sang as they marched south behind the banner of St Cuthbert. Trustingly, they had sworn allegiance not only to the Holy Church but to their king, who they felt must surely have been led astray by his advisers.

Henry VIII repaid this loyalty by massacring them. The

gallows of the North were heavy with their bodies. Although those marching on the Pilgrimage of Grace were too strong to confront militarily, he was able to weaken the impetus of the rebellion by playing on their divided allegiances. And within eight years, all the monasteries and convents in England and Wales had been dissolved anyway. They had died in vain.

Henry described it as 'a tragedy'. When he did so, he was not thinking of the deaths of the humble peasant pilgrims or indeed the monks who he also put to the sword. He was thinking of the decline of the royal houses of the North like the Percys of Northumberland, whose fortune and influence were thereby diminished. Not of the bodies of the poor that the widows of Richmondshire had to cut down from the gibbets.

☆

I had deliberately timed the departure from Richmond to arrive at Catterick Races when a meeting was being held. What I had not been able to predict was the brilliant sunshine. The racecourse was bathed in colour, even though it was almost the last race of the year. It was a fabulous scene, like one of Raoul Dufy's famous paintings at Deauville: the jockeys in their colours leading the horses round before the weighing-in; the good burghers of Yorkshire in their tweeds and dashing yellow shoes (the gentlemen), and a smattering of fine hats and racing-cut jackets (the ladies).

I've always enjoyed the races, although as an occasional visitor only. When I was younger, my idea of a perfect day was to be at a racecourse with a pretty girl and plenty of other friends, some drinks and, preferably, some winnings, although I rarely managed to pick a winner.

Jethro clearly could not come inside even though the Coast-to-Coast path passed a stone's throw from the racetrack.

I would have liked to have shown him how fast a thoroughbred horse can motor; it might have motivated him for the flat section we now had ahead of us beyond Catterick. Although I reassured Jethro he shouldn't get jealous. A thoroughbred horse would have been useless for crossing England. That was a job for the equine equivalent of a mountain bike, not a Tour de France racer.

I did walk the course beforehand, both to see if the going was firm – although this would make little difference to my bets, which were usually made on the basis of an amusing name, the jockey's colours or appealing odds – and to see the lake at the centre of the racecourse. Someone had told me that it entertained a surprising array of wildlife, and it was true: I saw a pair of nesting swans on the little island and, along with the heron gulls, some dazzling white egrets living in splendid isolation from the world.

Egrets are some of my favourite visitors to these shores, not least because they have only started arriving in my lifetime. Impossibly white and elegant, they are the supermodels of the wading world, striding with impossibly long legs down the catwalk of any shore. Apart from a dozen horses thundering by every two weeks, no intruders or stalkers could disturb them here.

Just alongside the racetrack, they were working to widen the A1. This would not have been of particular interest if they hadn't in the process uncovered a staggering number of Roman artefacts: some 200,000, according to the archaeologists who had put on a temporary display. The A1 follows the line of the old Roman Dere Street – and then, just as today, a large army camp was stationed nearby. What fascinated me was the evidence of how the Roman legionaries whiled away their time. There were plenty of oyster shells and decorative horse ornaments for the races that even 2,000 years ago were already being held – and, the thing that amused me most, some dice that were loaded. Now that was one way to win a bet.

By the time I got back, the first race was about to begin. I always like the rough and ready mix of a small course. Catterick was by no means a fashionable, or for that matter large, meet;

the starts had to suffer the occasional indignity of being delayed for the TV schedules if a bigger race was taking place elsewhere. But it was certainly one of the busiest in the country: twenty-eight fixtures a year put it second only to Doncaster.

There were thin, wiry men in trilbies, chain-smoking and clutching race cards on which vital information had been scribbled; a clutch of larger beer-drinking builders, for whom this was a bar with racecourse attached; and a solitary small woman wearing an old-fashioned 1920s flapper hat in grey felt, who peered anxiously through her binoculars as the first race began.

I overheard a conversation beside me on the stands between two men who had not seen each other for some time. They were both in their sixties, I reckoned, and talked in slow, deliberate Yorkshire accents.

Man One: 'On Friday, I went to see a doctor about 'prostate. He gave me 'pill to get my testosterone levels down.'

(He pronounced 'testosterone' to rhyme with 'macaroni'.)

Man Two: 'I thought they were down anyway! And at your age you should count yourself lucky to have any testosterone at all.'

Man One: 'Well, they did gall bladder first. Then they did 'prostate. And I've got polyps.'

Man Two: '*Polyps*! Oh I know all about polyps. *Blud-y* polyps! Last blood test before I went for my bowels, t' nurse said, "You're a regular little polyp-factory, you are."'

Man One: 'A "polyp-factory". I suppose I've been called worse than that!'

There was a pause for consideration and a sip of beer, before he continued.

'But I tell you what, I've got problems with 'legs as well. To do with my varicose veins. They've diagnosed something called thrombophlebitis.'

Man Two: 'Yer what?'

Man One (with some pride): ' "Throm-boph-leb-itis". It's affecting both legs. Left leg worse than right. By some way. I shouldn't really be standing on it now. But what am I supposed to do? Just stand on one leg like a *blud-y* flamingo!?'

It was the sort of conversation that left me needing a drink. Particularly as Mexican Mick had not lived up to the promise of his name and had come in towards the end of the pack.

At the racecourse bar, a couple were fussing over their race card, and I got talking to them as I waited to order. Both were strikingly tall. They were Scottish and, it turned out, owned one of the horses. The woman was nervous and excited.

'We've come down from Scotland. He's our first thoroughbred horse and he's only been in two races before.'

'But,' added her husband, 'he won the first and did well in the second. There was a £14,000 prize for coming first. And winning that first race quadrupled his value. So, it's been good business. He's in terrific form at the moment.'

They were having a drink before going to see their horse in the owners' enclosure. After that run of luck, I was surprised they weren't drinking champagne.

'Originally, we wanted a horse for the jumping,' said the wife. 'But we've gone over to the dark side.'

I looked questioningly.

'Flat racing,' and she laughed.

The husband nudged his wife. Their horse was being led into the enclosure. It looked calm and composed.

Only five horses were in the next race. Their horse was the favourite. Surely, I thought, even with my notorious bad luck, I should have a good chance with an each-way bet. Particularly with an insider tip-off. If his form was that good. Although as the odds were short, it would only be worth doing with a reasonably large stake.

The race track was left-handed, sharp and undulating, just over a mile round, with a three-furlong run-in. I stood in the sunlight at the top of the stand and used my bird-watching binoculars to watch the horses as they shimmered round in a brilliant line against the horizon, the jockey's colours and silks flashing green and purple, turquoise with a star and sapphire blue. I remembered Siegfried Sassoon's phrase about a horse that had won a race: 'He had become the equine equivalent of divinity.' The racecourse served a remarkably fine rosé, and a few glasses of that had warmed both my spirits and my hopes.

The commentator on the PA was building up to the customary crescendo as he galloped with the horses into the final straight. One phrase penetrated my well-*chambré*'d mind: ' . . . and right at the rear, the favourite seems to be showing very little interest in proceedings'.

It was time for a reality check: to head back to the much more reliable Jethro and start crossing the Vale of Mowbray — not so much flat racing as flat plodding. But I knew that we would shortly be coming to a memorial to a most remarkable story.

*

Chapter 10

# Confabulation: The Man Who Lived to Be 169

The age at which mules are fit for transport work is four years for
light work, five years for hard work. They are better at six, and
work satisfactorily until eighteen or twenty, sometimes even longer.
                    The War Office, *Animal Management* (London, 1923)

The churchyard of Bolton-on-Swale has one singular distinction: an obelisk commemorating a man called Henry Jenkins,
who, it was claimed, died at the fabulous age of 169. There was
another memorial inside the church, and he had become famous.
In many ways, the mythology that had grown up around him was
as interesting as the historical evidence, of which there was little.

He had certainly died in 1670, and was described then as 'a
very aged and poor man'. He had been a servant to Lord Coniers
of Hornby Castle at one stage in his life and later worked as a
fisherman before becoming destitute. When he died, Jenkins was
receiving alms.

The astounding assertions of his longevity – most of them
made in the centuries after his passing, not at the time – rest on
his contention that he was born in 1501. He also claimed that he
could remember the Battle of Flodden Field in 1513, and helped
carry a horse-load of arrows to Northallerton for the archers. A
Victorian antiquary pointed out that if he had indeed lived to
be 169, and followed his legal obligations during those years, he
would have needed to change religious allegiance eight times
between the reigns of Henry VII and Charles II.

The parish records did not extend back to 1501, so there was no evidence for his birthdate; and of course, there were no records for those who had helped in the battle of Flodden Field.

But my own father had given me an insight into what may have happened here. Like many of those suffering from dementia, he had turned to what experts call 'confabulation'. Confabulation is a disturbance of memory, defined as 'the production of fabricated, distorted or misinterpreted memories about oneself or the world, without the conscious intention to deceive'.

In conversation with somebody, particularly a stranger, my father would often feel the need to produce a story; but as his memory was failing, could not remember any. So instead, he would invent one.

I was with him down by the Thames as we sat at a table by the riverbank with some friends who had not met my father before. 'Of course, we had to repair the jetty,' he told them, 'when the Thames froze over a few winters ago.' My friends knew little about the Thames but felt they had missed the story of it freezing over; as indeed they had, unless you went back a few centuries.

Confabulation is very different from lying. There is no intention to deceive and the person is unaware the information is false. They are accessing a random part of the memory bank, in which the distinction between knowledge and lived experience has broken down: some mysterious kink in the hippocampus. Moreover, it is easy for someone with dementia to have a confused memory of having told such a story once before; they will then go on to repeat it with even greater authority.

This was perhaps the most striking feature of confabulation – that because the person does not know they are lying, they present their story with startling conviction. Jenkins' claim to have been present at the battle of Flodden Field was testimony he gave in court when called as a witness to a local case. It would have seemed unthinkable to contemporaries that an elderly, humble man receiving alms would have the temerity to lie in such circumstances.

In an age like the seventeenth century, when dementia was clearly present — *King Lear* is almost a case study — but not precisely diagnosed, Jenkins' claim to have taken part in a battle 150 years before his death would have been taken at face value. And any disquiet would have disappeared long before the following century, when his long life began to be canonised.

In a way, the process of confabulation is continually taking place within our own national history. We forget those truths that are inconvenient: that Churchill allowed a million Indians to die by not sending a relief ship during their famine; or that we needlessly bombed Hamburg and Dresden to shreds, with more loss of life than at Hiroshima and with no corresponding military gain.

Instead, we lull ourselves to sleep with reassuring fables: how brave and right we were to retake the Falklands, even if almost half as many combatants died as previously lived on the islands — and each of those inhabitants could have received more than £1.5 million as a relocation package, given the cost of the war. How while the Spanish Empire was a dark satanic force that spread misery to South America, the British Empire brought democracy and fairness to much of the globe. And that while the southern states of America might have tolerated slavery, it was never something of which the British really approved.

After a while, we will have told these stories so often to ourselves that we come to believe them to be true.

Kazuo Ishiguro's *The Buried Giant*, one of the greatest novels about England yet written in the twenty-first century, shows the whole country struggling under the deadweight of collective amnesia — a mist of forgetfulness, as he calls it, cast by a sleeping dragon.

Just as his protagonists can only make sense of what is happening — can only begin to remember — by making a journey, so my North-crossing was clarifying my thoughts about England

and the last few decades. Nowhere was this more true than in the countryside, so often an ignored province for metropolitan politicians. When Tony Blair lunched with Gordon Brown in Islington – or for that matter when their Conservative successors chewed the marbled fat at the Connaught – I doubt the conversation ever turned to the price of milk or wheat. Or the people who made what they were eating.

Talking to farmers and those who live in the wilder stretches of the North was a deeply unfashionable pastime, but it was teaching me much that I had forgotten myself – or perhaps, had never known.

*

Between Richmond and the Yorkshire Moors lies the Vale of Mowbray, a broad stretch of 'agricultural land', a bland phrase that can conceal a great deal.

Land. The farm that you've always lived in. On the one hand, there can be the reassuring sense of roots – of something you're part of. But then there is the darker side; the sense that you also can't get away from it. That those same roots have got you by the ankle and are pulling you underground.

You look out at fields and you may have a sense of satisfaction, of ownership, of achievement, perhaps of family continuity; but you may also have a sense of nagging anxiety. That there is always more work to be done. Something waiting to go wrong, which can happen all too easily on a farm.

As a diversion from the plod across the plain – Amanda Owen had warned me that the Vale of Mowbray was the most boring stretch of the Coast-to-Coast, with too much tarmac and too few views – I went to meet an old friend who I hadn't seen for years. He lived on his farm a little south of our route.

Hugo Hildyard was a few years older than me; I had known him at school and then, when he had gone on to study English Literature at Cambridge, I had followed him there, in part on his advice.

Our age difference now was immaterial, but as a boy, of course, it had seemed substantial. I looked up to Hugo and admired him. He was sardonic, intelligent, quick-witted and slightly rebellious, all attractive qualities in a schoolboy – just as they were at Cambridge, where he enjoyed life enough for a contemporary, Conrad Williams, to use his name for the central character in his novel *Sex and Genius*.

But I had not seen Hugo for many decades, and had always wondered if he had changed at all and what had happened to him. He was waiting for me at the end of the remote farm lane, older, of course, and with a farmer's permanent tan, but, it struck me at once, remarkably similar to how he had been as a boy. And as to what had happened to him, the answer was 'a lot'. He had founded a clothing company that imported clothes from India, and married a well-known art dealer, Fiona Stachowiec, who had in her turn founded the Lisson Gallery. But he had also taken on the family farm, which his father had bought in 1950. His mother, who still lived there, told me his father had not realised how heavy the clay was when he bought it, how unproductive it could be. And Hugo's wife had died some five years before, while their son was still a teenager.

Hugo now lived at the farm with his Argentine girlfriend Florencia Clifford. She was such a good cook that they were opening up a restaurant together in York called Partisan – which, if the meal we had that evening was anything to go by, would be a spectacular success. I liked Florencia at once, not least for her South American candour, something I was used to from my travels there; she was outspoken – for instance about the fact that Hugo had invited various other friends round to join us on the evening that I arrived.

'That's so English. The two of you haven't seen each other for thirty years. So the first night that you do, you get round lots of other people, rather than talking to each other.'

She was right. It was very English. But it also worked.

Hugo's friends came round. We drank a great deal, and had some good conversation. Everyone cooed and fluttered over Florencia's 'roasted aubergine with pomegranates in a tahini sauce', especially me after a substantial but relentless diet of 'chorizo and Cheddar', our muleteers' lunch. But then in the morning, when the guests had all left and Florencia had departed to cook for a group convention up on the Yorkshire Moors, Hugo and I had a further conversation, just the two of us, sitting in the garden with his fields beyond.

The economics of farm life, he told me, were harsh. Hugo's father in his day had employed three farm workers to help. Hugo did everything himself: a lot of work, even with improved farm machinery. He could be harvesting from dawn to dusk. And it was in some ways a never-ending battle. There was, for instance, the mounting problem of black grass, little commented on outside the agricultural press; but then we have become a nation increasingly divorced from what actually happens on our farms.

Black grass (slender meadow foxtail, or *alopecurus myosuroides*, to give its correct name) is a tall grass that comes up through barley and wheat, and can easily swamp the crop – not least because it has developed a strong resistance to pesticide. A neighbour of Hugo's had been forced to plough up a third of his land and keep it in constant rotavation, in the hope that the black grass seeds would finally be eradicated. But only a few need to survive for the cycle to begin again. Black grass was fast becoming a serious national problem. The money needed to develop an effective pesticide would run into the billions, and would be unlikely to show a commercial return.

Hugo had barley, beans, oilseed rape – although the first crop had failed this year, so needed replanting – and some willow down near the river, which he harvested every three years for biomass fuel, an enterprising idea and a green one. He also had cattle. The farm was only about 300 acres, not large by today's standards.

Nearby, the other small farms had all consolidated. In the local village of Scrayingham, with its population of a hundred people, the old farmhouses had lost their land, so to speak; or rather, the estate had bundled all of it into one big holding of thousands of acres to achieve economies of scale. The farmhouses themselves were now rented out by the estate – indeed, that was where they made most of their money.

This was a pattern that was being repeated everywhere I had been. In some places, there had been talk of keeping smaller fields near a rural community as a barrier between them and the big commercial prairies beyond. Modern tractors were so wide and could travel so fast – at forty to fifty miles an hour – that parish councils were speaking of the need to build rural bypasses around villages.

'As a way of life, in some sense this is finished,' said Hugo, with a wave of his hand at the small fields beyond the garden. 'There will only be the big commercial farms in the future. That's the financial imperative.

'I haven't tried to persuade my own son to keep the farm going. To be drawn to "the romance of farming". Better to make money some other way, and then have a lovely house in the country.

'Some years I've made a bit of money. But very few. And that was often because of the European subsidy, which provided a baseline for support. One which, as we're leaving the EU, may no longer be available.

'Barley was selling at £144 a tonne thirty years ago when I started farming. These days it's selling at just £100. Wheat went up to £200 and the government told us to get used to it staying at that price. Now it's down to £120.

'It's the age-old problem. If yields one year are good, then the law of economics means the price you can sell at is going to come down.

'There are farmers near here who have hundreds of thousands of pounds' worth of debt. Some of them don't even own the land, but the banks will lend to them anyway. A lot of them get depressed, particularly in winter. I know because they've told me.

'Sometimes I feel I've sacrificed a lot for the farm. And for what? Everything has always gone back into it, including time. When my wife died, I realised it was important to do things now. Things I would like to do, like travel.

'It's animals that bind you to a farm. If I didn't have cattle, it would be easier. And while machinery has got more expensive, it has also got more effective. With some of these new seed drills, I could plant all my crops in a week and take the winter off – if I didn't have any animals. Get a contractor in to spray the crops occasionally while I was away. I know that with some of these big arable farms up the road, there's nothing much happening from November to February. They could all go off to the French Alps skiing if they wanted to, for all it mattered.

'My son pointed out I could sell fifty acres and make enough money to pay off everything. It had never really occurred to me.

'If this restaurant takes off, then maybe I'll contract out all the land to one of the neighbours. But probably not. It's very difficult to sever the bonds.'

I wanted to ask Hugo if all the years of farming had been worth it, although that seemed presumptuous. I was impressed by the sheer physical effort he had put into the farm over that time – despite some serious illness, for instance, just a year before – and said so.

'I have always liked to work hard. There are times, though, when it's difficult to do it on your own. Just simple things like linking up machinery. Much easier to do it with two of you. But needs must.'

I talked to Florencia later. 'Hugo's very strong. But he's not getting younger. And last year he was ill, partly from spending long hours on a tractor, so I hope the restaurant takes off. The first time Hugo brought me to see the farm, I cried at the thought of coming to live here. The house was very run-down. We've done a lot to fix it up just in the last few years. But that was from money we got elsewhere. The farm itself would never have provided that.'

✻

'There's no such thing as a happy farmer' has long been a countryside adage. And of course, farmers moan, even those prosperous enough to afford top-of-the-range pickups and a month's skiing in Courchevel. But over the last few years I've come to share farmers' frustrations, albeit in a minor way, and to be more sympathetic to their complaints.

On our smallholding back home, all of five acres, we have enough pasture for a few alpaca to roam and crop the grass. We originally acquired these curious and lovely animals when we bought the place and I realised that the only alternative was to cut the grass myself – on a disturbingly regular basis, as it grows fast. Not a compelling option when I could be lying in the hammock having necessary and creative thoughts, as I described them to Irena; the sort of thing a self-respecting writer should be doing, not cutting the bloody grass.

And, I argued, even if I did want to do the cutting myself – which I didn't – there was far too much for a regular garden mower, let alone a scythe of the sort the Quakers were practising with. We would need to buy an expensive sit-on mower for thou-sands of pounds. Whereas the alpaca came at a fraction of the price and were charming reminders of our travels in Peru.

Tough and self-sufficient, they have needed little maintenance since we bought them, other than an annual shearing. They are also good at scaring foxes away from the chickens. I had originally wanted to call them sensible, pragmatic names like Pedro, Sandro and Flymo, to reflect their Andean origins and grass-cutting function. But with teenage girls in the household, more whimsical notions took over, and they have ended up with names like 'Aspen Moonflower' and 'the Archangel Gabriel'. Luckily no neighbours live close enough to hear me calling them.

We have all become fond of the alpaca as they wander the not-very-capacious grounds, peering at us inquisitively from above long necks, and eating both the grass and anything else they can get hold of. Like goats, they are omnivorous. I've seen them strip an entire rosemary bush, not to mention climbing roses, thorns and all; they can leave the low-hanging boughs of an apple tree quite bare. What they like most is to nip a flower bud off, like an appetiser.

Well – *almost* omnivorous. The one thing they won't eat is pasture covered by weeds. And we have a lot: invasive weeds, of the sort that sweep across our modest meadows, colonising whole swathes and making the grass unpalatable. Creeping buttercup that looks attractive, but which livestock hate. Creeping thistle that doesn't even have the virtue of looking attractive. A plague of giant spiny teasels that advance across the clay soil like triffids, emerging with speed in late summer. Even the woodland isn't safe, carpeted by spreading brambles that prevent the alpaca from reaching their favourite branches.

Nor is chemical control an option. Alpaca are quite capable of jumping temporary fences unless they're built like Camp Bas-tion. And we would not want to risk them eating any stray glypsophate-coated leaf as an *hors d'oeuvre*. So a lot of the weeds have to be topped or removed by hand.

As I've learned the hard way, a successful weed is one that has developed a root system that resists any form of control. The taproots of spiny teasels can become formidably entrenched. Creeping buttercup is more insidious, with fragile tendrils that melt away into the soil to reappear later. The roots of creeping thistle go ten feet deep and then spread laterally underground. Try digging that up. You can keep topping a thistle, but it will be a long time before it refuses to come back.

The battle modern farmers have with increasingly invasive and herbicide-resistant weeds — and on a massive scale across their hundreds or thousands of prairie acres — is one I can appreciate. Yes, it was more difficult for Job with his plague of locusts. But not that much more difficult. Job never had to deal with creeping thistle. Let alone black grass.

✳

Jasper, very sensibly, was not with me for this stage of the walk and nor, reader, you will be relieved to hear, are you. An account of travelling the rest of the flatlands that lie between Richmond and the Yorkshire Moors might have the brisk austerity of late Samuel Beckett or Cormac McCarthy's *The Road*; but it would not be a pleasurable experience. A great deal of it was on tarmac along small lanes.

Wandering along, I started to get that song in my head that both Nancy Sinatra and Kirsty MacColl had made famous: 'These boots are made for walking / And that's just what they'll do / One of these days these boots / are gonna walk all over you.' I had been a bit inhibited at singing aloud when we had been with Jasper (as he had a much better voice than I did), but now I could let rip. Admittedly, I wasn't sure it was good motivation for Jethro, who, like me, needed some. Even though I loved that line, 'You keep lyin' when you oughta be truthing.' Why had 'to truth' never entered the language?

However, waiting for us across the Vale of Mowbray rose the massive bulwarks of the Cleveland Hills that edged the Yorkshire Moors – foursquare, like Mordor: the last and final section of my walk and in some ways, perhaps the wildest.

*

Osmotherley was the perfect entry point for the Yorkshire Moors, with its wide, handsome streets and houses in toffee-coloured stone. The little post office sold copies of *Yorkshire Life*; the cover proclaimed an illustrated lead story on 'The Boycotts at Home'. Hydrangeas and montbretia flowered boldly outside the houses. The hydrangeas were blue on one side of the street and pink on the other, perhaps from some local 'war of the hydrangeas' played out by careful adjustment of soil acidity.

I stopped off for an early pint at the Golden Lion to give me strength for the afternoon's walk ahead – and was hoping for a packet of crisps.

'Cheese and onion! We don't do *cheese and onion*.' The barman looked as if I had asked for canapés.

'We only do *plain* crisps here.' Very proud of it he was too.

I had no idea what to expect from the Yorkshire Moors. Never having been before, my only preconception was of a vast open space across which Brontë heroines roamed to a Kate Bush soundtrack. But after the flat Vale of Mowbray, I was looking forward to getting up to the heights again.

What I hadn't anticipated was the lushness of the vegetation as I ascended from Osmotherley. Along the edges of the Moors were forests of birches underpinned with exotic giant ferns and verdant azalea. Rowan trees – the mountain ash, to give them their more evocative name, and perhaps the most emotive of all Britain's ancient trees – stood out with their red berries against the grey and the green of everything else: an incorrigible display of optimism in the face of Yorkshire weather.

I passed a birch tree blown over by the wind. The roots had lifted to create a natural cavern for wildlife underneath; like a Buckminster Fuller eco-dome, the voles and small animals of the heathland could congregate in a wonderful hollow space, with small amounts of daylight and ventilation coming through the roots from above.

Once I reached the top of the Moors, the heather was at its best. Natural England, the government agency, had a complicated scheme by which landowners who managed and burned sections of their heather were given large grants – which they hardly needed, as they would do that in any case to help the grouse, who liked young plants. Another case of 'and to those who already have, will be given more'.

But then, what could you expect from an agency whose very name – Natural England, a suitably emollient rebranding that Tony Blair came up with – asked more questions than it answered? It presumed the countryside had a natural state to which it must always be returned. Whereas there has never been any such thing as a 'natural England', from the earliest of prehistoric times, and it would be far better to have an honest admission of this. There has only been a managed and manipulated England, with land-scapes from the Dales to the Moors responding to agricultural change.

With purple heather in the foreground and the blue plains stretching away to either side, those same moors were giving me a grand view. Even Wainwright when he came this way let out the odd breath of exhilaration. Around the western edge, head-lands extended in a sequence of rounded, alliterative peaks: Carlton Moor, Cringle End, Cold Moor and Clay Bank Top. To swing up and down from summit to summit along the stone-lined

Cleveland Way must surely rank as one of the great walking experiences in England.

And yet, on a fine day I passed only one other person. There is a myth that we are a nation of walkers: a myth to a certain extent perpetuated by travel writers like me, as it is in our interests to presuppose a readership. Of course we were once – in prehistoric times when we drove cattle from one end of the country to the other, or more recent centuries when British armies marched phenomenal distances. But now, if truth be told, we prefer to cycle if we want to see the countryside.

The aspiration, when I was young, to walk one of the long-distance footpaths with a couple of friends and a tent, and have access to beer, pubs and other teenagers, well away from the prying eyes of parents, has long gone. Simon Armitage had told me that when he walked the Pennine Way he had a similar experience, and met few others.

In many ways, I can understand why. Cycling has always attracted me; and after a few weeks plodding along with a mule, it attracted me even more (although a mule tandem might have proved hard to design, let alone ride). When Edward Thomas did some of his 'walking books', such as *The Icknield Way*, a hundred years ago, he got so bored he cycled large sections – even if this never made its way into the text.

But it also seems a shame that walking is on the decline. We are lucky in England to have a quite unrivalled system of footpaths. Christopher Somerville, our foremost national gazetteer of the walks of Britain, who must have tramped more miles along them than just about anyone else alive, has also written about Ireland and told me that there, with no tradition of footpath access, you are forever walking on tarmac and along lanes. In France, there are intimidating signs saying '*Chasseurs – Privé*' along every country road; an irate Frenchman with a shotgun does not make wandering off-piste an alluring prospect.

We, on the other hand, now have the 'right to roam' all

over the uplands of Britain. We just don't take it. As a nation, it seems, we would rather take a low-cost flight to the sun or get on our cycles. But when we do remember again the pleasures of walking across our own landscape, the hills will still be waiting for us.

I felt a little tired of walking myself, particularly after the Vale of Mowbray. It would be good to report that days spent crossing the flat agricultural plain had left me with a sense of Zen-like simplicity, or mindfulness, or connectedness with the Earth. But in fact, it had left me with a profound sense of boredom: boredom which had only fallen away now that I had reached the Moors and could become excited again.

It had also given me time, though, to consider again why it felt so appropriate to be travelling with a mule. I had always liked the way characters in Philip Pullman's *His Dark Materials* trilogy had an animal that represented their inner self: a dæmon. By that yardstick, Jethro was my perfect companion. Other writers might have a horse, or if fleet of foot like Robert Macfarlane, perhaps a deer – while Benedict Allen had often compared himself to a camel, and William Dalrymple's dæmon would surely be an Indian elephant. But a mule was more my sort of animal: intelligent, I hoped, yet with a streak of stubborn cussedness that sometimes got it into trouble.

At the moment, my dæmon was having problems. Jethro was finding some of the stone-laid track difficult to negotiate; while I had likewise to do some adroit navigation, as for reasons that were unclear, the Cleveland Way kept turning from a footpath to a bridleway and back again. What exactly did councils expect riders to do when a bridleway suddenly ended? Carry the horse on their back?

There was one terrific moment as the path swung round from north to east just after Beacon Hill, and the view extended in a broad swing of the compass from Swaledale on my left to the coast on my right. The white industrial buildings of Teesside, far from looking like dark satanic mills, seemed more like celestial apparitions in the shaft of sunlight that illuminated them.

This part of the track felt very ancient, as if there was a geographical logic for so many people to have come this way; to skirt around the edge of the wild moors, but keep above the valleys, as both a drier and faster way to the coast. As I entered a small copse, there were gnarled birches, ferns in the dry-stone walls, stunted oak seedlings and so many tangled roots spreading across the path that they almost tripped Jethro up. If this place had been a book, it would have been a manuscript whose pages of handwritten vellum blew out with dust as you opened them.

Another ancient place awaited me. After a day of rounding the headlands of the Yorkshire Moors, I arrived at Clay Bank Top and the Wainstones. The Wainstones — not named after Wainwright as a giant cairn in his honour, although he appreciated them — were monumental natural rocks that looked like menhirs stacked carelessly together on the side of a hill. Some had been carved with the characteristic cup and ring markings of the Bronze Age.

After the rolling heather and the moors, they came as a shock. It was impossible not to imagine how the prehistoric travellers of the Bronze and Iron Ages, with their fetishising of stone and its provenance, would have found this a place of power and significance. No wonder they wanted to leave their mark here.

It was almost sunset by the time I arrived with Jethro, and apart from one couple walking the dog up from Great Broughton below, I had the place to myself. Leaning back against one of the giant stones, sheltered from wind and with the sun going down over the west, I felt a quiet contentment at having come so far; along with the momentary sensation that I was catching at the hem of all those travellers with pack animals who had passed this way for thousands of years.

Once more I had a magnificent view of Teesside curving away below me, with the old ICI and steelworks plants fringed by the distant North Sea. But now we were close to sunset. And there were fires burning. The flames were pullulating from the chimneys down at Wilton like the entrance to hell, the smoke blowing away and dissipating in the thin half-light that streamed off the estuary. An estuary that had been used for shipping since prehistoric times, and had seen millennia of human habitation.

There's nothing like having walked hundreds of miles to help take you back to an age when that was the only way to reach a destination. For I have often noticed a presumption that we invented travel; or certainly, that in the prehistoric age people tended to stay put.

More and more evidence shows that nothing could be further from the truth. DNA testing of skeletons is showing us how far Bronze Age man could travel in a lifetime. And the route I had now taken across the country would have been one used extensively in the prehistoric past. Archaeologists estimate that half the stone axes found in Yorkshire were quarried from sites some way to the west, in the Lake District; there would have been constant traffic between the two areas.

Another false presumption is that the Yorkshire Moors have always been just that: moors, open and wild. However, like Dartmoor to the south, they originally had a thin covering of trees, which was deforested and cleared remarkably early. Bronze Age man liked to wield his axe. The process of forest clearance accelerated during the second millennium BC. By 1000 BC, much of the country as we know it had already been cleared, including the Moors. So the Yorkshire Moors were settled and farmed earlier than we might expect, given what seems a hostile agricultural environment. But then, as one archaeologist pointed out to me, it would have been difficult to work the heavy clay of the valleys below without hefty iron ploughs, so the uplands had more appeal.

However, the shallow, infertile soils of the Moors and Dales could not sustain long-term cultivation. By 1200 BC, some upland areas had turned into the sort of bog we had encountered above Ravenseat; the sort of bog in which a man could disappear while carrying a rucksack and his girlfriend took photographs.

This may have been due to significant climate change after 1500 BC. The temperature fell, the growing season contracted, and altitude limits for crops came down.

There is another intriguing idea which archaeologists are still investigating: that a volcano in Iceland called Hekla erupted with great force in 1159 BC and sent so many millions of tonnes of dust into the atmosphere that it created the Bronze Age equivalent of a nuclear winter. Acid rain was produced, affecting both crops and livestock.

A much smaller eruption at a different Icelandic volcano a few years ago brought havoc to aviation across Europe. Hekla itself has continued over the millennia to cause problems for both Iceland and its southern neighbours: in the Middle Ages, it was described by Europeans as the 'Gateway to Hell'.

I thought of Hekla now, as I looked down at the chimneys of Wilton flaring their nostrils. The twin towers of the Cracker were torching out smoke. I watched as the smoke drifted out towards the estuary to be lost in the mists of the North Sea. The faint shapes of ships were silhouetted like smudges on the water towards the horizon, part of the Teesside traffic with northern Europe.

It occurred to me that Britain has always been part of Europe – indeed, only some thousands of years ago was attached to it by a land barrier when that sea did not exist. Yet our national identity had been re-spun. We had chosen in a referendum to leave. Shorn of Empire, we had a choice either to be part of a collegiate Europe or to go our own way.

I had voted to remain in Europe – but I could see that we had done what a mule would do every time, for better or worse: strike out on our own with bloody-minded, sturdy independence, with a quick kick to the crotch of a government that had lost touch with its dispossessed. We are not really a herd nation.

Brexit was now stamped right through the north-east's heart, like the kiss-me-quick candy-rock they sold on Scarborough beach. They had voted for it more than anybody else. And the people of the north-east were some of the most dissatisfied people in the country, with reason. The steelworks I was looking at down at Redcar had been decimated. Real unemployment, not that massaged by the statistics, was at a record high.

The process of confabulation about leaving Europe had already begun in the national consciousness. Many who voted for Brexit 'hadn't meant to', or had not understood its implications. Immediately afterwards a new prime minister, Theresa May, had proclaimed 'Brexit means Brexit'; but no one quite knew what either word meant. We were confused, disorientated, and would be for some time.

Brexit had been an accident, even if it had been an accident waiting to happen. The usual aftermath of an accident would unfold in the long years afterwards: shock, legal confusion and the undying conviction that it must have been the other driver's fault.

But of one thing I was sure: in the years and decades to come, the memory of what had happened – 'the story of Brexit' – would morph into something rich and strange and unrecognisable today, whether as triumph or tragedy. We would re-tell the story to ourselves until we had created a historical fable, with some familiar and reassuring narrative. The real reasons would become as diffused and lost as the sea-mist that was billowing out from Teesside below me. And whatever story we decided on for this confabulation, we would recount it to others and to ourselves so often that we would come to believe it to be true.

Glyn Maxwell had put it beautifully: 'England is the same, / cheering to order, set in its new ways / it thinks are immemorial.'

The chimneys were flaring alternately red and gold in the last of the evening light. The waters of the distant sea had become so dark as to look like oil washing against the land. A short-eared owl flew up from behind me, its white face luminous like a clock dial, and gave a hunting call as it flew off along the escarpment of the Moors looking for the last of the day's prey. I felt a shiver run down my spine.

✻

Chapter 11

# How Not to Get Married

The pace of mule transport is from three to four miles an hour, the mule being a quick walker. A short stepping, active pace is preferred to a long striding action.

The War Office, *Animal Management* (London, 1923)

I had arranged stabling for Jethro just off the Yorkshire Moors in one of the villages that line their flanks. We met up with Jasper, who was going to accompany us again for the final stages of the journey across the Moors to the sea. It was good to see him. I had missed his company and quick wit.

A cousin of mine, Elizabeth Kirk, came to see us as she was interested in Jethro's ride across the country and lived nearby. Elizabeth was the most remarkable person. She instantly impressed Jasper – not an easy thing to do – with her knowledge of horses.

Now in her eighties, Elizabeth had ridden over much of England and had dedicated herself to opening up old bridleways that had been closed. In North Yorkshire alone, she and her friends had managed to get a hundred miles of bridleway added to the 'definitive map', the legal document which every county council has to keep about the rights of way in their area. And during a long lifetime of diplomatic campaigning, she had helped restore some forty bridleways around the country which had fallen into disuse for all sorts of reasons.

Until I had tried to get Jethro across England, this had not been an issue I had needed to confront so urgently, and it had puzzled both Jasper and me as we struggled with stiles and lack of access.

I told Elizabeth my story about the bridleway that kept turning into a footpath from the day before, and she explained how some of these problems had come about in the first place.

The 'definitive maps' in use today were mainly drawn up in the 1950s. At the time, the Ramblers organisation was strong. It had built up momentum since the early part of the century, when Edward Thomas had been so preoccupied with historic rights of access to the countryside. Since the mass trespass on Kinder Scout in 1932, it had also gained a political edge. The Ramblers lobbied effectively to keep many footpaths open and for them to be included on these new 'definitive maps'.

However, the organisations representing the nation's horse-riders were far less effective, perhaps because riding in the country is not such a communal activity. Moreover, riding was at a low ebb after the Second World War, and local authorities, then as now, were keen to minimise the perceived maintenance burden of bridleways.

Among countryside riders, there was also an assumption that routes which had always been used as bridleways would somehow remain so, whether legally or not; a false assumption, as unless given official status, they could easily be treated like a footpath and 'grubbed up and ploughed out', as Elizabeth put it. Around 65 per cent of the footpaths in the North York Moors National Park had originally been bridleways but were no longer so – a quite staggering proportion, mirrored elsewhere in Britain and one about which the wider public (like me up until this point) were often blithely unaware.

By 1979, the situation had become so bad that concerned riders like Elizabeth set up the Byways and Bridleways Trust to protect our network of ancient minor highways. 'We got a lot of stick from people for "making a fuss" – but we were right!' And while she had been a formidable negotiator, writing many letters to local councils, she had also sought much wider publicity for the issue.

Only that year, she had ridden with friends for 300 miles from Devon to Dorset to draw attention to the way in which many a bridleway had an electric fence slung across it, or was so over-grown it was impossible to use. The local council remonstrated that the South Dorset Ridgeway was almost entirely a bridleway, so why didn't they take that? Elizabeth pointed out in reply that the whole point of the exercise was to draw attention to small local bridleways: precisely the ones most at risk.

'What gets me so annoyed,' she said, 'is the assumption that somehow horse-riding is an aristocratic, upper-class pastime. Which is why councils can ignore bridleways. But there's the shop-girl on her pony and the nurse who wants to ride after work as well. And it's just not safe on roads any more. If we're not careful, we'll end up with a generation of riders who are too scared to go out of the stables and the training ring.'

Jasper agreed wholeheartedly. 'Exactly. The whole point of riding is to be able to take off across country. Or you might as well not get on a horse in the first place.'

Like Tolstoy or the celebrated Tschiffely (who rode from one end of the Americas to the other for his book *Southern Cross to Pole Star*), Elizabeth seemed to have spent a large part of her own life in the saddle. Only ten years ago, when still in her sprightly seventies, she had ridden with some friends from the Yorkshire Moors right down to the Brecon Beacons in South Wales. And in earlier times, she had taken part in horse endurance events, riding fifty miles a day – although with characteristic modesty, she pointed out, 'that's nothing these days. They can easily do a hundred.'

Elizabeth was a great advocate for the New Forest pony, particularly for the larger, sturdier ones that can reach just over fourteen hands in height.

'It's too much to take a thoroughbred right across country.

They can go wrong so easily. And it's such a long way to go. You're doing the right thing in taking a mule.'

She inspected Jethro with an experienced horsewoman's eye and pronounced herself satisfied, particularly with his unusual colouring. Jethro, perhaps conscious that he was in the presence of a connoisseur, demurely bowed his neck to let her stroke him.

Elizabeth asked about the route we were next taking across the Moors, which was not always straightforward. Our natural, most direct route lay along footpaths not bridleways. She warned us to be careful when walking in any old mining areas, as her horse had once slipped up to the girths in the loose washings that had been left in the chambers of a similar hazard.

'Of course, what we would really like to see,' said Elizabeth, 'is the Right to Roam Act extended to riders as well as walkers.'

The Countryside and Rights of Way Act that was brought in for the new millennium in 2000 – popularly known as the 'Right to Roam Act' – allowed walkers untrammelled access to open country, like the Moors. But it didn't do the same for horse-riders. And as Elizabeth pointed out, there was no reason that a sensible rider shouldn't be able to pick their way across the Moors in any direction, as they would certainly have done in previous centuries. However, there was a new complication.

'When the definitive maps were being drawn up in the 1950s, off-road mountain bikes weren't invented. Cycling was never a concern. Whereas now, of course, it's become a predominant one. And it's difficult to differentiate between cyclists and horse-riders in any legislation, but they often have different needs.'

I could see that the owners of shooting estates might not like the idea of cyclists beating through the heather, even in low gear;

although who knows, that could be as cost-effective a way as any
of managing a shoot.

After some tea, Elizabeth headed back to her house before it
got dark as, while still driving in her eighties, she didn't like to
do so when the light was going. I was impressed by how much
time she had given to this cause during her long life, while also
having a family and running a small farm on the edge of the
Yorkshire Moors. Let alone that she was still riding for hundreds
of miles.

What I liked most of all was her air of quiet deliberation about
these issues. She was not a tub-thumping, bossy horsewoman of the
Thelwellian school, who made grown men quake in their boots.
Instead, it was her very reasonable and patient articulation of the
sorry state of affairs that I suspected made her such a formidably
effective campaigner. And having tried to get Jethro across the country, it was a campaign with which I now had every sympathy.

It was also a campaign with a deadline. All the revisions to
the definitive maps based on historic evidence had to be in place
by 2026. At that point, any 'unrecorded public rights of way'
would be extinguished by statute, even though the maxim 'once
a highway, always a highway' has stood the test of time in England
since 1189. Ten years might sound like a reasonable window of
opportunity, but county councils react to legal challenges at glacial speed. There were an estimated 20,000 bridleways and byways
which needed to be reclaimed. Elizabeth and her colleagues were
facing a formidable challenge.

☆

We drove back up onto the Moors in the old Dodge horse van,
which only just managed the steep gradients, and parked up at
Clay Bank Top. As we got going for that day's walk, we met a man

and a boy who had come up from Middlesbrough, the man told us, 'to get out of the town for some peace and quiet'. They looked very urban in tracksuits and hoodies. The boy was his nephew.

'That yours, is it?' the boy asked about Jethro.

'Well, we wouldn't have stolen it, would we!' said Jasper, with some asperity. 'That's a leading question.'

'And is it a male?'

'Jethro used to be a male. But he's had the snip.'

'Poor old sod,' said the man.

'Mules are sterile anyway. Because they're a cross between a donkey and a horse. So they can't breed between themselves.'

'Well, that's a bit of a disadvantage. Must take the wind out of his sails.'

The man came up quite often to do a five-mile circuit around Bloworth Crossing, he said. But it was the first time on the Moors for his nephew, who looked unsure about proceedings – although he was interested in Jethro.

'Are you sure it's not a donkey?' he asked. 'And how do you get it down? Or do you just throw it?'

'Throw it? Well, for a start he's a "he", not an "it". And he's a mule, not a donkey. And he's got a name – Jethro.'

'I know,' said the boy perkily. 'That's why I asked the question. "D'ya throw?" "*Je-thro*". Get it?'

We groaned. It had been a while since we had been in the playground with the tough ten-year-olds.

'So what's your name?' we asked the kid.

He looked hesitant. 'Bob.'

The man laughed. 'No, it's not. It's Joshua. You're just embarrassed by it.'

'It's Bob. And tomorrow it's going to be Jeff. Did you know that Michael Jackson died on the toilet?'

'I run a business down in Middlesbrough,' interjected the uncle, to get us back on track. 'It's go, go, go down there. Then you come up here and they all stay down there. It's all peace and quiet. I've been coming for twenty years. My dad used to bring me when I was a kid, when I was just seven – up to the Wain-stones and round. And now I've brought him up. Although he keeps asking embarrassing questions about my girlfriend.'

'So can you ride him?' interjected the nephew, who was displaying more and more *Just William* characteristics.

'No, he's too small. We're doing what people used to do,' explained Jasper, who liked the romantic history of muleteering. 'We're travelling with a mule as a pack animal. That's how you could keep going for days in the past.'

'So what you're doing is "olden-days style"?' said 'Bob'. Or 'Joshua'. Or 'Jeff'. His ten-year-old face wrinkled in distaste.

'Yes, I suppose we are,' said Jasper.

'Now that *is* sad. No offence. But that is *really, really* sad.'

Jasper looked crestfallen. 'Is "sad" one of those words like "sick" that these days means it's actually good?' he asked me, hopefully.

'No, Jasper. I'm sorry,' I told him, 'it means "sad".'

'And your mule's got stupid ears,' said 'Bob'. He laughed knowingly.

The kid was obviously too young to have seen Clint Eastwood's *A Fistful of Dollars*, with the immortal line, 'My mule don't like people laughing. He gets the crazy idea they might be laughing at him.' Or he would realise what happens next.

It was time to come back off the ropes.

'You're wearing a smart pair of green trainers,' I told 'Bob'. 'They must be the smartest trainers on the Moors.'

I knew my ten-year-old psychology. There is nothing they dislike more than having attention drawn to their clothes. Or to be told they're smart.

'Thank you,' he murmured bashfully.

Jethro, Jasper and I walked on with our heads held high. Nobody messed with us in the playground. If I had found one under my poncho, I would have lit a cheroot.

As we climbed up the Moors on the northern side, the remarkable profile of Roseberry Topping came into view in the distance, looking like a miniature Matterhorn. The young Captain Cook had grown up nearby and was said to have climbed Roseberry Topping as a boy, which gave him his taste for adventure.

'It's quite phenomenal among these rounded hills to have this sharp fang sticking up like a canine tooth,' said Jasper.

There was a reason for its distinctiveness. The Topping's original, more conventional sugarloaf shape collapsed in 1912, possibly because of all the mining that had been done, or due to erosion from the incoming weather.

Jethro was moving well along the difficult path up the heather. Jasper was pleased with the progress our boy had made during our journey. He was even carrying a little bit more in his saddlebags: some Yorkshire pork pies, among other essentials, which I had sourced in Stokesley, and of which I had high hopes.

'Look at him,' said Jasper. 'On his dainty little dancer's feet, he's tangoing up the whole way!'

Yet again, we had been lucky with the weather. It was one of those sunny days that sometimes come to Yorkshire when you can see for miles and miles, and it truly did appear to be 'God's Own Country'. Up on top and crossing to Urra Moor, there was a carpet of heather rolling forever away from us – one of the largest expanses in Europe.

Over the ridge, we chanced upon a group of Lycra-clad cyclists sprawled in various attitudes of recovery and lassitude. With their legs hidden, they seemed to be rising up from under the heather. The group reminded me of Signorelli's famous resurrection fresco at Orvieto, in which young men in equally tight hose emerge from the ground as angels trumpet the Second Coming; but I thought I'd get talking to them first before I suggested this comparison.

They were experienced cyclists doing a mountain bike leaders' course. Their own leader cast an expert eye over Jethro. 'So how many gears has that got?'

'Twenty-four. Although some of them are rarely used.'

Jethro took advantage of the conversation to go and nibble some of the heather while stocks lasted.

'Where have you come from?' asked the leader in a friendly way. We explained how we had travelled over from the Lake District.

'Haven't come across a mule before. But I did have a close encounter with a horse in Mongolia once.'

His pupils looked up expectantly from the heather as their man in the green jersey began his story.

'I was crossing Mongolia . . . '
'As you do,' interjected Jasper.
' . . . and I went to sleep with my bicycle chained to my tent with a padlock. I woke up in the middle of the night when the whole tent, with me in it, started to move at great speed across the Mongolian steppe. A horseman had come along, taken a fancy to my bike, tied it up to his horse and galloped off, not realising that the whole tent was attached to the bike as well. So I came too. It was a bit of a bumpy ride for a few moments before he realised what had happened and let go.'

That was the advantage of a mule. They were extraordinarily hard things to steal. I remembered once travelling in Morocco with some mules out of Taroudant – as you do – and coming to a small market town with my guide, Ali. We left our mules in a clearing outside the town where everyone else had as well. None of them were tied up or secured in any way.

'Don't they sometimes get stolen?' I had asked Ali, naïvely.

He looked at me with pity. 'Have you ever *tried* to move a mule that wasn't yours? It's hard enough to move a mule that *is* yours.'

Ali was right. It was the ultimate vehicle protection device. A mule was its own natural immobiliser. Nobody could ever steal one. Thieves had to stick to horses and bicycles.
Ahead lay Bloworth Crossing, from where we could take the

disused railway track to Blakey Junction. We could see how it wound its serpentine way across the top of the ridge, keeping to the contours.

The Rosedale Ironstone Railway had been the most remarkable, if short-lived, achievement of the nineteenth-century mining boom on the Moors. The iron ore needed to be transported down to the big blast furnaces of Teesside. Roughly ten million tonnes were taken on the railway between 1861 and its final closure in 1929. The rails had long been taken up, but the cinder path still ran straight and true across the landscape, and made for a remarkably efficient way of travelling with a mule.

As we marched at some speed along the old railway track, I was surprised by the deep and green valleys that cut through the Moors to either side as, in my ignorance, I had always presumed they would be one continuous upland plateau. I was particularly taken by the beautiful green bowl of Farndale to the south, fringed with a purple lip by the heather and shaped like a shallow oyster shell. This was another valley that at one point had been threatened with flooding for a reservoir, but had somehow mercifully escaped.

Ahead lay a lone building on Blakey Ridge. We knew this, with some anticipation, to be the Lion Inn. I was hoping for a lost rural pub in the middle of nowhere, of the sort that had blackened timbers and a few pickled eggs to go with the beer from the cask. We were, after all, almost in the centre of the Yorkshire Moors, and had walked for miles without seeing a soul. But I was wrong. The place was jumping. It had one of the largest dining areas I had seen for some time and a fruit machine in the corner. The menu alone ran to six pages. And all this because there was a car park.

The Lion Inn lay on the Castleton Road, one of the few north–south axes that run across the Moors, so was a magnet for motorists as well as stray walkers (let alone mules). It was clearly not a locals' pub. While Jasper escorted Jethro to his accommodation for the night, I decided to head down into the enticingly green valley of Farndale and the Feversham Arms, in search of fresher alcoholic pastures.

*

It was still early hours when I met Dave Maynard, a large, cheerful Yorkshireman who took great pleasure in the fact I could only understand two out of every three words he spoke. He was sitting with his wife, Sue, in the snug single room of the Feversham Arms.

Dave had worked around Farndale and the valleys of the Yorkshire Moors for all his life. Initially he had worked for individual farms, but as these had consolidated into a few large farms, with fewer workers, he had gone freelance with his own fencing business.

He remembered often getting snowed up as a child in the remote farms where his father lived.

'It were nothing to get blocked in for three weeks in winter sometimes. The snow would get so high, you couldn't use the gates, so you would just step over the walls. The dogs would have to tell you where the sheep were buried. They would stand over them in a deep drift as they could smell them through the snow. Gave a lot of local employment as well, for the snow cutters. All the local men would get work cutting. It was too difficult to get the snowplough up.

'We had some hard winters in the 1970s, I remember. We once got locked in for six weeks. Now, that was difficult. My mother had to shift to make the food last. Although we always got big sacks of everything anyway. Big sacks of potatoes and flour.

'It was different in those days, because there were so many travelling salesmen. They would come to you. Not often, mind – maybe once a month – but that was all you needed. The Clarks van would come with clothes and shoes; Colin Challoner with the groceries. Even the postman would always have a few sacks of potatoes on the van. If you live in Farndale nowadays, you have to drive to get everything you need. And there are a lot of incomers who work elsewhere. So they bring their stores with them.

'Time was when there were lots of small farms and everyone knew each other, so Christmas would last until Easter because everyone had to have a party and invite everybody else round. That took a while. Of the twelve or so farms on one side of the valley, there's only three left now. Of course, there are a lot more gamekeepers on the grouse moors. That's where the money is. There's one estate that used to have maybe two or three keepers when I was a boy. Now they have seven or eight.

'That said, the poachers these days are a bit rougher. It's not just a few locals looking for one for the pot. It's men up from Middlesbrough with lurcher dogs, wearing balaclavas.

'Isn't that right, Sue?' he asked his wife.

'What I think's a shame,' said Sue, who had recognised Dave's question as purely rhetorical, 'is that it is so difficult for young farmers today. There aren't any starter farms of 100 acres for them to begin on. I don't see how a young farming couple can get started at all, now that farms are so big.'

'Some days I used to do sixteen- or seventeen-hour shifts,' said Dave. 'Quite often in the summer. I've no regrets, though, about working here all my life. I mean, it's a grand office window, ain't it.' He waved outside at Farndale.

Dave was interested in the mule trip.

'Be careful with the boggy areas up on the Moors. You can always tell the horses that know the Moors, as they'll avoid the bogs. I've always done a lot of riding and if you go slack-reined, the horses that know the area will find their own way round. But the horses that come from off-Moor will just wade in and go up to their chests.

'What's your mule like? Is he clever and obedient?'

'Well, he hasn't gone into a bog yet,' I said, loyally, and skirting part of the question. 'And he's come all the way from the Lake District, so he's not done badly.'

'Oh, aye. You can do owt if you get your head set, as they say.' This last was delivered in such a gravelly accent, with consonants backwashing across each other – '*Y-c-n do-owt-if-ye gyr-ed soot*' – that I had to ask Dave to repeat it, as he knew I would.

'You haven't understood a word I said, have you?' he said with a broad grin, before Sue and he left.

The pub started filling up. The Feversham Arms was small and homely, so it didn't need many people to make it feel like a full house. Everyone in the bar joined in the one general conversation. The landlady, Rachel, told me that the same locals tended to come in every night. They all knew each other's jokes so well they started laughing before anyone reached the punchline.

The conversation got more raucous as the evening wore on, fuelled by Black Sheep and, in my case, Jack Daniels, for which I had conceived a sudden yearning. A black-haired fellow called Norman was holding forth about how plastic drainpipes were useless if you were trying to climb down from housewives' windows because they broke so easily. From which the conversation flowed quickly and easily to how many times everyone present had been married.

'I've been married three times,' said a bald gentleman called Steve.

'Yes, and you've bought a house for every one of your wives,' said Rachel. 'I've often thought I should marry you myself.'

'Three times! Three times!' shouted Andy, a voluble character who had enough facial hair to stuff a pillow and whose volume control had been turned up to eleven. 'One's been quite enough for me!'

Once they had established that I had been married twice, so stood somewhere in the middle of the pecking order, and after another round of drinks, the talk turned to weddings.

I had a showstopper up my sleeve, and proceeded to use it. My mother had a favourite tale about how she had attended a wedding at which the bride arrived even later than was customary. Turning to the congregation, she had begun a speech straight away, without waiting for the service to start. At first her audience were unfazed — we live, after all, in an age when couples make up their own rules as to how they get married — but after the bride had thanked them all for coming, she delivered her bombshell.

'And I particularly want to thank the chief bridesmaid,' she announced. 'Because by sleeping last night with the man who was to become my husband, she showed me exactly what sort of a man he is.' And with that, she had flounced out of the church.

It was a great story and I had told it before, so could include some curlicues and flourishes that kept my pub audience alert and wanting more.

A farmer's son called Darren was intrigued. 'So what did the fellow do who was still standing at the altar waiting for her? Must have been a bit awkward.'

'And more to the point,' said Norman, 'what did the chief bridesmaid do? I bet she could have done with a drainpipe to escape down!'

Andy started laughing again. He had a laugh so loud it was like a foghorn in the small room of the pub. It certainly would have scared any American werewolves out roaming the Moors.

'And that was your mother's story,' he boomed. 'So it must be true!'

Steve bought me another Jack Daniels. Rachel's dog was brought into the room to sniff at me to check whether I was up to scratch. I felt a benign warmth spread through my body from both the fire and the conversation, although the alcohol was helping as well.

They had a few rooms at the pub and I thought it sensible to sleep over, as Jasper was with Jethro. After the extra shots of Jack Daniels, I was in no condition to be heading back, and it was getting late.

The next morning, I woke not feeling at my brightest. Even a substantial breakfast – 'that'll fill you up' – and copious coffee didn't help.

I opened some email on my laptop, as there was a whole raft of things that had floated by while I was travelling across country – including the delivery of the vintage ice axe, bought in that exuberant moment back at Jeff's place. A note had come from FedEx, who I assumed had been trying to drop what must have been a large package at a house that was empty during the day. And my wife was hardly expecting it.

Except it wasn't a real delivery note from FedEx. It was an exceptionally strong virus which threatened, with menaces, to blow up my computer unless I paid money in Bitcoin to some address on the dark web. All my files had been locked, a message on the screen announced, with an algorithm of the most powerful sort known to mankind. In a generous, caring sort of way, the hackers gave me a full three days to pay off the ransomware or all those same files would be wiped. Forever.

It was the sort of thing that only ever happens when you have a hangover. I envied those nineteenth-century drovers who had come this way with their pack animals. They could have a drink and not have to worry about email. The experience taught me a valuable lesson: never handle a computer unless strictly sober.

I turned off the laptop and let it look after itself. Outside, a country lane led back up the hill. The tarmac was shining with a light sprinkling of rain that had fallen during the night. October was coming to an end. As I walked along the lane, a northerly

wind was bringing down a cold burst. The tops of the hedgerows
had been stripped bare and only the shoulders were still covered
in hazel leaves. Rosehips shone out bright red from the bare
branches, while green wreaths of morning glory were draped in
swathes across the boughs. The hedge was under-planted with
ferns and the last shoots of angelica, perhaps my favourite herb,
and one I had seen in remote valleys of the Himalaya as well as
English country lanes like this. The oaks along the lane were
ageing with the year so much more gracefully than the other trees,
still keeping their handsome structure with just a hint of fading
to the leaves, like old roués.

Who needed data anyway, I thought to myself. And I was
certainly not going to pay a bunch of internet pirates some exor-
bitant ransom. They could go and take a running jump off the
plank into cyberspace. Not least because I had, in a rare moment
of foresight, backed the whole thing up only a few days before.
At this happy thought, I whistled as I walked.

✻

Chapter 12

# The Moors:
# Zombies Versus Steampunks

*The mule's one drawback from a military standpoint is their
tendency to stampede under fire.*
            The War Office, *Animal Management* (London, 1923)

As I strolled back up to the Lion Inn to meet Jasper and
Jethro, I bumped into a young farmer called Peter Mawson
standing in a small yard off the lane. Beyond him was a field
with pigs circling round their open metal arcs in a proprietorial
way. They were some of the first pigs I'd seen on this entire journey
and I told him so.

It turned out that Peter was an 'incomer' who had moved to
the Yorkshire Moors only a few years ago, when he was already
forty. To those who might quibble that forty is not so young, it
made him a stripling compared to many of the farmers along
the valley who, as he pointed out, were in their seventies. Peter
was tall, and looked fit and energetic.

Like almost all the other farmers I had talked to on my long
journey from one coast to another, he was also extremely talkative.
Farmers have a reputation for being grumpy and taciturn – but
given a little encouragement, I've always found they can talk the
hind legs off a donkey (or mule).

Born on Teesside, Peter had spent most of his working life in
first the Air Force and then in marketing for various London-
based companies – including National Car Parks. It seemed an

odd preparation for what he was doing now. With his partner Nicola, he had moved to this small farm in the upper part of the Farndale Valley to rear rare-breed sheep and pigs.

I was surprised by this.

'Quite a change. And a very bold leap. If you don't mind me asking, how did you learn to do all this?' I gave a wave at the pigs behind him.

'Internet. You can learn everything on the internet these days. And I didn't rush into it either. The first couple of years I did a lot of contract work for farmers around here to see how they managed. Learned a lot that way. Both how to do it – and how not to do it.'

I knew that incomers could be treated with some suspicion on the moors. One of Hugo's friends at the dinner the previous week had told me that when he had moved into one of the small villages there, the local pub had refused to serve him. So I wondered how Peter had found it.

'I was very, very careful. But I did what I used to do in the military: hang back and not say too much at first. I soon realised a lot of them had fallen out with each other, so I've been wary of getting into arguments.'

He certainly hadn't chosen the easy way to farm. The sheep were Whitefaced Woodlands, an unusual rare breed that Peter had researched as being particularly suitable for these hillside conditions.

A few were wandering in a field in the distance. Their fluffy white faces made them look very pretty. If a Texel was the action hero of the sheep world, then these were more like dizzy blondes, the starlets. And there weren't many of them around. 'Only 900 or so in the world,' Peter told me. His pigs, though, were British

Saddlebacks, an old-fashioned type that were becoming more common again.

This meant he could market and sell the meat himself. He talked me through the economics.

'If I take a lamb to market, I get about £65 for it. If I arrange to have it cut up and then sell the joints myself, I can get three times that. Of course I've got to pay the abattoir and butcher about forty quid an animal. But I'm still quids in, by some way.'

And this was where Peter's previous experience in marketing paid off. He had set up a website and found nearby specialist shops who wanted upmarket, locally sourced meat. He also heavily promoted his 'hogget', year-old lamb that was often tastier than the six-month lamb so heavily sold by supermarkets.

It sounded a niche market. I had never even heard of hogget before.

'Well, there absolutely is a market for it. You just have to spread the net to find it. As Steve Jobs said, "Sell to people who believe in the same thing as you do."'

It was the first time a farmer had quoted Steve Jobs at me. But what Peter hadn't done was to try to sell any of the meat directly to customers himself as a farm shop.

'Because we're in the middle of nowhere. No one's ever going to find us. And having a farm shop comes with all sorts of other hassles – like someone always being here to run it, for a start. You were lucky to catch me in the yard. Usually I'm off and away in a field up there,' and he waved towards the hillside.

He invited me in for coffee to a farm kitchen that was startling in its simplicity and cleanliness. Two Apple Mac laptops faced each other across a stripped beech table, but Peter's partner Nicola was away beating for a grouse shoot, which she did regularly.

'You soon discover that's where the real money is around here: grouse. They've started letting a few sheep onto the moors again to get more of a mix – and because they help keep the grouse worms down – but grouse shooting is still what pays the bills. And there are some huge estates up on top.'

Peter spoke, I discovered, as a man whose own farm was only forty-two acres, one of the smallest I had come across on this journey. Although I had learned to be careful when asking farmers how big their land was. It was considered impolite. As Peter said, while he was happy to tell me, 'it's like asking someone how much they have in their savings account.'

He was particularly interesting about the old European subsidies that would now be disappearing.

'Young farmers voted for Brexit. And that wasn't just turkeys voting for Christmas. It was because they were fed up with the old system where farmers could trundle along without doing much and collect Euro handouts. The whole thing was like a pension system round here. Whereas if we had a level playing-field, then farmers would have to get on with it again. Which means more of a chance for young farmers to come in with a bit of energy and ambition. That's what they did in New Zealand – get rid of subsidy. Now they've got the most efficient farming industry in the world.'

He told me a good story back out in the farmyard, as I was leaving.

'Some of the old boys had a rough shoot that went over my land. A very rough shoot. And I was just walking across the yard here when I heard shots pinging off the roof tiles.

'So I went down and told them, "What did I say? You can shoot on my land, as long as you don't shoot at the house, or over my animals." I said, "I'm not falling out with you" – I was careful to say that – but I spent two years in the military in Northern Ireland. I didn't want to end up getting shot in my own back yard in Farndale!'

I suspected somehow that Peter would always be served in the local pub.

✳

Once reunited with Jasper and Jethro, our small mule train headed on from the Lion Inn along Blakey Ridge. But although it was still morning, the sky ahead was turning black. When we came over a rise, we could see why. They were burning the heather. A long line of men stretched away to either side, their pickups left on the Castleton Road. The flames were intense, and sent up smoke so thick that the sun was diffused to a hellish glare of orange and red and purple through the haze.

Jethro seemed unperturbed. He walked on with his head down in a determined way. Our route meant that we would need to walk right through the smoke. It enveloped us like a dust storm in the desert. Sometimes patches cleared enough so that I could make out the silhouettes of men lined up against the horizon, beating the flames. And I had a sudden vision of warfare; of what mules like Jethro had endured on the Western Front.

For while the British might have ostracised mules at home as unwelcome reminders of their Catholic past, they had no objections to using them abroad in the pursuit of war. The Duke of Wellington relied on 10,000 local mules for the Peninsular War in Spain; the rocky terrain made it almost impossible for wheeled vehicles. Mules took part in British Army campaigns in the Crimea, Afghanistan and Abyssinia in the later part of the nineteenth century. So great was the need for them in the Boer War that 67,000 were imported from the USA. Mules played an important part in the many campaigns waged by the British on India's North-West Frontier. Younghusband took mules with him when he invaded Tibet.

But it was in the carnage of the First World War that mules were used by the British on an industrial scale. A quarter of a million were deployed on the Western Front alone.

There is a monument to animals killed during warfare on one of the lonely traffic islands in the middle of London's Park Lane. At its centre, two life-size bronze mules plod towards a gap in a stone wall, burdened down with the parts of a gun. It is a rare recognition of the contribution made by mules to British military success – and of the price they paid.

The mules were kept in appalling conditions. One bad mistake was to clip their coats so that, come winter, they had no way of keeping properly warm, as the rough horse blankets they were given quickly became sodden and rank. Many died of pneumonia. The British soldiers asked to look after them had no previous experience of mules – and that ignorance was often fatal. As a result, the War Office decided to include a chapter on mules in the *Animal Management* book they issued to troops. It remains one of the very few British manuals on how to look after mules, and my old maroon-bound edition had proved invaluable for this journey.

The heavy 2.5-inch steel guns which for over a century were the mainstay of British artillery – and which were romanticised by Kipling in his poem 'Screw-Guns' – frequently worked the poor mules who carried them to death. These guns would be taken apart to be carried, usually by a team of five pack animals, so were broken down into the wheels, carriage, axle and other constituent parts; but even in sections, they were an enormous weight to bear. Given the appalling conditions of the war, many mules died before they even came within range of the enemy guns.

More mules had constantly to be imported, from the USA and India in particular. British soldiers often became very attached to their charges, the 'long-eared old darlin's' that Kipling eulogised, and valued them for their sense of self-preservation. There were numerous stories of mules that refused to advance into what later was revealed to be a minefield or other form of danger.

Most of the few mules in England after the war were bred by soldiers who had learned their value and overcome the deep British prejudice against them. But as ever, it was the horses we remembered mainly, not the mules.

No one had written a book – let alone a West End play and blockbuster film – called *War Mule*. Horses were the officer class; mules, the poor bloody infantry, and foreign to boot.

✻

A little further on we passed the so-called Millennial Stone, erected in 2000, but designed confusingly to look like a prehistoric monument: the sort of thing that would puzzle any post-apocalyptic archaeologist of the future. At least no one had needed to wheel it into place like an ancient megalith. Instead, all five tonnes had been lifted by crane from Spaunton Moor and transported by trailer to its current position.

It seemed a bizarre exercise in prehistoric nostalgia. If erecting a monument to the year 2000 AD rather than BC, something modern might have been more appropriate. Perhaps a shining titanium cube? Not least because there are a great many genuine prehistoric artefacts littered over the Moors already.

There was only one appropriate adjective for the moorland that stretched ahead of us: sere, a word meaning 'dry' that has wonderful provenance. According to the dictionary, '*sere* has not wandered very far from its origins – it derives from the Old

English word *sēar* (meaning "dry"), which traces back to the same early root that gave Old High German, Greek, and Lithuanian words for drying out and withering. The adjective *sere* once had the additional meaning of "threadbare", but that use is now archaic. The noun *sere* also exists, though it isn't common; its meanings are "a dry period or condition" or "withered vegetation".'

A small bird flashed past across this sere, empty land. No, I don't know what it was. If I had been a serious natural history enthusiast – a Chris Packham or a Mark Cocker, both of whom I admire – I would have recognised it in a glance; or indeed not needed to look, if I could hear the call and knew the likely species in this particular habitat. But like the majority of the public, while I can identify most birds on a garden feeder, I am less good on the small brown birds in hedgerows or on open moorland.

Nothing is more irritating than nature writers who assume universal knowledge of all the species they are talking about, especially rare ones. The most accessible naturalist in the last twenty years has to be the wonderful Bill Oddie, not least for his immortal observation that when someone rings him to say, 'I've seen a very strange bird in my garden', it will always be a jay; and for his premise that most of us start off knowing very, very little. I was no exception.

George Orwell was deeply suspicious of natural history writing or, as we now brand it, 'nature writing': of those for whom 'the world centres round the English village, and round the trees and hedges of that village rather than the houses and the people'.

In a review of a contemporary natural history book, he went on to say:

There is no question that a love of what is loosely called 'nature' – a kingfisher flashing down the stream, or a bull-finch's mossy nest, the caddis-flies in the ditch – is very widespread in England, cutting across age groups and even class distinctions, and attaining in some people an almost mystical intensity.

Whether it is a healthy symptom is another matter. It arises partly from the small size, equable climate, and varied scenery of England, but it is also probably bound up with the decay of English agriculture ... The fact is that those who really have to deal with nature have no cause to be in love with it.

Review of *The Way of a Countryman* by William
Beach Thomas, *Manchester Evening News* (23 March 1944)

He ended with the damning comment that, for such writers, their 'ideal picture of rural England might contain too many rabbits and not enough tractors'.

If Orwell had taken this journey, he would not have wanted to write about which birds were in which hedgerows. He would have wanted to talk to people; to take the temperature of the road to Whitby Pier. And like me, I suspect he would been appalled at the disconnect that now reigns in the North, just as it does in the rest of the country. The way in which so much of the middle class are unaware of the depths of the pockets of deprivation, both in the countryside – where they are particularly easy to ignore – and in small market towns like Richmond.

That big country house on the top of the hill, whose owners arrive at the weekend in an SUV laden with shopping bags, could be a thousand miles away from the small cottage at the bottom, whose occupants may rely on a moribund bus service. And there is no longer any reason for the two sides to meet. The wealthy couple in the big house feel no sense of responsibility for what happens in the rural community. They are merely visitors. And this is not just because they do not want to be engaged: many of the old focal loci of the countryside – the church, the gathering for the harvest and even the beleaguered rural pub – have faded. The closest contact its inhabitants sometimes have is on a country lane when the wheels of their cars or buses swish past each other.

We turned down by Rosedale Head and the old shooting box at Trough House, a cottage for day use by estate owners, which looked a good deal more substantial than some that their tenants enjoyed for the whole year. I felt we were beginning to head for home. The path curved away past the strange jumbled tumuli of Great Fryup Head, named not after the great British breakfast but the Norse goddess Freya.

I saw a man ahead with a small gun dog. What was unusual was that the dog had two saddlebags strapped round it. I caught up with the dog's owner, Paul, but before I could ask him about the saddlebags, he had his own question, which he asked in an agitated way.

'Did you see it?'

'See what?'

'The adder. There was an adder just back there, coiled up on the track. A big one. I almost stepped on it. It was lucky that Millie was walking behind me as she quite often goes in front. Because if she had got to the adder first, she would have worried it and that could have been nasty.'

I had not seen the adder, although I was pleased that an advance party had flushed it out. It was obvious Paul had been doing the full Coast-to-Coast, as he had a large backpack and a determined expression. He was also wearing a balaclava, which would have been sinister on some people, but which his benign features made less threatening.

He told me that he was doing the Coast-to-Coast as a way of recovering from a stroke. This struck me as 'kill or cure'. Paul added that his gun dog, Millie, was carrying all her own supplies in the little saddlebags. Although not that little. They were about the same size as Jethro's.

'The trouble is, she's very young. It's fine when we're walking, but if we stop for a moment, she feels she has to defend me and that causes problems in campsites. So I'm just camping wild wherever I can.'

We reached a small rise from which we had our first view of the sea. But Paul didn't linger to take it in. He pushed on, as he wanted to reach Grosmont by nightfall. And I had my own plans for that same night.

✻

Hallowe'en. With remarkable accuracy, I had timed our arrival near Whitby for the annual Goth Festival which takes place in the town Bram Stoker used as the English setting for *Dracula*. I even had my black leather costume in the horse van. But I could not persuade Jasper to attend – nor for that matter, Jethro – so I lit out for the territory that night on my own.

Whitby at dusk had the most dramatic of silhouettes. The twin piers stretched out their embrace around the inky pool of the harbour. On the headland above, the ruined abbey called out for a full moon, the creaking of a coffin-lid and the whoosh of Dracula's cloak as he made his way down to the quayside; although the Count would have been disappointed by some of the tawdry fruit-machine palaces now lining the waterfront.

What might have given him more pleasure were the costumes. The town was full of pilgrims to the annual Goth Festival, which had grown and grown in popularity since its inception in 1994. Dark figures in heavy brocaded frock coats brushed past me as I made my way against what was still a brisk and chill northerly wind.

The fish and chip shop on Silver Street was packed with

black-uniformed Goths eating their lightly battered cod with silver and purple varnished nails. They looked like crows tearing at the white flesh. A woman with her back to me had a row of silver steel spikes coming out of her padded shoulders, like an armadillo on steroids. A man had a chain with a locked padlock round his neck; I wondered if he had put the key in a safe place. There was a curious slithering noise in the shop, like fish that had been caught in the bottom of a trawler; it took me a while to realise that it was wet PVC clothes rubbing on benches.

As I sat at my own bench to open up a styrofoam tray of fish and chips, I found it disconcerting that no one was talking. The Goths were all locked in silent tableaux, like some old German Expressionist film in black and white, gazing intently either at each other or at the fish and chips in front of them.

Two teenage girls broke the silence. They were dressed in start-ling symmetry: one in white leather jacket with black trousers, the other in black leather with white trousers. Both had red lip-stick that could have stopped traffic at fifty yards.

'I just wanna tell her to fucking man up,' said one, loudly.

I winced, as did the Count Dracula lookalike opposite me on the bench. It is always painful when the young use a split infinitive.

'That's what she should do. Fucking man up. I mean, what does she think she's on about with the fake tanning? You only have to look at her hands to know what's happening.'

A little further up the hill, and the wind and driving sleet got so bad that I took refuge in a pub, the Elsinore. It took me a while to de-mist and get my bearings, but when I could focus on the other inhabitants they seemed subtly different from the Goths I had seen in the chippie. For a start, they were not all wearing black. Many looked more like they belonged to the set of a Jules

Verne or *Chitty Chitty Bang Bang* movie: Victoriana with a twist. One man at the bar was wearing a bowler hat with a red sash, a pheasant feather and what looked like a small ormolu clock stuck jauntily in the brim. He was talking to a buxom lady in a bright red corset with arm-length fishnet gloves, who was unostentatiously and with a complete lack of embarrassment tucking herself back in where she had popped out a bit at the top.

When I ordered a drink, a lean, grey-haired man wearing cinder-goggles, a tartan waistcoat and calf-length boots looked at me appraisingly. He had a slightly cadaverous face that reminded me of gruff Inspector Blakey from that old TV series, *On the Buses*.

'So is this all part of the Goth Festival?' I asked, hesitantly.

'Goths!' the man spluttered. 'They don't come in here at all. We're not Goths! We're steampunks. This is a steampunk pub now. It used to be Goth.

'The Goths hate us. Particularly the über-Goths. They're the worst.'

He slowed and stared at me as he sipped his bitter. I sensed he was the sort of man who would get a pint to last as long as he could.

'But then the über-Goths hate everybody ... In fact, quite often they hate each other as well. That's what happens when you wear black and only come out of your bedroom at night. And listen to darkwave.'

Blakey relapsed into morose silence. A woman nearby wearing head-to-toe tartan and a bowler hat came to my rescue.

'Yes, steampunks are much more cheerful. We like to get out and about.'

She introduced herself as Lady Elsie, and I discovered she was a stalwart of the Victorian Steampunk Society.

'We've been a splinter group of the festival for the last ten or so years. I think the Goths are a bit annoyed that we've been growing. In fact, many of us used to be Goths but then got bored with taking ourselves so seriously.

'Steampunk is all about time travel with attitude. So it can be Victorian but it can also be post-apocalyptic, like *Mad Max*. You see those replica cinder-goggles everyone's wearing round their hats? I've got some of the originals. Worth a lot now. They were what you wore in third class on Victorian railways, as you were in open carriages behind the engine so you needed them to keep the ashes and smoke out of your eyes.

'We're not as coded as the Goths. I mean, these days most department stores even have a section called "Goth"! For teenage girls who are into emo and all that stuff. Black eyeliner, white make-up, a bit of PVC or leather. Whereas the whole point about steampunk is that you dress in stuff you *can't* buy in a department store. I'm a costume designer in real life, so I know all about dressing up.'

She was wearing a fabulous Victorian necklace, or rather set of necklaces draped over each other.

'Do you have a Nerf gun with you?' asked Lady Elsie suddenly.

I had to admit that I didn't.

'Don't worry, you can get them two for one at Toys R Us. We like to accessorise Nerf guns with a lot of metallic paint and other stuff. They can end up looking amazing. Then you could join us for the steampunk versus zombies battle we're holding tomorrow.'

I felt the conversation was accelerating out of control.

'What's a steampunk versus zombies battle?'

'We try to survive the zombie apocalypse when they come at us. Although usually there aren't any survivors. The zombies attack en masse. It's hard to get away or shoot them fast enough. Unless you've got a good aim with a Nerf gun and have practised. Also, you need a lot of ammunition. The zombies just have to touch you and you become one of them.'

For the meantime, Elsie invited me to a fringe musical event the steampunks were holding at a venue dubbed 'Steampunk Central', just by the car park. As the alternative was to go to the main Goth concert and listen to The Mission, Heaven 17 and Sigue Sigue Sputnik – all eighties bands who only ever played in my nightmares – I happily joined their group as they trundled up from the pub. They were walking slowly, as you do when wearing steel-studded calf-length boots with four-inch heels. I noticed a large amount of cross-dressing going on; the men in corsets and high heels were finding it particularly hard work getting up the hill.

'You should have been here during the day,' said a woman, I think, who looked like Anjelica Huston wearing a bright red wig. She was trundling three chihuahuas in a pram, all wearing diamante dog collars. 'There were so many Goths and steampunks crossing the bridge down by the quay that they almost had to close it. A lot of the locals don't like the festival. But it brings a lot of business here. And who else would come to Whitby at the end of October?'

She had a point. The wind was whipping in from the North Sea so hard that some of the frock coats were blowing vertical, revealing either fishnet stockings or military Sergeant-Pepper-style trousers. I was the coldest I had been all trip, even dressed in my old motorbiking leather jacket and trousers which, I now suspected, were a fashion mistake. What if any of the steampunks mistook me for a Goth? I should have done my research and accessorised more. My daughter Daisy had once told me that my dark glasses were steampunk, as they were round glacier goggles – but I could hardly wear those at night, stumbling along the cobbles.

Up at Steampunk Central, things had cranked up. There were enough corsets on display to start a burlesque club. One striking woman in a black fishtailed whalebone dress sashayed down the aisle towards her man who had mutton-chop sideburns and was propping up his chin on a bone-handled cane. A karaoke group called 'Brass Zeppelin' were massacring some old heavy metal songs with cheerful aplomb. Deep Purple's 'Smoke on the Water' was having the life thrashed out of it.

The barmaid recommended some Theakston Smooth Dark, which sounded like the right sort of drink for the occasion, and I settled into a table behind two bald men wearing angel wings. Towards the end of the musical entertainment, one of them noticed Lady Elsie, who was making her way to the stage in order to announce some forthcoming steampunk events – and to prepare her troops for the battle against the zombies the next day.

He stood up, blocking her way so that his angel wings were waving in front of her. 'I'm terribly sorry to bother you, but I don't suppose you know any taxidermists in Whitby?' he asked. 'Or even Scarborough? It's a bit urgent.'

Not for the first time, I thought how very strange the English could be.

*

It was our final day and we were heading towards the coast and Robin Hood's Bay, the traditional end of Wainwright's walk. The sun was shining and the sea was almost in our sights. Did the breeze already have a tang of salt spray?

We had got Jethro out of the horse van with some elation that morning. Was it my imagination or had he danced down the ramp with more than usual elan? Certainly, he looked every inch the pack mule. Over our journey, the Colorado riding blanket had even acquired that faint sheen of equine sweat, which was the difference between a fashion ornament and a working garment. He still wasn't carrying much in his saddlebags – but to be fair to him, by this stage of the journey there wasn't much to carry.

Jasper seemed in jaunty mood as well. His beret was set at a rakish angle. He spotted some peregrine falcons in the distance.

'Quite late in the season for them. Although someone once said that a pigeon can look a bit like a hawk at a distance. Well, in fact, *I* once said that.'

Passing High Hawsker, a friendly fellow popped out of the village hall to say hello. 'Have you got a carriage for him?' he asked, pointing at Jethro.

This was the first time anyone had suggested hitching Jethro up to some wheels. I wasn't sure he was ready for it.

It turned out that the man once had a donkey called Trudy, and had used her to pull a small cart; she had lived to the ripe old age of thirty, although she never liked the cold and sea spray of the coast. Given his experience, I introduced him properly to Jethro and explained that we had come 200 miles from the other coast, in Cumbria.

'So what are you going to do when you get to Robin Hood's Bay? Because you'll have to get Jethro all the way back again. And he'll be double fare on the bus.'

'Well, he's only eight,' pointed out Jasper, in his best and most beguiling Irish accent. 'He should get a half ticket, by rights.'

'I tell you what, though,' said the man. 'The hotel down by the water's edge in Robin Hood's Bay should give you a free drink for getting a mule across. Worth asking at least.'

It was exactly the incentive we needed. We set off with added sprightliness to our step.

I asked Jasper if he agreed that Jethro was looking unusually frisky today.

'Well, he's got fitter, like all of us.'

'Do you mean to say you weren't fit at the start of all this, Jasper?'

'Well, not as fit as I am now! I mean, people always ask, do I train for these long-distance walks? But to be honest the best training is just actually to do them and play yourself in.'

I agreed. 'Yes, particularly as walking only makes you fit for walking. You can be a champion jogger and be a rubbish walker.'

Jasper wondered what Jethro would make of the sea again, given it was many weeks since we had seen it last; whether he'd be confused and think it was the same sea, and we had just gone around in a big circle. 'What was the point of that trip? The stupid idiots.'

'I mean, we've all muddled along and got to know each other better on this trip,' added Jasper. 'And I'm sure Jethro thinks he's trained us, not the other way round.'

It was true that we were walking at mule pace a lot of the time. A bit brisker than a normal human one, like being on an exercise machine. And for this last section of the walk, we found a fine bridle path, an old cinder track which had once been used for a railway, so we were motoring.

Our first sight of the sea was not as revelatory as might be expected. Given the haze and cloud, it was difficult to make out quite where air ended and water began, although a distant ship gave us some bearings. Then a lovely hedge of gorse and hawthorn shielded it from us completely.

We reached some houses on the outskirts of Robin Hood's Bay. The descent into town was steep, and had to be negotiated past a great deal of traffic. A lady called Linda, who was out walking with a friend, spotted us and asked if we had been doing the Cleveland Way with Jethro.

'No, no, we've come a lot further than that. We've done the Coast-to-Coast, or at least a version of it, with bridleways.'

'He hasn't done the Coast-to-Coast?' she said, pointing to Jethro. 'Really! Right, well, listen, if you go down to the bottom by the sea, there's a pub down there called the Bay Hotel. It's my pub! There's a book for you to sign . . .'

'What's his name? Jethro? Then maybe Jethro should put in a hoof print,' interjected her friend.

' . . . There's a book for you to sign,' continued Linda firmly. 'Tell them Linda said that Jethro can have a certificate on me for nothing.'

'I thought you were about to say we could have a pint on you for nothing,' I said.

'Ooh, I wouldn't go that far. Don't be ridiculous! A publican giving out a free pint! There are rules, you know. I'd never hold my head up high again. But Jethro can definitely have a free certificate. I'll ring them now and tell them.'

A thought occurred to her and she suddenly looked worried. 'I mean, obviously you can't actually take him *inside*.'

We carried on. Another lady asked, for the very final time on our walk, whether Jethro was a donkey or a mule, and what was the difference anyway. A sign in the local greengrocer's shop said that, 'Due to a very naughty blackbird, no fruit and veg can be displayed outside'. Jethro was spooked by seeing his reflection in the greengrocer's window and started backing up, which was alarming given the narrow road and traffic. I realised he had never seen a mirror before. But Jasper and I managed to calm him.

A few more turns of the cobbled streets and we were down by the North Sea. We led Jethro to the edge of the waves, which were dancing up the launching ramp for the trawlers.

'Shall we try to get him to dip his feet in the sea?' I suggested.

Jasper gave that same funny whistle he had done many weeks before in the Lake District to get Jethro to dip his head. Jethro ventured forward until an incoming wave lapped at his hooves.

'Well done, you've done well, Jethro. Well done, Jasper. We've all done well. And there's the pub right here with that pint which has got our name on it.'

'Several pints, with our names on them,' said Jasper.

As if she had heard our voices, a barmaid materialised at the door of the Bay Hotel. 'I've just been informed by Linda that you've done the Coast-to-Coast with a donkey.'

'Is that the certificate to say he's done the Coast-to-Coast?' I asked. 'Because if you're filling it out, can you put "Jethro the mule" not "Jethro the donkey"? Or he might get upset.'

# Acknowledgements and Epilogue

To Anna Hemmings and the staff at RSPCA Lockwood, and to Helen Brodie, Yvonne Phennah and other members of the British Mule Society.

My thanks to Annis Sokol for her helpful advice in advance of the journey.

To those who offered hospitality and pasture to Jethro and to us as we made our way across country, including my sister Katie Tait and her husband Alex, Catherine Ducker, Charles Hunter and Jocasta Shakespeare, Catherine Bell, Harry and Susan Wilmot, Jeff and Fiona Ford, Peter and Joanne Bland, Jason Gathorne-Hardy, Melanie Fisher, Hugo Hildyard and Florencia Clifford, John and Jude Haslam, Elizabeth Kirk and Margaret Barton. To Graham Rogers for our discussions about Swaledale.

My particular thanks to Jasper Winn for his kindness and generosity in joining me on the journey. For of course, it's not really *One Man and a Mule*, as the keen-eyed reader will have spotted; Jasper was with me for much of the time, although not for the entire trip across country. The full title should have been *One Man and a Mule and a Friend Some of the Time and a Dodge Van*. But for some reason, the publishers objected.

Jason Gathorne-Hardy did buy the horse van, although part of the purchase price was made up of paintings, so I ended up with some fine bird drawings of his – bringing the nature of our original meeting to a satisfying full circle. He painted the Dodge in royal red and green racing colours before driving it around Westmorland to paint from, often in the rain.

The RSPCA were delighted to see the new slimline Jethro back in such fine fettle after our journey across England. The publicity he received from his 'Jethro the Mule' Facebook page was enough to find him a more permanent home. He has been adopted by Greta, who works at a vets' practice, so he is by definition well cared for. He shares an 'en-suite paddock' with a couple of geldings and has attracted interest from the vicar for the local Nativity play; it seems there is considerable debate in biblical circles as to whether Mary arrived at the stables on a donkey or a mule, depending on how you translate the Hebrew. Whether Jethro will be well behaved on stage is yet to be seen. Greta and her husband Nick describe him as being 'very opinionated' and 'impossible to catch', so not much has changed there.

I've been able to visit Jethro while writing this book. He always looks at me in the way the English do on such occasions – with a friendly if slightly quizzical expression that leaves the changes in both our circumstances unspoken. And he is too tactful to mention that his Facebook page still attracts more interest than mine; although he prefers to keep his current location a secret, in order to keep paparazzi away.

I am grateful to my agent Georgina Capel, the editorial team of Trevor Dolby and Lizzy Gaisford at Preface, and all those at Penguin Random House who helped with the production of the book; to Rachael Beale for her considerable editorial help in preparing the manuscript, to John Gilkes for the fine map and to Bryan Ledgard for his portraits at the Whitby Goth Festival.

And special thanks as ever to Irena and all my very supportive family.

**From:** John Pettifew Clark
**To:**     Crowmarsh, Eustace
          [mail to:ecrowmarsh@penguinrandomhouse.co.uk]
**Subject:** Hugh Thomson – Mule Book

Dear Eustace,

Good to catch you briefly on the phone at your Frankfurt meeting. Quite understand you didn't have time to talk. Can't help thinking, though, that it's a shame the tradition of publishers' lunches is on the wane – a text and a Pret a Manger chilled sandwich is about as good as it gets these days.

Anyway, my thoughts on Thomson, for what it's worth. As you know, I still find him insufferably irresponsible, and question your wisdom in letting him loose on the reading public. At least you've taken my advice after the last book (or perhaps he did himself, as you managed to leave my letter at the end of the MS, much to my embarrassment – try not to do that this time), and hitched him up with an animal: one uniquely suited to his own character, in the same way that dogs always choose their owners.

Admittedly, given his own stubbornness, undiplomatic forthrightness and fondness for pies, he seems to have met his match in Yorkshire. Indeed, actually quite liked it. And there are fewer gratuitous insults than in the last *Green Road into the Trees* outing. Although does he really need to tell us he voted to remain in Europe? Probably lost half his readers at one fell swoop. Or rather 51.9% of them.

What worries me is that this could be shaping up to be a trilogy, like his books on South America. I suspect he will head even further north next and over the border to

Scotland, which could be fraught with problems. The Scots don't mind the English appreciating their wild places, but they will certainly mind Thomson talking about the actual people he meets and tweaking their tartan-covered tails. They're notoriously thin-skinned.

Just warning you now. Personally I'd dump him completely and get one of these new nature writers who seem to sell so well, and confine themselves strictly to beasts and birdies and the lyricism of the landscape – even if their books are bought more to display on the oak dresser than actually to read.

The copy-edited manuscript is attached. I have followed normal UK and Penguin Random House publishing practice in my editing and instructions to the typesetter. I have also tried as before to remove the author's frequent solecisms, repetitions, anachronisms, incorrect use of quotation marks when quoting from partial sentences, and use of prepositions to end sentences and sometimes – unbelievably – even whole paragraphs. I can't believe the man went to – and presumably received some education from – a well-known public school, although I understand they kicked him out before he could finish. Quite right too. I would have as well.

Still think it would be good to have another lunch at the Garrick sometime?

Yours

John

John Pettifew Clark

PS And don't forget to take this out! I sometimes wonder if you bother to read these editorial notes at all.

# Index

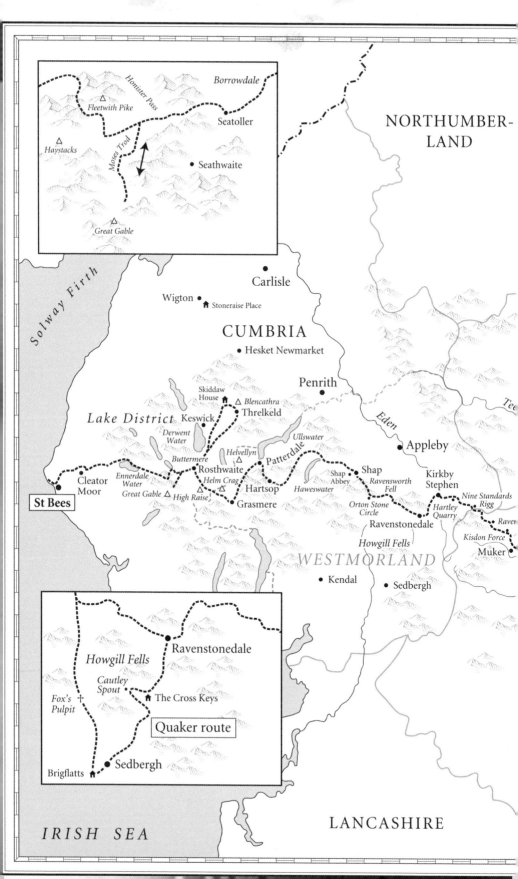